THE PERMANENT CRISIS:
COMMUNISM IN WORLD POLITICS

A Blaisdell Book in Political Science

CONSULTING EDITOR

Andrew Gyorgy

INSTITUTE FOR SINO–SOVIET STUDIES
THE GEORGE WASHINGTON UNIVERSITY

The Permanent Crisis

● ● ●

COMMUNISM IN WORLD POLITICS

KURT LONDON

Institute for Sino-Soviet Studies
The George Washington University

BLAISDELL PUBLISHING COMPANY
A DIVISION OF GINN AND COMPANY
Waltham, Massachusetts • Toronto • London

To Jean

Foreword

Kurt London is one of the most successful and assiduous "revisionists" I have ever known. Revising his earlier volume of *The Permanent Crisis*, first published in 1962, he has rewritten and reformulated such a vast proportion of the first edition that the reader is now delightfully confronted with a brand new book. This volume effectively raises and significantly answers a myriad of questions deeply troublesome to scholar and student alike. The central dilemma in the author's search to outline the "backgrounds of conflict" and to delineate the diverse ideas and forms of world politics can probably be reduced to the following question: How do we rationalize the irrational, and how do we systematize the hopelessly unsystematic in the peculiarly and uniquely murky field of contemporary world politics?

The author attacks the problem from several vantage points — by the use of both conventional scholarly means and unconventional research techniques. Power, economics, security, policy planning, intelligence, diplomacy, and propaganda (not necessarily in this order) are some of the major facets through which insight can be gained into today's two principal ideological and power conflicts — namely the relatively short-term Sino–Soviet dispute and the distressingly long-term East–West confrontation, more popularly labelled as the Cold War. Indeed, these are the major conflict areas which add up to our epoch's current and "permanent crisis."

In this volume the disturbing "psychopathology" of today's international relations (to cite the author's felicitous phrase) is lucidly and candidly analyzed. The author employs several useful political science techniques but does not indulge in an overreliance on any single method. Thus, the book can serve as a useful guideline to the expert observer of world politics as well as a valuable teaching tool for our faculty colleagues and as a pleasurable textbook for the mushrooming number of students in courses in international relations and comparative government.

ANDREW GYORGY

Preface

This book attempts to focus attention on the far-reaching changes in the character and substance of world politics and to suggest the contributing causes for these changes. The first edition was written between 1959 and 1960, and was based not only on academic research but also on practical experience in the field of communist affairs and international relations. While much has been changed in the present edition, I have had no reason to abandon the original thesis.

It still is my contention that the unprecedented phenomena that have occurred since World War I have not been sufficiently understood. The ideological struggle and the scientific progress, interrelated as they are, have created conditions that require a re-thinking of our world outlook and, concomitantly, of policies and methods to cope with the new situation. Our environment is changing rapidly, but while the communists have broken with the past and try to build a society with entirely new concepts of life, perverted as they are, we seem to have imposed upon ourselves an intellectual containment of sorts. Yet containment is stagnation: the *status quo* is an illusion because, so long as this planet exists, there will be change. Life *is* change; death is the alternative.

Since World War I, world-shaking events have gnawed away unceasingly at the conventional political thinking which, regrettably, is still deeply ingrained in the minds of too many free-world students of foreign affairs. Tradition-bound societies, opposed to change, are loath to depart from their established reasoning. But the emergence of revolutionary totalitarianism and the new technological developments have brought about conditions that compel us, in the interest of self-preservation, to discover their nature and adjust our political logic accordingly.

It has been my experience, both in government and academic circles, that surprisingly few foreign affairs specialists are willing to admit that nationalism, as we understand it, no longer is the nub of political reasoning in our confrontation with the communist world. Certainly, this factor has not vanished, and on the surface it seems to have become stronger in the sixties. But under communism it has acquired a different meaning. This nationalism is tempered by doctrinal interdictions, particularly by the concept of socialist internationalism which is at the core of what is now called Marxism–Leninism in its Soviet and Chinese versions. Modification of Soviet behavior and greater freedom of movement in the Eastern European states seem to have re-enforced the opinion of those who have always tended to downgrade or deny the importance of ideology and have claimed that nationalism, not political doctrine, remains the decisive rationale even in communist-ruled countries. Were this indeed true, we would have to deal not with revolutionary but with traditional states and could look forward to an eventual accommodation or convergence. I believe this analysis is incorrect in Soviet bloc affairs and even less so in the Chinese puzzle.

In the pre-totalitarian, pre-nuclear age, the conduct of relations among nations was a relatively simple procedure, especially after the regulations adopted at the Vienna Congress of 1815. As a rule, the political issues were clear enough; one nation knew, more or less, what to expect from another. Not so now when we are confronted with a complex political philosophy, a secular religion of sorts, whose proponents are imbued with the belief that all those unwilling to accept conversion should be liquidated — given favorable conditions. This has become an unpopular point of view, but I have seen no real evidence that the communists have changed their beliefs. What Moscow has changed are the tactical means to achieve its strategic ends. Mao's China has not done even that.

* * *

I am greatly indebted to Professors Hiram M. Stout, Andrew Gyorgy, Ralph K. White, and John Hardt, all of The George Washington University, who gave me the benefit of their advice for this revision of *The Permanent Crisis*. I am particularly grateful for the invaluable research assistance and suggestions by Mr. Michael Zinovieff, formerly of the Institute for Sino–Soviet Studies. Miss Sally Jensen has done a splendid job in preparing the manuscript. And again, as so often before, I bow to the editorial talent and the unflinching encouragement of my wife Jean.

KURT LONDON

Contents

1. OUR POLITICAL HORIZON   1

The Changing Aspects of International Relations   1
The International State "System" and the Ideological Schism   8

2. FOREIGN AFFAIRS IN A DIVIDED WORLD   13

Foreign Policy   13
Psychopathology in International Relations   19

3. THE INGREDIENTS OF POWER IN THE NUCLEAR AGE   32

Metamorphoses of National Power   32
Domestic Backgrounds of Conflict   62

4. COLD WAR ECONOMICS   72

Political Economy — Bipolar   72
Foreign Aid   76

5. TO HAVE AND TO HOLD: PROBLEMS OF SECURITY   86

Isolation, Autarky, and Neutralism   87
Balance of Power   89
Collective Security   91
Arms Control and Disarmament   93
Protective Alliances   98
International Organization   115

6. WAR AND PEACE IN THE NUCLEAR AGE 121

7. THE MAKERS OF FOREIGN POLICY 132

Who Has the Power in the West? 132
Who Has the Power in the East? 145
Who Formulates Security Policy? 151

8. FOUNTAINHEAD OF POLICY PLANNING: INTELLIGENCE 163

Theoretical Aspects 163
Organizational Aspects 174

9. BIPOLAR CONDUCT OF FOREIGN AFFAIRS 187

Vanishing Diplomacy 187
East–West Negotiations 193

10. PROPAGANDA VERSUS DIPLOMACY 199

Concepts and Types 199
POLITPROP: *The Amalgamation of Policy and Propaganda* 207

SOME CONCLUDING REFLECTIONS 217

BIBLIOGRAPHY 226
INDEX 237

Our Political Horizon

The Changing Aspects of International Relations

Political terminology has lost its absolute values since the entrance of ideological states upon the scene of world politics has created uncertainty as to the meaning of words and concepts. Truth has become relative and, like other ethical terms, is bent to fit an ideological framework or to serve the purposes of psychological warfare.[1] Political science, especially in the study of international relations and foreign policy, can no longer assume universal acceptance of its traditional concepts. The established principles of international ethics, codified in a body of international law, are not universally honored. Different interpretations of political terms in a divided world make understanding between East and West difficult, if not impossible.

There exist two main groups of contestants: the traditional and the revolutionary. Traditional nations consider policy problems within the ethical framework of established principles — tempered by the bitter experience of centuries of war and agreed upon by a community of nations belonging to the same culture complex. This makes it easier to discover a common basis of understanding despite the existence of rivalries and other conflicts. It is perhaps this fundamental similarity of world concepts which has set a natural limitation on the policy objectives of the traditionalists. Not even the great nineteenth-century empires pursued world domination as a feasible goal.

Contrariwise, revolutionary states recognize no such limitations. They reject the principles of international relations developed by the traditionalists, claiming that such principles are established in the interest of the "ruling classes" and do not, therefore, constitute the

---

[1] Q. Wright, *The Study of International Relations* (New York: Appleton-Century-Crofts, 1955), p. 21.

legitimate aspirations of the peoples. They tend to become *ideological* empires and, like the medieval church, acknowledge no limit to their aims. They are obsessed by messianic zeal to convert the heathen even though they may find it convenient to couch their catechism in seemingly conventional terms. The revolution, be it fascist or communist, determines their attitudes toward other nations and projects its dynamics into their policies. Different from the traditional nations, ideological states seek to impose their systems upon an unwilling world by any means, fair or foul.

It is of utmost importance to recognize the fundamental contrast between the foreign policy goal of a traditional power and the revolutionary objectives of the opponents of long-established order. Many, if not most, of the difficulties that beset Western policy-makers result from their failure to realize that *a revolutionary government has no foreign policy in the conventional sense.* Instead, it aims to reshape the world in its own image and seeks to liquidate all opponents that stand in the way of this goal. The position of a traditional power in the state system, as we know it, may be compared with that of a corporation which tries to surpass its competitors, but has learned from economic history that their destruction may be a Pyrrhic victory; that in a sound economy competition is designed, not to wipe out the rival, but to stimulate better methods of production and merchandising. But the attitude of a revolutionary, totalitarian state resembles that of a monopoly which, having liquidated competition in its own field, seeks to gain control of enterprises beyond its original interest. Its goal is to establish an economic empire that will dominate financing, production, and consumption without opposition.

As a result, "diplomats can still meet but they cannot persuade each other. Instead, diplomatic conferences become elaborate stage plays which seek to influence and win over public opinion in other nations; . . . they are less a forum for negotiation than a platform for propaganda."[2] It is one of the deplorable facts of life that men of traditional background and upbringing cannot easily perceive the meaning of revolutionary methods in international relations which they find

[2] H. A. Kissinger, *Nuclear Weapons and Foreign Policy* (New York: Harper and Brothers, 1957), p. 318.

enigmatic, inexplicable, and baffling. If they do realize the deadly danger confronting them, they react too slowly, often lack understanding of ideological motivation, and are sometimes unable to cope with the cat-and-mouse game which is second nature to the revolutionists. And yet, "when an established order is confronted by a revolutionary power, its survival depends on the ability to see through appearances and to keep the implied challenge from becoming overt."[3]

A revolutionary power, due to its dictatorial, integral conduct of foreign affairs, can easily embarrass traditional states, which, being governed by the slow-working democratic system of checks and balances, are unable to make quick decisions except in wartime. For the same reasons, it can maintain the initiative in the field of world politics. If it is psychologically skilled, it can exert a formidable influence on popular opinion. It can strive for a "relaxation of tensions" or "peaceful coexistence" and implement this tactic with minor measures, which may have considerable propaganda value, without affecting its fundamental attitudes. It may expect the peoples in democratic countries to accept these "concessions" at face value and relax their vigilance. In such an atmosphere, the democratic peoples may well demand that less money be spent for defense and general preparedness which is exactly what the revolutionary leaders desire. They can and will reverse their "relaxation" at a moment's notice and confront the traditionalists with blunt warnings or brute force. They will try to exploit such a situation by blackmailing their adversaries into further weakening their position.

Thus it appears that the cliché of the "two camps," coined by the communist world, is indeed a reality, not only in terms of power but also in ideas and beliefs. Complex as world politics are, it is no oversimplification to draw the line between the bipolar power aggregations, regardless of the diversities within the opposing camps and the existence of an allegedly non-committed "third world." "Contradictions" within the "socialist camp," such as the differences in ideological interpretation, strategy, and tactics existing between the Soviet Union and Communist China, must be viewed against a background of common revolutionary experience and hostility toward Western

[3] *Ibid.*, pp. 319–320.

"imperialism." It is true that the communist world has undergone important changes since 1956, the year of the Twentieth Congress of the Communist Party of the Soviet Union (CPSU). Polycentric communism has brought a measure of independence to the domestic affairs of the states of Eastern Europe; Moscow and Peking are embroiled in an acrimonious cold war and the parties outside the "socialist camp" are no longer bound by the dictates of either Moscow or Peking. Nevertheless, most communist leaders certainly realize that the future of their secular religion depends on unity and are aware of the necessity to regain it.

There are considerable political and economic differences inside the Western alliance systems. But, troubling as they are, the West — and its non-European allies — recognize the vital need for the continuation of these systems opposite the communist orbit. Nation-individualism is more characteristic of the West than the East, but, France excepted, there is growing evidence of willingness to subordinate differences in the face of the acute danger threatening Western civilization. (The Common Market is a telling example.) The efforts are uneven and sometimes grudgingly made, but even the most individualistic and rationalistic statesmen appear to realize that division within the Western alliance systems is exactly what the communist leaders desire. General de Gaulle's illusions of national grandeur, which are outdated in their conception and dangerous for the Western world, are only a little less troublesome for the West than is the Moscow–Peking conflict for the East.

As to the "uncommitted" areas, predominantly located in Asia and Africa, they are not in a position to exert power-based influence upon the two opposing camps. Their role in world politics is formidable by indirection. The conversion of these uncommitted areas to the ideological views of Marxism–Leninism and their subsequent incorporation into the "world socialist system" are the goal of both Moscow and Peking. The prevention of such a catastrophe is recognized by the West to deserve high priority. Indeed, communist mobilization of neutralist manpower and economic resources would be intolerable for the West, which would be content with an absolute and genuine neutrality should an anti-communist position be unattainable.

The existence — and in some instances the influence — of the third world has not altered the picture of bipolar power concentration. Some of the more developed states are peacefully intent on improving their living standard. Others just emerging from colonial domination convert their pent-up resentment into a violent, destructive nationalism which is materially unrealistic. Still others tend to develop a revolutionary character along Marxist lines and are, therefore, unfriendly toward the West. Indeed, the social, political, and economic conditions within the neutral zone differ widely, and the only common goal discernible is the consolidation of their sovereignty, national prestige, and economic progress.

The differences between the contemporary aggregates of states and the earlier, constantly shifting combinations of nations can no longer be explained in terms of power politics alone. The division of the world into competing "camps" is due largely to the insertion of communist ideology into the relations between nations. Without this motivating force, neither the Soviet Union nor Communist China would have become what they are now: a constant menace to the free world and producers of a permanent crisis.[4]

Therefore, we cannot afford to base our decisions exclusively on Western ethical concepts when dealing with nations which do not recognize them. Indeed, since the hostile "socialist camp" is the primary source of danger, even our attitudes and policies toward kindred nations must be governed by an appraisal of communist intentions and capabilities. Nor can such an appraisal be limited to a discussion of power in the political, economic, military, and technological spheres; it must also deal with the intangibles of ideology and its effect on human nature.

One may question whether "human nature, in which the laws of politics have their roots, has not changed since the classical philosophies of China, India, and Greece endeavored to discover these laws."[5] It is precisely because communist experiments have proved man's mind *can* be changed, that a re-evaluation of the entire concept of international relations is urgently needed.

---

[4] For a concise statement of the functions of ideology, see J. W. Spanier, *World Politics in an Age of Revolution* (New York: F. A. Praeger, 1967), p. 76.

[5] H. J. Morgenthau, *Politics Among Nations* (4th ed.; New York: A. A. Knopf, 1967), p. 4.

Environmental changes have subjected human nature to enormous pressures for millennia. These changes were partly the work of nature and partly man's own doing. Experimental psychology has proved that they have a modifying effect upon man's mind; in turn, the mind exerts great influence on the body. This interaction may produce inevitable changes in human nature. It is true that man's physically-conditioned urges, such as hunger and love, remain constant; they are dependent on the biological facts of life. But where man expresses himself through intelligent action, he is flexible; otherwise life would stagnate. Man's thought is composed of both inherited and newly-acquired elements, tempered by experience. In this way he develops and keeps in flux; he may either progress or retrogress, but he can never stand still. If he does, he begins to die.

The pressures and influences that have befallen humanity since World War I extend beyond economic hardships, physical destruction, and political upheaval. They have three basic causes:

1. the birth of the era of political ideologies — secular religions which aspire to regiment our planet's inhabitants into a collective happiness;

2. the development of new techniques of communications that have shrunk the earth to a fraction of its former size; and

3. the breakthrough into the very secret of matter that holds the universe together — or may split it asunder.

The secular religions seek to demonstrate that previous concepts of life are no longer acceptable and that traditional philosophies of government must be destroyed to attain a kingdom of heaven on earth. They not only stir the consciousness of the underprivileged who greatly outnumber their luckier fellows; they also raise the hopes of would-be reformers who delude themselves that social justice can be enforced. The technological breakthrough, on the other hand, found humanity unable to digest its meaning. Our understanding of the philosophical implications of nuclear energy or the conquest of space lags far behind our technical advancement. The result is confusion and fear, vastly exacerbated by the ideological schism which stimulates further technical progress but inhibits adequate appreciation of its true value and meaning.

Like the natural sciences and the nascent science of the human mind, the social sciences, especially the discipline of international relations, are in flux. Compared with the changes that have occurred since the middle of the twentieth century and may occur in the coming decades, the Renaissance revolt against scholasticism was trifling indeed. We must keep our minds open to these changes even if our hearts rebel against them. Unfortunately, we have not done so. Our thinking remains conditioned largely by concepts which, although most useful during the hundred years between the end of the Napoleonic wars and the outbreak of World War I, have become increasingly useless. They are completely outdated since the rise of modern totalitarianism and, more specifically, since the Soviet Union, after World War II, became a world power and the stronghold of the "socialist camp" and since the communists conquered the China mainland.

✓We suddenly found that we had no intellectual communication with our communist adversaries. Instead of studying their scriptures and trying to understand the ideological fountainhead of their actions, we shrugged off this motivating force as a facade for political manipulation. We blithely proceeded to think along the lines of old-fashioned diplomacy, power politics, and Christian ethics, ignoring the fact that none of these concepts appeared in the communist dictionary. In short, we continued to analyze world affairs through the medium of our Western minds, and, thereby, more often than not came to wrong conclusions.

We became slaves of emotional oscillations engineered by the masters of the Kremlin. A friendly word from them made us see the world in a rosy glow; a scowl indicating a "tough line" wrapped us in gloom. Had we studied the principles and practices of communism, we would have known that these ups and downs are tactical devices, while the foundations of Marxism–Leninism change little and the ultimate objective of all communist-ruled countries — world victory of communism — not at all. We still pay scant attention to long-range developments, immersing ourselves in current events. Again, if we do any contingency planning, we do it with small regard for the communist psyche because, alas, we have not digested the meaning of the new and unprecedented world environment which Moscow and Peking have created.

It is therefore imperative to take leave of the nineteenth-century pattern of political thinking still all too evident in the West. We have been static long enough; we must determine which of our traditional concepts are obsolescent and replace them with new, dynamic, and practicable ideas. We shall have to formulate our thoughts with the realization that we must contend with a hostile ideology of great propagandistic effect and material strength and keep in step with a runaway technology whose power and meaning are as yet largely unknown quantities. Unlike Marxists, we do not pretend to be able to predict the political things to come. But we can prepare ourselves for change, consider the alternatives, and in so doing modify our traditional view of world politics to fit the requirements of the free world in the decades ahead.

The International State "System" and the Ideological Schism

In modern times, repeated attempts to create supranational organizations for the purpose of maintaining peace and productive cooperation have led first, to the establishment of the League of Nations and later, of the United Nations. The League foundered under the first impact of totalitarian *hybris* which, in the absence of the United States, was not strongly opposed by France and Britain. The success of the United Nations was limited from the outset by the ever clearer distinction between the revolutionary and traditional elements representing the two opposing camps. This fact has thus far prevented the United Nations from becoming the strong stabilizer which would make possible an interacting, cooperative world community.

In times past, lack of communication and geographic, political, or religious barriers effectively isolated certain regions for centuries, for example, the Islamic countries, Japan, and Tibet. During the nineteenth century, most of these barriers fell as improved communications stimulated the exploration of new horizons. In the twentieth century, technology developed too rapidly to permit national governments to adjust their political thinking to the new conditions. The ideological imperialists were far quicker to recognize the enormous advantages offered by the new techniques, but they used them negatively, to hinder rather than foster relations with nations and governments of whose philosophy they disapproved.

Still, even in a divided world, intercourse is maintained between those states whose governments "recognize" each other. Basically, relations among states occur on four levels: political, economic, social, and cultural.

The more friendly peoples feel toward one another and the more interests they share, the more lively and intensive are their exchanges; the more strained their relationship, the less frequent their interaction at official and unofficial levels. But even when official relations are frozen, as in the case of non-recognition or war, instances still occur when communication must be established, if only through the "good offices" of a third, neutral power or a humanitarian institution such as the Red Cross.

As in a community of individuals, in a community of states many types of relationships exist which are affected by variations in national power and the endeavor to balance this power. The objective is to achieve a maximum of political and economic stabilization and thereby minimize the danger of war. There are few lone wolves among the states. Rugged nation-individualism was possible a century ago and, with limitations, perhaps even at the turn of the century; specifically, it could exist in large countries whose natural resources and economic independence permitted autarky and isolation. When our planet began to shrink as distance was overcome and radio waves penetrated everywhere, nations could no longer "go it alone." They were compelled to seek alliances to strengthen their position and protect their interests. None of these associations was formed for perpetuity; conditions changed — and so did treaties. There are relatively few instances in which states maintained a sympathetic attitude toward one another over a long period of history.

For this reason, a bewildering number and variety of alliances have been formed and broken since the nation–state came into its own. Prior to the arrival of revolutionary states on the world political scene, these alliances grew out of common interests not only *for* a cause but also *against* the possible threat to that cause from other powers. Unlike friendship between individuals, political alliances brook no sentiments. It is true that friendly nations are often drawn together by bonds of identical or related cultures or common historic experiences. Such sentiments are likely to enhance political agreements. But on the whole, the organization of alliances is undertaken on purely realistic grounds. So it has happened that alliances — temporary ones, to be sure — have been formed between governments whose political philosophies were diametrically opposed, who basically loathed one another, and whose peoples had little, if any, understanding of each other's culture and way of life.

In past history, bilateral agreements were the most common. They still serve commercial purposes, but no longer suffice to preserve the "balance of power." With the growth of the nation–state and the increase in the number of states, multilateral agreements have become more frequent. Witness the alliance of Prussia, Austria, and England against Napoleon, or the alliance of Germany, Austria, and Italy prior to World War I which was countered by the *entente cordiale* between France, Britain, and Russia. In World War II, the British Commonwealth and France were allied against Nazi Germany, Fascist Italy, and Japan and were later joined by the USA and the USSR. In all these instances, countries with varied or antagonistic points of view were aligned to safeguard their survival as nations against determined and ruthless aggressors. But once these aggressors were disposed of, the alliances became casual or were permitted to lapse altogether. Even the "holy alliance" of nations victorious over Napoleon, which could be cited as an exception, turned out not to be a productive organization, but basically one which used pious verbiage to suppress the growing liberalism engendered by the rise of nationalism. Its greatest merit probably lay in the formulation of rules for diplomacy agreed to by the Congress of Vienna in 1815.

The technological advances of the twentieth century, climaxed by the development of nuclear fission and rocketry, have radically altered previous concepts of international relations. In conjunction with innovations in communications media, these advances have led to accumulation of such enormous power for mutual destruction that "balance" has been replaced by "deterrence." Although limited local and non-nuclear wars have occurred with regrettable frequency, major war no longer is a useful instrument of foreign policy. It cannot lead to victory for one of the contenders and means destruction for all concerned: it is politically senseless. While tragic mistakes and miscalculations can never be ruled out, the possessors of nuclear weapons almost certainly will exercise extreme caution in unchaining them, although they occasionally rattle them to apply psychological pressure. Under such conditions — reflecting neither war nor genuine peace — the contest is fought primarily on ideological, political, economic, and cultural battlegrounds of global proportions, unconfined by territorial borders. This has led to protective alliances among groups of nations which, more or less, share political and social philosophies. As a result there has developed a political bipolarity whereby nations have congregated around the two super-powers, the United States and the Soviet Union. It would be a mistake to assume that the Sino–Soviet conflict or the differences between Washington and Paris have altogether eliminated polarization. The components of each "camp" still are akin in terms of basic concepts and long-range goals. The pluralistic approach to implementation of these goals has not entirely eliminated common beliefs and common hatreds. Besides, Mao Tse-tung will not live forever and neither will Charles de Gaulle. Both are causing disturbing diversities within their respective groups but it is doubtful that these would impair their basic kinships, especially in case of emergency.

It has been said that bipolarity of the fifties has given way to greater diversification in the sixties, not only because of divisive trends inside the two opposing power aggregates but even more because of the increasing number of new and uncommitted states, especially in the Afro–Asian areas. In the competition for the greatest appeal in these states, an indirect or latent increase in power unquestionably has accrued to the new countries due to their tactic of playing one camp against the other, one nation against the other, often succeeding in obtaining aid from both. Nevertheless, it would be a mistake to regard this "neutral zone" as a newly-emerging power constellation, adding a third element to the political tug-of-war. Most of these states have neither political nor constitutional stability, and even India, which has inherited a working administrative apparatus from Britain, suffers from economic hardship and chronic social chaos. The countries of Black Africa have not yet become genuine nation–states. Most of the North African, Near and Middle Eastern states are so consumed by the flames of raging nationalism and hatred of Israel as to neglect their socio-economic stabilization. They are political adolescents.

There is no indication that, apart from India, any power or combination of powers could amount to more than a pawn in the struggle between the giants. Many of these crosscurrents become evident in the United Nations, where the divergencies of the contesting and neutral groups come to grips but cannot be reconciled until the struggle between tradition and revolution is resolved. No international police can cope with the basic malaise of the ideological struggle.

It may be true that the international political processes still aim to promote national interests and to settle resultant international differences. Nevertheless, since Eastern and Western concepts of the meaning of national interests differ because of the ideological schism, these problems can no longer be resolved by means of traditional diplomacy. Negotiations between "bourgeois" statesmen and revolutionary leaders have proved to be of little value. The latter's employment of various types of pressure and deception is prevalent in combination with "indirect aggression" (subversion), ideological struggle, economic "competition" and penetration, massive propaganda, and the continuous armaments race.

In a world where brute force is too risky an instrument for obtaining desired goals, the crucial problem, more than ever before, is the approach taken by one government toward another, the line of reasoning for measures taken, and the long-range philosophy behind attitudes, intentions, and planning. In other words: foreign policy. It is necessary to dedicate some space to this phenomenon on whose quality and implementation depends the fate of the world.

Foreign Affairs in a Divided World

Foreign Policy

Since the emergence of the ideological empires, foreign policy has two aspects. Traditionally, a nation's foreign policy determines its course of action vis-à-vis other nations. In the non-communist world, it remains a program designed to achieve – by peaceful or any other means short of war – the best possible position and security for a nation. This program reflects the political, economic, and social philosophy of the country and seeks to translate it into principles and attitudes which will, it is hoped, produce those national aspirations the policy strives to achieve and maintain.

War was once an indication of political failure, unless it was used to attain objectives which could be achieved in no other way. Hitler's aggression is the best modern example of such a policy. For pre-nuclear, totalitarian powers, war was indeed, as Clausewitz wrote, a continuation of policy by other means. They purposely sustained a martial spirit among their peoples, and their well-prepared offensive strategy brought them extraordinary initial successes. In the democracies, war was and is considered not an end in itself but rather an unavoidable defense measure against encroachment on vital interests. Democratic foreign offices are fundamentally departments of peace. Only if they fail to preserve the peace do the departments of war take over.

Thus, it could be said that traditionally the prime objectives of foreign policy are to maintain external peace and further internal prosperity. More specifically, the fundamental policy goals of every sovereign nation are to preserve territorial integrity and political independence, and to maintain or improve the population's standard of living. These are, of course, the rock-bottom requirements essential

13

for the continuation of national life. As such, they are premises rather than objectives. Over and beyond these requirements, national foreign policy formulates and tries to achieve its aims in accordance with historic aspirations, socio-political and economic philosophy, and physical conditions.

A workable foreign policy is never static. Therefore, to base a policy on a *status quo* is an illusion which leads only to disappointment, if not disaster. A nation is born, lives through adolescence, becomes mature, and may die unless it seeks rejuvenation. Standstill, "disengagement" from political developments, or isolation are deadly diseases for any nation.

Every traditional sovereign nation has minimum objectives, but aims at a maximum of security and prosperity. Between these extremes, its policy must maneuver. If flexible and non-dogmatic, it may develop alternative solutions while remaining within the framework of its national philosophy. If rigidly conceived, its adjustments to world conditions remain tactical only and contribute nothing to the maintenance of peace. But whatever the aims and means of a foreign policy, they are, of necessity, limited by a nation's power and power reserve. The estimate of such power must be based on relative rather than absolute values, taking into account the actual and potential power of other nations. Without a realistic comparison of its own resources with those of other countries, a nation cannot reach an objective estimate of its own strength.

The era of the modern nation–state was marked by the struggle for power. Power for what? For the satisfaction of power itself? For the wealth that accompanies power? For the political and economic influence power can produce? A definitive answer is impossible. All or most of these elements probably were involved. But one significant attribute of national power politics stands out: the natural limitation of its objectives. Nations tried to accumulate more wealth and territory (contiguous or colonial) and to expand their spheres of economic interest without serious competitive interference. They neither planned to conquer the globe nor attempted to subject other peoples to ideologies that were foreign and unacceptable to them. While they may have believed in their superiority, they did not proclaim their political creed to be the only one capable of providing a panacea for suffering humanity. They rarely used inhuman methods to "persuade" subject peoples of the validity of their doctrine.

Yet, it is exactly this approach to international thinking that the totalitarian, ideological states have cast aside since World War I. After World War II, when the rightist "isms" were liquidated and the leftist ones had acquired tremendous influence, the concept of power changed because its motivation was different. Power was no longer an end in itself, but an instrument by which to achieve ideological pre-eminence that could facilitate political, economic, and/or military victory. It is logical that under the impact of these trends relations between revolutionary and traditional powers have changed, both in form and content. *For the ultimate policy objectives of the ideological states are unlimited.* At a time when that bugaboo of the communists, "capitalist imperialism," no longer really exists, the ideological imperialism of the "socialist camp" seeks world conquest. Therefore, the foreign policy of its members is essentially international rather than national. We must examine why.

Ever since the publication of Marx' and Engels' *Communist Manifesto* in 1848, communist doctrine has always emphasized its international validity. Communism is a state of political and economic affairs that cannot come to full fruition unless it conquers the globe. The concept of revolution is local only in the beginning; its final aim is world revolution. This is conceived as a chain reaction, stemming from the more or less rapid disintegration of capitalist countries (stimulated by native communist subversion) and further enhanced by outside communist-inspired maneuvers, not necessarily military in character. Once capitalist governments are on the verge of disintegration, a *coup de grâce* can be delivered without undue risk, leaving the field free for a take-over. Khrushchevism, more aware of the meaning of nuclear power and afraid that a *coup de grâce* might trigger destructive retaliation, proclaimed that the inevitable demise of capitalism's last stage, imperialism, renders military action unnecessary. Peaceful competition will demonstrate the superiority of Marxism–Leninism, and by emulating the "socialist" countries, imperialism will disintegrate without battle.

Both the doctrinal factors and the political organization of communist party rule must of necessity lead to a foreign policy concept totally different from that of non-revolutionary governments. It is not foreign policy in its traditional sense, but a combination of schemes and stratagems, conceived for the sole purpose of carrying out eventual world revolution. Traditional amenities are employed merely for the sake of appearances. The customs of diplomacy may be followed outwardly, but the pattern is set and the aims determined. The communists regard retreats and concessions as temporary. They adhere to agreements only so long as they serve communist objectives. The nature of basic Marxist–Leninist principles, anchored in the concept of a dialectical materialism, has produced a view of international relations which is determined by revolutionary views of state and society and, therefore, remains rigid so long as these views prevail. Flexibility is tactical, even strategic when necessary, but it does not detract from the fundamentals, a fact which renders negotiations with the communists virtually hopeless unless the interests of the negotiators happen to coincide — for whatever reasons. Yet they are essential, not so much because world opinion demands them, but, because personal contacts on the conference table may prevent holocaust. Besides, one must never close the door on the hope for future changes.

It may be objected that pluralism in the "socialist camp" (which was pioneered by Yugoslavia's break with the Cominform in 1948, became polycentric communism after Khrushchev's denigration of Stalin at the Twentieth Congress of the CPSU and has received considerable stimulation by the Sino–Soviet conflict since 1960) has led to an erosion of the principles which characterize the Marxist–Leninist secular religion. Indeed, Tito's example of "national" communism and the improved chances of Eastern European states to move from satellite status to eventual sovereignty have brought about organizational changes in what used to be a relatively monolithic communism. The question, thus, is whether the end of the monolith should be considered as the end of international communism.

There are now different types of communism which are determined not only by national backgrounds but also by the power a communist state has at its disposal. It is a truism to propose that the extent of such power decides the extent of the ideological influence. There are two communist giants in the world: the Soviet Union, a super power, and Red China, a potentially great power. Both are ruled by communist parties, different as their interpretation of Marxism–Leninism may be. Without these states, especially the USSR, world communism would lose its significance. Therefore, it is important to keep in mind that a strong Soviet Union and a Communist China growing in strength remain the predominant factors in contemporary international relations. Whether or not individual states in Eastern Europe or Asia demand and obtain more sovereignty, whether or not they manifest rising nationalism is not as significant as the position taken by Moscow or Peking vis-à-vis non-communist foreign policy. Although communist pluralism appears to lessen the danger of a unitary world-wide communism, it does not remove the hazards to Western policy makers of dealing with opponents whose views are radically different.

The nature and scope of foreign policy in the newly-independent countries will differ, to some extent, from that of the conventional West and even more from the Marxist–Leninist position of the communist states. Having emerged from either semi-independent or outright colonial status and being determined to preserve their freedom of action, they now grope for policies which will enable them to steer clear of the Scylla and Charybdis of the East–West confrontation, although their sympathies are often directed toward one of the two sides.

Driven by highly emotional and often immature nationalism and the obsession to play an important role in international affairs, they are torn between Western concepts of government, with which many of them were imbued, and aversion to the former master who set them free. Ignoring their debt to Western teachers and disregarding the dangers to their precious independence from communist encroachments, some of these states are flirting with the East because it flatters their nationalist ego and offers them economic and military aid, ostensibly with no strings attached. Biased in their political analyses and suspicious of Western "neo-colonialism," they seek to gain advantages from both sides, hoping to remain outside the fracas and steer clear of the issues at stake. Apart from a few African areas such as Congo–Brazzaville, Mali, or Zanzibar and some of the Arab states which quite openly sympathize with communist states, most third world countries seem to have adopted the policy to seek help from both sides but remain politically apart from either.

The contest between political philosophies is harsher today than it was when distances were so great and communications so slow as to render accommodation and isolation easy. The division of the world into groups with irreconcilable beliefs and the remoteness of genuine compromise exacerbate the problems of the free world statesman, whose "opposite number" is permitted by his government's ideological position to function as no more than a mouthpiece for the ruling party and who cannot contribute creative thoughts toward lasting peace. Moscow's concept of "peaceful coexistence" is strictly opportunistic: it presupposes continuation of the ideological and economic struggle by any means short of open warfare. For communists, genuine peace presupposes the liquidation of bourgeois and imperialist nation–states and the investiture of communist world rule. Until these conditions prevail, "peace" is no more than a temporary accommodation between two social systems.

Thus, despite attempts at détente and a greater measure of autonomy for former satellites as well as for communist parties outside the orbit, there continues to exist an ideological stalemate that is hardened by nuclear deterrence. The great powers are aware that a general war would cause sufficient destruction on both sides to render it unprofitable; military victory has become an empty phrase. This is predicated on the continuation of approximate equality in nuclear potential and facilities for delivering weapons, and the assumption that no new technological developments on either side will arise to upset the delicate balance. In terms of foreign policy, these conditions have created a set of circumstances without precedent in human history.

Such are the conditions which determine the relations of nations and blocs in a divided world, which have produced a state of permanent crisis. They force the Western statesman to abandon the thought pattern in which he was reared and which has become obsolete. They confront him with a situation in which he must cope not only with elements measurable in accurate and even scientific terms, but also with imponderables of an ideological and psychological nature which introduce areas of uncertainty.

Psychopathology in International Relations

Relations between nations are maintained by governments. Governments consist of individual human beings; nations are composed of individuals. Consequently, the organization of foreign affairs, the philosophies which guide inter-state relations, the policies which determine the character of world conditions, and the mode of implementing such policies — all are devised by human minds. The machinery of government may seem unfeeling, and the course of history as relentless as that of a Greek tragedy; nevertheless, world politics is man's creation and man is an imperfect animal. Of the many reasons for his shortcomings the most important is rooted in his psychopathological tendencies but, strangely enough, few concerted attempts have ever been made to relate this aspect of psychology to international relations. Those pioneering works which do exist are mainly specialized studies on personality and character; more emphasis appears to have been given to research in the field of behavioral sciences. However, the application of this research to the international scene is scant, dealing as it does with statistics and public opinion reactions, with little systematic assessment of findings in terms of world politics.[1]

The psychopathology of international relations requires an interdisciplinary approach to research. It must borrow from medicine and psychiatry and from the social, political, and behavioral sciences; it must embrace anthropology and genetics as well as human relations and public opinion; it can neglect neither economics nor such sciences as biology and climatology. This may sound complicated and costly, but the significance of psychological factors in world politics is so great and the need for their understanding by statesmen so long neglected that further indifference to this field may have appalling consequences. For, since war is no longer the traditional instrument of foreign policy, the conduct of international diplomacy in a divided

---

[1] Cf. H. D. Lasswell, *Psychopathology and Politics* (New York: The Viking Press, 1960; first published in 1930). Lasswell's pioneering work presents vivid case studies, but all of them have to do primarily with domestic, not international, affairs.

world requires far greater insight than ever before into the psychological motivation of opposing statesmen and leaders.

Within the scope of this study it would be impossible to suggest practical approaches for developing psychopathology of international relations as an integral science. One can only indicate the major problems which arise from the psychological makeup of individuals and people of one nation in their dealings with individuals and peoples of other nations.

In bringing such problems into focus, we must distinguish between individual and mass. True, the latter consists of individuals, but remains amorphous, just as its faces are indistinguishable. It cannot act with considered judgment. It can only follow trends and, in so doing, hypnotize or compel unwilling individuals to go along. The individual may be influenced by the mass but, once lifted out of the mass, can also influence it. Although a component of the mass, he has a personality of his own. His psychological background is specific; that of the mass is mixed. The fact that an interrelationship exists between him and the mass must not lead us to conclude that the nation's leaders and its people can be measured with the same psychological yardstick.[2]

The old adage that man is wholly the product of his environment no longer finds full acceptance in either Western or Eastern science. In the earlier days of Soviet Marxism, scientists leaned heavily on the Pavlovian theory of conditioned reflexes, which developed into the generalized thesis that environment in itself decisively shapes human personality. Somewhat later, Lysenko's genetic theories tended to confirm Pavlovianism in the eyes of the communists. (Pavlov, a world-famous scientist long before the revolution, received the Nobel Prize for medicine in 1904. Lysenko, Stalin's protégé, developed the ideas of the horticulturist Michurin; his temporary eclipse, following Stalin's denigration, appears to have ended.) It is easy to understand the appeal these theories had for the followers of Marx and Lenin:

[2] Cf. R. K. White, "Images in the Context of International Conflict: Soviet Perceptions of the U.S. and the U.S.S.R.," in H. C. Kelman (ed.), *International Behavior: A Social-Psychological Analysis* (New York: Holt, Rinehart, and Winston, 1965).

the creation of the New Communist Man depends on a proper conditioning and training system.

Post–Stalinist Soviet science went further. From Stalin's blunt and naive image of creating obedient servants of communism through coercive conditioning and environment *per se,* Soviet politicians and scientists progressed to an increasingly sophisticated examination of individual and group and the relationship between the individual and his environment. This required the reinstitution of such outlawed sciences as psychology and sociology. It also meant an inter-disciplinary approach toward solving the problem of how to create entirely new trains of thinking and reacting by establishing new culture patterns. If the Soviet scientists succeed in modeling new generations on the basis of genetic and cultural changes, they will have set a precedent for an extremely dangerous procedure and may be able to erase from the minds of future generations even some psychological and cultural characteristics which today are still deeply rooted and displace hereditary predispositions from these generations despite the possibility of increased contacts with the West. Should such be the case, those psychological and intellectual links between East and West which do exist would be further distorted and the fragile basis of mutual understanding gradually eliminated.[3]

Western science has never denied the importance of environment, but believes that it is only one of the factors shaping man's mind. We consider man to be, in large part, the product of his genetic past, and judge his personality by taking into account his ancestral traits, both physiological and psychological. Physiologically, we observe his body type, glandular system, nervous constitution, and overall stamina. Psychologically, we probe into his earliest childhood to determine the effects of parental influence and other human relations on the formation of his conscious and unconscious mind. We analyze his personality not only by itself, but also take into account what we know of his antecedents and psychosomatic status. By knowing his background and the circumstances which fashioned his personality, we can understand him better. A variety of clues enables

[3] Cf. H. Cantrill, *Soviet Leaders and Mastery Over Man* (New Brunswick, N. J.: Rutgers University Press, 1960).

us to evaluate him objectively. The aim is not to mold him into a type desired by others but to free him to grow in ways that are natural to him as an individual. We have no intention of making a "new man" out of him, only a healthy one.

Leaders responsible for the conduct of foreign affairs are not supermen. They are subject to the laws of human heredity and environment. They have reached their exalted position by dint of talent, work, political connections, sheer accident, or some combination of these. And yet, ordinary mortals though they be, they hold in their hands the fate of millions, by indirection perhaps billions, of people. Aside from the fact that the most important decisions concerning the fate of the world are made by fewer men in dictatorships than in democracies, the vital and final word is almost invariably given by one man, usually on the counsel of or with the support of a few close advisers. The personal character of these men determines, more often than not, the form and content of a decision.

Do leaders necessarily act as representatives of the national community which produced them? The answer to this question must be qualified in terms of bipolar divergencies. In general, nationalism is an ever-present influence in the lives of non-communist statesmen. Under communism, the leveling process of the Marxist–Leninist ideology purposely seeks to establish a common denominator among the nations of the "socialist commonwealth" which the communist leaders hope will eventually become an association of nationalities rather than an alliance of nation–states. These leaders may represent their countries, but even more they are spokesmen for the communist orbit. Nationalist traits may still be present in the leaders of the generations that made the revolution; the new generations are more familiar with proletarian internationalism than with nationalism in the Western sense.

Nevertheless, in countries both East and West, leaders are imbued with the traditional prejudices and stereotypes of their homeland, whether the reason be nationalism, ethnic culture, or political ideology. All were exposed for a long period of time to psychological influences which sperm the formation and retention of prejudices. As a result, they may be inclined to accept at face value "derogatory information" about other countries while taking for granted the superiority of their own.[4] The nature of this "information" almost invariably leads to generalization, for example: "the British are perfidious and a nation of shopkeepers;" "Americans have no culture and are materialistic;" "the French know best how to make love;" "the Russians are cruel and backward."[5] Only the intellectually mature remain free of such clichés even though they may be sufficiently Machiavellian to utilize popular prejudices to political advantage. Stereotyped prejudices insert emotional issues into international controversies, a fact which often has been used to stir up hatred of one country for another; the Machiavellians, past and present, may well fear that if people understood each other, their governments would be hard put to force them to shoot one another.

Apart from being the product of national (ethnic) upbringing, most political leaders cannot rid themselves of the psychological ballast of early impressions which generate insecurity or hostility contributing to the "major determinant(s) of prejudices."[6] We know that insecurity, fear, hostility, unjust treatment, or inflexible education "contribute to our emotionality."[7] Probably no member of past and present generations has remained entirely free of such traumatic experiences. Much depends upon the strength and frequency of these experiences, and whether or not the opportunity arises later in life to sublimate them, to become intellectually and emotionally aware of them, or, should they grow to bothersome proportions, to psychoanalyze them away. Unremedied traumatic experiences may produce rigidity of character. In choosing a leader or reacting to a superimposed one, people are inclined to interpret such rigidity as strength of character, unaware that inflexibility, far from being synonymous with strength, often indicates a tendency toward authoritarianism, if not self-deification.[8] Such leaders refuse counsel, admit no mistakes

---

[4] Cf. W. Buchanan and H. Cantril, *How Nations See Each Other* (New York: Harper and Brothers, 1953), p. 111. See also *passim* G. W. Allport, *The Nature of Prejudice* (Cambridge, Mass.: Addison–Wesley, 1954).

[5] Buchanan and Cantril, *ibid.*, Chapter 5, "National Stereotypes."

[6] G. Saenger, *The Social Psychology of Prejudice* (New York: Harper and Brothers, 1957), p. 111. See also G. W. Allport, *ibid.*

[7] Saenger, *ibid.*, p. 71.

[8] Cf. T. W. Adorno and others, *The Authoritarian Personality* (New York: Harper and Brothers, 1950).

(and therefore correct none), and remain generally intractable. Without overgeneralizing, one might also say that pathologically rigid personalities are rarely intellectual creators, nor are they particularly original thinkers. Whatever new ideas they propound are seldom their own. Nevertheless, history proves that such personalities were all too often given popular preference. It is scarcely an exaggeration to submit this as one of the main reasons for the unending series of wars or warlike situations, and for the political servitude into which peoples were forced or sold themselves because of illusory promises and visions.

In contrast to the compulsive personality whose mind had no opportunity — or refused — to grow toward greater flexibility and realism stands the rare individual with a comparatively mature mind. Either he was lucky enough to have been saved from the environmental factors making for authoritarian rigidity or he succeeded, through his own volition and strength, in overcoming them. He is one of the few who has conquered himself and perhaps one of the even fewer who knows himself. He is not a conformist in the sense that he necessarily subscribes to current fads and fashions. He has the courage to disagree with the majority. He is not necessarily popular; his non-conformity makes him suspect. A man of considerable intellectual achievement and free from stereotyped prejudices will encounter difficulties in running for elective office. For the intellectual and emotional level of the mass is determined by a common denominator; the mature-minded leader is above and ahead of it, and his chances for finding a common platform are slim. Political genius is perhaps rarer even than artistic genius; concentration on one art is circumscribed by its particular medium and demands neither the universal knowledge nor the versatility expected in the charismatic leader of men.

The consumption of statesmen is one of high rate but relatively few of those utilized are individuals of depth and understanding. One should perhaps be grateful that there is no prevalence of obsessed and over-ambitious authoritarians, but one can never be certain whether they will develop into evil or benevolent tyrants. The majority of leaders probably balance in the middle of the scale. Their personalities are neither as good nor as bad as those of the protagonists of extremism. Since they resemble more the "ordinary" people, their attachment to the mass is usually stronger and it follows them more easily. Without belittling their merits, one might conclude that the world today is governed by average individuals, many of whom are psychologically impeded and intellectually mediocre. There are exceptions on both sides of the scale, of course, but when it comes to quality in statesmen, the exceptional should be the rule.

At this stage, it is again necessary to differentiate between leader personalities of communist and non-communist background. Communist ideology and upbringing have greatly influenced the character and minds of dedicated leaders. These aspects of the psychopathology of international relations have unquestionably added a new dimension to psychology and the study of human personality. The nearest example approximating the fanaticism of convinced communists is perhaps that of the medieval church or of Islam. Both religions were militant, *de facto* or *de jure*. Both penetrated the minds of men to the extent of becoming a way of life and conduct. Both were ever present so as to determine all action and reasoning. Both were highly organized and superseded regionalism. Both developed a hierarchy, whether the seat of power was the church proper or was delegated to the temporal rulers who served also as religious leaders. Communism, being a secular religion, contains all these characteristics and magnifies them: its "clergy" rules the state and has absolute power to proclaim, interpret, and implement the dogma. These factors, spiritual and temporal, substantive and organizational, have in the past produced dedicated and fanatical leaders just as they do today.

Convinced communists cannot be measured with traditional psychological yardsticks. The old leaders who made the revolution and whose aggressive hostility can be couched in familiar psychological terms are dying out. Their successors are the products of revolutionary education which in depth, intensity, and consistency heavily outweighs possible adverse influences on the part of old, unreconstructed family members. The generations that follow may be even further removed from pre-revolutionary thinking and fall gradually into the "scientifically" determined pattern of the New Communist Man. Since communism, according to neo-Leninist concepts, cannot be achieved without a change, both in the nature of man and in his environment, systematic attempts are being made to train the new generations in a specifically developed type of formal — principally utilitarian — education, part of which is mental discipline (dialectics) and adjustment to communist society. This technique of conditioning has been developed for some time by social and natural scientists. It begins at birth; it never ends. The Soviet educational theses, proclaimed in conjunction with the Seven Year Plan at the Twenty-first Congress of the CPSU, demonstrate at least some aspects of the Kremlin's ambitious plan to prepare the people for the "transition to communism."

The effect of this training on international relations, unless qualified and mellowed through outside influences, may be catastrophic from the Western point of view. Although it remains to be seen how successful will be the communist efforts to remake men in their image, even a degree of success would tend to widen the abyss between traditional and communist man. This conceptual schism may become too deep for sensible communications, especially if traditional man does not prepare himself, psychologically and ideologically, to face his antagonist in an advantageous position. How can he do that?

He must no longer be satisfied to study power relationship as such. He will have no choice but to delve first into the ideological premises for the new society which is in the making. Then he will have to learn to derive psychological conclusions from the ideological findings. But in order to comprehend the psychic makeup of his opponent, he must first become better acquainted with his own psyche. Finally, he must face the fact that a new civilization is developing and, repulsive though it may be, he must analyze it objectively and then propose such adjustments as appear imperative in order to save his own civilization. The foreign offices of the future will need information and guidance from interdisciplinary staffs which can supply policymakers with advice they cannot possibly obtain from routine intelligence. Indeed, the world is divided not only ideologically and politically; a psychological dichotomy is evolving also. This fact may become the greatest obstacle to political accommodation, greater even than ideology, since the latter can be adjusted if need be, while psychological dispositions, once firmly acquired, cannot. Under these circumstances, the study of psychopathology of international relations becomes a matter of Western security.

We have thus far discussed the psychological aspects of individuals who direct the course of foreign affairs. We must now examine some psychopathological traits of the mass that is being led and with which the leaders have certain direct or indirect reciprocal relations. The mass consists of elements encompassing many intellectual and cultural levels. But the greatest impact made by the mass on the leaders and their policies is not derived from its superior levels.

With these qualifications in mind, it must be stated that mass reactions generally are characterized by stereotypes and prejudices originating from both ignorance and distortion of facts. Pertinent literature on social psychology offers clear evidence to this effect. Since a goodly number of individuals who form the mass are intelligent beings, the question arises why mass actions more often than not are irresponsible, particularly when they are spontaneous.

In part, the answer is that emotions are contagious among people living in the same communities or within the same countries. Danger of contagion outside these boundaries among people with similar interests is enhanced through modern means of mass communication. These emotions usually are elementary: "Fear, anger, hatred, enthusiastic acclamation may . . . spread with terrific speed and ever-increasing intensity."[9] The danger is aggravated by the fact that these emotions are uncritical, and therefore unreasonable. The individual can always stop, look, and listen; the crowd cannot, and, as a consequence, is unable to control its emotions. "Hence the notorious fickleness and irrationality of mobs."[10] The psychologist would link the mass to manifestations of an infantile unconscious mind. In this mind is the need for an all-knowing, all-powerful father, be he adored or hated. Only in these terms can the peculiar attitude of the mass toward a leader be explained; he symbolizes the protector who must be protected "presumably because of his being vital to one's own

---

[9] G. W. Kisker (ed.), *World Tensions: The Psychopathology of International Relations* (New York: Prentice-Hall Inc., 1951), p. 53.
[10] *Ibid.*

safety or existence";[11] but against him there also may arise the wrath which manifests a child's dread or hatred of the father. The mass may feel lost and endangered without a father-leader, regardless of whether he is a dictator or a democratically elected official.

Superimposed on such basic psychopathological reflections are the hard facts of political and ideological realities, as well as the differences between the psychological makeup of communism and that of democracy. As psycho-ideological indoctrination and education become more firmly ingrained in the brains of the new communist generations, these differences will be more pronounced. The psychological reasons for this are the varying degrees of security and insecurity of peoples under free and tyrannical systems.

Insecurity of non-communist masses may develop from lack of confidence in the government; doubt about job continuity persisting in a fluctuating economy; and the tensions caused by competitive struggle for social and financial status. In order to compensate for the lack of mental security, people strive overwhelmingly for the very conformity they would loudly condemn were it enforced under totalitarian rule; they tend to join "respectable" groups and become "organization men,"[12] acquiring all the prejudices and clichés these groups promote. They willingly sacrifice many freedoms for the security of the welfare state.

A comparison with the communist mass reveals that its insecurity exists for different reasons. Under Marxism–Leninism, conformism is a must; jobs, as a rule, are readily available, even compulsory. But the manipulations of police-state organs create fear; the alleged warmongering of the "imperialists" seems ominous; and improving one's lot requires great effort and dexterity of maneuvering which are not every man's talent. Joining organizations is compulsory or necessary for career advancement; human relationship is beclouded by distrust which penetrates even the seclusion of family circles. However, the progress of psychological and economic stability and consolidation of the bloc's power have reduced the use of tension by fear so char-

[11] *Ibid.*, p. 55.
[12] See W. H. Whyte's fascinating and depressing study, *The Organization Man* (New York: Simon and Schuster, 1956).

acteristic of communist rule until the death of Stalin. Much more emphasis is now given to positive motivation for the achievement of such objectives as "overtaking America." Nevertheless, the communist masses, particularly in Red China, will continue to be kept on edge, although the psychological climate has changed the character of tension and will change it even further until the education of the New Communist Man is achieved. It is barely possible that the outcome may be a greater degree of security for peoples under communist rule, thereby putting non-communist peoples at a disadvantage.

Under both parliamentary and dictatorial systems, responsible individualism seems to be vanishing. The result is an increasing trend toward collective organization. A collectivized mass is easier to handle when it is either well controlled or sides with its leadership, but it can be highly destructive if neither contingency prevails. Realizing this, the democratic leaders take precautions against the danger; they know how to prevent it and have the means to act. Non-communist leaders have no such recourse; they must try to keep the mass in line by catering to its desires or by persuading it to endorse their policies. In either instance, the influence of the mass on international relations is seldom salutary.

The major differentiation between the Eastern and the Western masses is the fundamental cleavage in interpretation of the concept of liberty. In the free world, peoples still have an instinctively strong feeling for the blessings of freedom, which have been distorted or repressed into oblivion under the totalitarian dictatorships. But the concept of liberty is inseparable from that type of individualism which accepts the hazards of fending for itself so as to retain the gift of freedom of decision. As responsible individualism diminishes, the concept of liberty becomes impaired. It is liable to degenerate in misuse; the freedom to behave as one pleases regardless of the effect on society is psychologically infantile and, therefore, destructive. Were Western man to forget this, the differences between him and Eastern man would be small indeed.

The Western concept of liberty, ideologically inseparable from responsible individualism, was little known in either Russia or China prior to the revolutions. It was stronger, though often underground, in such countries as Poland, Czechoslovakia, and Hungary. The communist rulers had relatively little trouble imposing a totalitarian regime upon peoples whose main concern was such necessities of life as food and shelter. Patrick Henry's outcry "Give me liberty or give me death" was far from their minds; all they wanted was to be left free to eke out a living for themselves and their families. Moreover, the ideological preachings of the revolutionary regimes promised them eventual paradise in return for long, hard work. Whether or not they really believed in this vision, it provided them with the hope which is vitally necessary to man.

The sum total of these psychological sketches demonstrates that the conduct of foreign affairs is full of intangible hazards because the "adult unconscious . . . reacts with anxiety to its own aggressive impulses. This reaction has many fateful consequences."[13] We know that anxiety originates from within and may stay hidden, even from the conscious mind of the anxious individual, due to built-in defenses against revealing it. Such anxiety may be increased by "aggressive impulses of rulers," and "when they lead to great anxiety, aggression is often further increased; aggression is then both the cause and the effect of the anxiety."[14] Anxiety often is exacerbated by a guilt complex which may build up in the unconscious mind and further complicate the nature of the individual, making him untrustworthy and impossible to deal with. These ills of the leaders are apt to be present in the components of the mass.

Perhaps statesmen should undergo a short, but intensive, period of specialized psychoanalysis before taking office for the purpose of understanding not only the political but also the psychological factors of international relations. They would also benefit by more knowledge of social psychology. This may seem to be an exaggerated proposal in an era when not even the philosophical basis for the opponent's policies, the ideologies, are properly studied and when, at least in the West, antiquated concepts of power diplomacy continue to affect political thinking. It is, of course, an impossible demand for communists, who do not recognize objective psychopathology and,

13 G. W. Kisker (ed.), *World Tensions: The Psychopathology of International Relations* (New York: Prentice-Hall Inc., 1951), p. 68.
14 *Ibid.*

in general, remain hostile to psychoanalysis since it does not fit into their doctrinal world conception.

The effect of psychic illness on the body and that of physical sickness on the mind is part of this problem. It has become an accepted axiom that the "psychological factors influencing physiological processes must be subjected to the same detailed and careful scrutiny as is customary in the study of physiological processes . . ." and that "psychological processes are fundamentally not different from other processes which take place in the organism."[15] Although physicians have developed a tendency to ascribe physical symptoms somewhat too easily to psychological causes if no other satisfactory diagnosis can be made, the close relationship between mind and body had been already recognized in antiquity. The physical health of a statesman is therefore as important a factor in international affairs as his mental health. But then, even the best of rulers is subject to afflictions — he may begin his term of office healthy but become ill, with the result that his judgment and stamina suffer to the detriment of his country's foreign relations; he may die an untimely death when he is needed most; or he may develop psychological deficiencies which becloud his motives and endanger his country's position in the world. No remedy exists for the prevention of these contingencies, except that communist regimes are far more ruthless in discarding men whose usefulness appears to have come to an end.

Thus, the peoples of the world probably will continue to be exposed to leaders whose psychological (and/or physiological) makeup should preclude their being in power; only rarely will they find themselves lucky enough to be governed by mature, benevolent, and healthy statesmen.

[15] F. Alexander, *Psychosomatic Medicine* (New York: W. W. Norton, 1950), pp. 11–12.

···· 3 ··

The Ingredients of Power in the Nuclear Age

Metamorphoses of National Power

In the past, the strength or weakness of a country's position in the world depended on its size and location, military and economic topography, climate, transportation and communication facilities, manpower, industrial assets, and natural wealth. In the twentieth century, technological developments, in conjunction with ideological crusades, have inserted new elements into international relations. The arrival of the nuclear age added to this change in values, in fact, made impossible the application of conventional estimates to existing and potential power of the leading nations.

Since ours is a period of transition in which the political mind must endeavor to adjust to scientific progress, some traditional elements of power still require attention. But they are suffused with new ingredients which either qualify former positions by downgrading them or rule out their pertinence altogether. In determining how these largely unprecedented phenomena displace traditional values, we are compelled to pioneer. In so doing, we must explore beyond the facts. For we can no longer measure power in visible terms only. We must weigh intangibles against appearances. We dare not fail to consider the tendency toward polarization; on the other hand, we must remain aware of the progressing eclipse of the nation–state system in favor of multi-national aggregates which are dedicated either to Western ethics, communist ideology, or other as yet unforeseeable faiths.

• PHYSICAL GEOGRAPHY – To begin with the most obvious of the traditional indicators of national power, physical geography, we can admit that even in the nuclear age a large territory is the *conditio sine qua non* of any country aspiring to great power. Largeness presupposes the existence of a vast manpower pool, natural wealth, and space for protective decentralization. But size in itself is not a symbol of power unless harnessed and organized. Vast lands such as pre-revolutionary China and the Ottoman Empire were not considered great powers. In both countries, weaknesses in political, social, and economic organization prevented the marshaling of potential strength. In contrast, middle and western European nations, smaller by far than the United States or the Soviet Union, were able so to increase their natural resources and develop industrial and military efficiency as to become world powers. The fact that they no longer are first-rank powers may be ascribed to technological changes and the emergence of the super-powers. In this sense, nations which possess sufficient square mileage and natural resources to sustain an advanced and balanced economy, in combination with a population both politically loyal and technically skilled, are influential beyond their areas.

Time was when a country's topography played an important role in the strategic estimates of governments. However, with technical improvements in communications, topographical impediments have lost some of their former significance. For a while, such factors as mountains and forests, deserts and swamps, accessibility to sea lanes, road nets, and strategic location of industry and agricultural centers will retain importance in times of peace or local conflict. But in the event of a general conflagration, even super-powers are vulnerable to missile attack or the effects of radioactive fallout, no matter how vast their territory and how impregnable their terrain.

The nature of its frontiers has traditionally conditioned a country's political position and attitudes. From time immemorial, easy access has seduced aggressors to embark on expansionist ventures. The central European plains are a classical example. This does not mean that natural obstacles have prevented attackers from trying to overcome all roadblocks; in ancient times, Hannibal crossed the Alps against enormous odds and succeeded in reaching the northern Italian plain. But, to some extent, natural obstacles caused aggressors to think twice and frequently persuaded them to forego their dreams of conquest.

Yet, in an age of jets, missiles, atomic submarines, nuclear developments, and space exploration, all these considerations lose much of
their former importance and are no longer necessarily decisive strategic factors. To be sure, in the period of transition — or rather of the
human brain's adaptation to hitherto unknown conditions — there
may be such exceptions as the vast reaches east of the Ural Mountains or the Mongolian deserts between the USSR and Communist
China. Similarly the Soviet frontier, the longest national borderline
in the world, lacks access to the major oceans.

The combination of size and difficult terrain has produced one
undeniable advantage: the possibility of strategic dispersal. Moscow
and Peking have organized a program of large industrial decentralization — in contrast to the heavy concentration of accessible American
and European industries — which impedes both the selection of vital
targets and the delivery of weapons.

The Western Hemisphere is separated from the Orient and the
Occident by two great oceans; theoretically, it is shielded by the
Arctic in the north and the Antarctic in the south. This is advantageous in conventional terms, but is not proof against jets or rockets.
Thus, the United States is accessible to long-range aircraft and vulnerable to missile attack as are its European and Asian allies. So far as
the great centers are concerned, the same pertains to the Sino–Soviet
bloc. It follows that no natural barrier, however inaccessible, constitutes an impregnable frontier. Whatever impediment it presents
to a would-be aggressor will be overcome within a few decades. From
a strategic point of view, the world is about to become an "open
society."

• POLITICAL GEOGRAPHY — A nation's territorial location determines
its geopolitical relationship with other nations. It will be necessary to
examine the nature and meaning of geopolitics, or, as some scholars
prefer to call it, political geography. But political geography is static
and merely defines relations between nations in terms of geography.
It assumes stable boundaries and describes present conditions without
contemplating future developments which may perforce alter the
map. Geopolitics is a dynamic exploration of space as the base of

political power, not merely at present, but especially in the future.[1]

It is not true that the German professor Karl Haushofer "invented" the science of geopolitics. Geopolitical thought was developed during the nineteenth century by British, German, and Swedish geographers. Haushofer was an eclectic who neither coined the term geopolitics nor created the science it describes. He, himself, never pretended to be its inventor and acknowledged his indebtedness to others.

His major predecessor was the German geographer, Frederick Ratzel (1844–1904), who regarded a nation as a biological organism whose only alternative to growth and expansion was stagnation and death. For him, expansion was not only natural for a healthy nation, but inevitable. It would involve a ruthless struggle without fairness or honesty. To what extent Nazi Germany seized upon and made use of his pernicious conclusions is a matter of history.

In 1904, the year Ratzel died, a British geographer, Sir Halford Mackinder, presented to the world an analysis of this problem when he spoke to the Royal Geographic Society on the "Geographical Pivot of History."[2] He observed that throughout history, land-locked peoples had repeatedly attacked littoral peoples in Europe and Asia alike, and that Europe and Asia should be looked upon as a single geographic unit. The center of this Eurasian landmass he called the "Heartland." Its possession, he felt, was crucial for the expansion of power, and the position of such littoral powers as Britain, France, and Italy would be endangered should Germany and Russia become allied as the "pivot peoples of the Heartland." Subsequent events did not prove Sir Halford all too wrong, except that the "Heartland" concept shifted farther east after Nazi Germany's demise. A meaningful alliance between the USSR and Red China would exacerbate the

[1] Cf. K. London, *Backgrounds of Conflict* (New York: Macmillan, 1945–1947), p. 77 ff. Literature concerning geopolitics was voluminous until the end of World War II. The following books in English may serve as source material: A. Dorpalen, *The World of General Haushofer* (New York: Farrar and Rinehart, Inc., 1942); R. Strausz-Hupé, *Geopolitics: The Struggle for Space and Power* (New York: G. P. Putnam's Sons, 1942); H. W. Weigart, *Generals and Geographers: The Twilight of Geopolitics* (New York: Oxford University Press, 1942); D. Whittlesey, *German Strategy of World Conquest* (New York: Farrar and Rinehart, Inc., 1942).

[2] *The Geographic Journal*, Vol. XXIII, No. 4, London, April, 1904.

danger to littoral powers, the USA included, since the potential of the China mainland is far greater than that of a divided Germany. Besides, since Communist China is also a littoral power, there would be a combination of the Eurasian landmass with littoral outlets.

In 1919, Sir Halford broadened his concept and wrote a book which was then only a moderate success in Britain and an unqualified failure in America.[3] Anticipating a globe shrunk by improved communications, he predicted a struggle for the geographical pivot areas. He enlarged his Eurasian "world island" to include Africa. He anticipated the unification of these enormous landmasses and boldly asserted that they would be dominated by those who controlled the Heartland, for, "who rules East Europe, commands the Heartland, who rules the Heartland, commands the world island, who rules the world island, commands the world."[4]

Haushofer was one of the few who grasped the full implication of Sir Halford's views. His affinity for this concept had been furthered by the Swedish geographer, Rudolf Kjellen (1864–1922), whose geopolitical terminology he appropriated, including the word "geopolitics." It is not surprising that he and his disciples believed a German–Russian entente to be indispensable and that the outbreak of war between Germany and the USSR constituted the defeat of his efforts to bring about such an alliance.

The significance of these geopolitical concepts has not been accepted as entirely valid by some political geographers. But Sir Halford himself believed as late as 1943 that his Heartland idea was sound[5] and modified it only by suggesting a counterbalance of the North Atlantic powers which indeed came to pass only six years later as the North Atlantic Treaty Organization (NATO). Sir Halford's opponents believed that his concept was exaggerated, that a combination of "Rimland" powers could conceivably dominate the "Heartland" and that he ignored the important political vacuum existing in such areas as the Middle East.

[3] Sir Halford Mackinder, *Democratic Ideals and Reality* (New York: Henry Holt and Co., 1919, reprinted 1942).

[4] *Ibid.*, p. 150.

[5] Cf. Mackinder, "The Round World and the Winning of the Peace," *Foreign Affairs*, No. XXXI, July 1943.

This is not the place to engage in a controversy as to whether geopolitics is a science or pseudo-scientific propaganda. Nazi use of geopolitics, or rather, Hitler–Haushofer's interpretation of the geopolitical concept for the purposes of a "Greater Germany," should not becloud the issue, which is whether the geographical position and expansionist potential of great powers can indeed put them into a pivot of commanding strength. For example, would unification of Soviet and Chinese Eurasian territories place these powers in a commanding position? Could it be assumed that in the event of the establishment of Sino–Soviet ideological, socio-political, and economic unity, the South and Southeast Asian countries would be able to prevent further expansion by the two great communist nations? In pre-nuclear times, these questions would have been answered in the affirmative. But geographic constellations as such have become less decisive in the second half of the twentieth century as technological breakthroughs change the face of the earth. Once the barriers of oceans, mountains, and deserts are easily and speedily surmounted, once distance is conquered, every country's political position — including its geographical location — must be re-evaluated by its leaders.

The technological revolution which began in earnest after World War I has made accessible remote countries of the world and opened the way for their peoples to demand a share of prestige and prosperity. In combination with the ideological revolutions, this may lead to shifts in, or new formations of, geographical power centers. Such developments would be furthered by the vast changes in communications. For example, communist pressure and nationalistic aspirations in the Middle East or the establishment of a northern Eurasian tier of a Soviet–Chinese bloc may conceivably enhance the geopolitical significance of Black Africa and South Asia. Western civilization, in receding from its cradle, the Mediterranean, has already established itself on three main bases facing the Atlantic: Western Europe, the Americas, and parts of Africa. Such developments cannot but rearrange the political map of the earth, shifting the emphasis of national, colonial, and global politics as radically as did the fall of the Roman Empire or the end of the worldly power of the medieval church. Certainly Mackinder's predictions would have to be revised if the Rimlands succeeded in maintaining their position.

• CLIMATE — The question of whether or not climate affects national power has been argued. It is here proposed that climate can produce both tangible and imponderable elements which contribute to or detract from a nation's strength.

To exemplify tangible factors: good food production and a comfortable mode of life typify the blessings of a good climate; zones of excessive heat or cold, unsuitable for industrial and agricultural endeavors, make for a much harsher existence. Europeans and Americans who work along the fringes of the temperate zones may partially overcome this handicap by means of technical devices but, on the whole, activities remain sporadic, continuity is lacking, and men wear out early in life. "The geographical distribution of health and energy probably depends on climate and weather more than on any other single factor. . . . This arises not only from the direct effect of weather upon human activity but also from the effect of climate upon agriculture, diet, disease, occupations, and general progress."[6]

It has been estimated that the healthiest climate is a yearly temperature range of 62.5° Fahrenheit. While fluctuations upward and downward from this zone probably would not prevent industrial and agricultural productivity, it is unlikely that the fate of the civilized world will be decided in equatorial regions or in the icy wastes of the polar regions. The main population and production centers of the great powers have always been located in temperate zones. "Where climate is stimulating and people's health is good, it is easy to be industrious. . . . They do not necessarily have more ideas than others, but their energy enables them to put the ideas into practice."[7] Soviet Siberia, bedevilled by excessive winter cold, attempts to wrest minerals and foodstuffs from the soil during the brief periods of mild weather; perhaps Montesquieu was right when he wrote in his *L'Esprit des Lois* that "man has more vigor in cold climates."[8] Nevertheless, even if Siberia should succeed, even if industrial centers now exist in the bleak Central Asian steppes, the locus of Soviet power remains in the more temperate European territories.

[6] E. Huntington and E. B. Shaw, *Principles of Human Geography* (New York: John Wiley and Sons, Inc., 1951), p. 399.

[7] *Ibid.*, p. 140.

[8] A. Missenard, *In Search of Man* (New York: Hawthorn Books, 1957), p. 205.

At the other extreme, under the impact of continuous heat the human body loses alertness and the mind tends to follow suit. It is, therefore, not surprising that only in temperate zones have powerful modern states developed and persisted. But even within these zones, the variation in temperature, the extent of precipitation, the number of days in which the skies are sunny or overcast, the vehemence of nature's outbursts, and the frequency of such "explosions" as hurricanes, floods, and earthquakes, create a variety of mental and physical characteristics which is pertinent to an estimate of a country's potential and therefore must figure in the calculation of policy-making and the "climate" of international relations.

To venture into the controversial field of climatic psychology: the topographical character of a territory, in conjunction with its climate, produces distinct emotional and intellectual traits. For example, striking differences are visible between people who live in mountainous regions and those who dwell on the plains; between those who spend their days in dense woods and those who live by the sea. Definite distinctions exist as much between continental and insular populations as between northern and southern peoples.

Thus the influence of climate and topography on life patterns contributes heavily to the formation of national character. It determines a nation's agricultural conditions and nutritional habits. If the soil yields generously under benevolent skies, the nation inclines to easier and better living; it may grow "soft." If the earth must be coaxed or compelled to produce by artificial means and inordinate expenditure of manpower, the hard-working people tend to be frugal, tough, and able to endure conditions which those living under more favorable skies cannot "take."

There is also the much-discussed question of whether or not climate creates a corresponding type of temperament. Certainly, the outward behavior of the northerner is more subdued and reticent than that of the more outgoing and volatile southerner. But while these appearances may characterize a national culture and create distinct sociological features, they probably will not affect decisively a nation's manpower potential.

Nevertheless, the connection between climate and national psychology cannot be ruled out. Let us remember the profound effect produced on human beings by such natural phenomena as high winds, especially the warm ones, known as mistral, sirocco, samum, or foehn. Nature's outbursts cause emotional outbursts in man. Certain countries subjected to these winds take legal cognizance of the fact that citizens are not fully responsible for acts committed while under the impact of these phenomena.

Or, let us consider the character differences between people who live in mountainous or isolated regions and those who dwell in accessible, undramatic open country. In the Soviet Union, the character of many national groups was forged by the vast expanse of endless steppes, violent changes in temperature, and long, hard winters. These groups consist of hard, moody, but basically stable people of introspective disposition whose emotions are as full of contrast as their climate. But others, living in the southern regions of the European Soviet Union, for example, Ukrainians and Georgians, bear little resemblance to their slow, subdued northern and eastern neighbors. They are less steadfast, less trusty, and have given Moscow more internal trouble than all other groups combined.

Elaboration upon the imponderables of climatic influences would lead us far beyond the framework of this study. Suffice it to say that research on the psychology of climatic effects on the psychosomatic state of a people is still a wide-open field and that statesmen and military leaders have consistently underestimated such influences upon the national mind. A nation's character can scarcely be analyzed without consideration of its natural environment; history and politics are linked to climate, and by themselves tell only part of the story. Knowledge of the national mind in a foreign country and realization of the role climate has played in its development would afford the policy-maker a psychological approach of particular usefulness for the implementation of his government's policy abroad.

Science has not yet developed methods to influence climate at will, thereby enabling governments to use such knowledge against political antagonists. Both the Soviet and Western press have intimated that climate could be changed provided the conditions controlling it could be modified. For example, displacement of polar glaciers by nuclear energy or diversion of the Gulf Stream would affect catastrophically the climate of the Western nations. One hardly need point out the disastrous consequences of willful climatic changes. To some extent, these fantasies are part of the East–West cold war, but they are based upon scientific speculation subject to serious research in the free world and the "socialist camp."

• THE NATIONAL MIND — The concept of a "national mind" has long been a matter of argument. It is surprising how many scholars disavow it, although every nation with a sufficiently long history evinces an individual character of its own. True, national character appears to be an intangible, which may or may not contribute to or detract from national power. But it is discernible in typical actions and reactions which may influence national behavior and, indirectly, national policy. It reveals itself in language and literature, in music and the fine arts, in customs and food. If a nation can produce a race imbued with a "typical" appearance, its people can possess collective "typical" feelings.

A nation's history causes certain stereotypes of behavior and attitude, sanctified by common experience and transmitted from generation to generation. These stereotypes consist of national *idées fixes* and psychological reactions. Such a heritage evokes a national uniformity not only in customs, but also in attitudes toward foreign peoples. Relations with neighboring states, for instance, often are based on quite illogical notions of friendship and enmity; and few persons, on reaching maturity, shed the established prejudices of their environment. Prejudice is, unfortunately, part of national character, and there is little chance of eradicating it. Thus far UNESCO has not succeeded in preventing prejudice from developing at its source — education. Some governments purposely obstruct remedial action against prejudices for ideological reasons. Indeed, the communists do all they can to exacerbate them. As a result, while personal contacts between citizens of the communist countries and those of the free world have somewhat increased, freedom of information scarcely exists.

Consequently, prejudice continues to shape national character and color the views of responsible policy-makers. Inherited atavistic attitudes, be they positive or negative, cannot easily be neutralized by rational judgment. Exceedingly few thinkers are independent enough to free themselves sufficiently from such mental ballast. Certainly no nation can do so without submitting to a revolution against traditional concepts.

To judge a nation according to one's own preferences entails risk. But there is danger too in estimating a country's position in the world without considering its national and ideological traits. A statesman knows that peoples develop similar views, preferences, and aversions when for centuries they have lived in the same general area, been exposed to the same climatic conditions, spoken more or less the same language, partaken of the same cultural traditions, experienced identical fortunes, and shared identical aspirations. No man can wholly escape his heritage; the policy-maker himself is subject to bias for this very reason, although his professional experience may afford him a wider than usual breadth of mind.

Communist negotiators as well as the party bosses are stifled by doctrinal thinking and preconceived notions of peoples, classes, and history. In this crucial area, the pathological mutation of the national mind, induced by ideological infection, is most glaringly evident.

Political ideologies have raised the question of whether secular religions will affect the national character of a people inasmuch as they affect its traditions and way of life. Most likely they will. It was submitted above that human nature can be changed; in fact it "is changing at an extraordinary pace."[9] Under totalitarian regimes and ideological imperialism, such changes naturally occur more quickly; what has taken centuries under traditional governments may take only decades under party dictatorships. The younger generations of Soviet citizens already differ in many ways from those who in their youth were imbued with the old Russian way of life. This is even more evident in Communist China, where, in an unbelievably short time, the traditions of millennia appear to have been upset. An ancient civilization is being replaced by a robot society whose character may bring about fundamental changes in behavior patterns and attitudes of individuals.

It follows that political philosophies have divided the peoples of

[9] G. Murphy, *Human Potentialities* (New York: Basic Book Publishers, 1958), pp. 5–6.

the world at least as deeply as religious schisms and far more than any of the issues which produced tensions in pre-ideological times. Ideological rebellion in one country necessarily affects neighboring states, for the objectives of communist revolution (the main rightist ideologies having been squashed in World War II) are global. The character of the ideological dictatorships in Moscow and Peking is reflected in the international dealings of the "socialist camp," just as the character of Western democracy has produced a corresponding kind of foreign policy and diplomatic behavior. Because international relations are conditioned by national beliefs, methods, and practices, it is essential that the policy-maker explore the effects of political ideologies on the national mind as well as the substance of the ideologies themselves.

The "ideologization of world politics"[10] has played havoc with the sociological and psychological maxims of old. There is no real precedent in history for this development; comparisons with medieval theocracies in the Christian and Islamic worlds are unsatisfactory. The communist mixture of rational and irrational elements and of pseudo-scientific distortions cannot reasonably be likened to antecedents. The West may scoff at the false premises of outdated Marxism, but the impact of the communist articles of faith, especially on the hungry masses in underdeveloped areas, continues to be strong. It suffices to realize that about one-third of the earth's population lives under communist rule and a large part of humanity in the Afro-Asian regions feels no antagonism toward communism as such. Although the totalitarian control system is tight and tough, millions of human beings have been subjugated by communist party rule. It is unthinkable that these millions could be held in bondage indefinitely without having faith in the proclaimed principles of "socialism." The average annual per capita income of the billion souls in Asia and Africa, Communist China excluded, is pathetic in comparison with that of some 500 million West Europeans, North Americans, and Australasians. These masses are concerned, not with democratic ideals, but rather with food, shelter, clothing, and a reasonable degree of security. Could

---

[10] N. D. Palmer and H. C. Perkins, *International Relations* (Boston: Houghton Mifflin Co., 1957), p. 84.

communism provide these necessities, they probably would sell their souls to the devil.

The consequences of the secular religion of communism have spelled doom to the traditions of international relations and diplomacy. Marxism–Leninism has become a tower of Babel in that it not only confuses the issues at stake between nations but also perverts concepts, meanings, and terms. It has divided the world into two major opposing factions, neither of which can comprehend the other's conception of language, life, ethics, and human relations. Political negotiations between representatives of these factions have thus been rendered exceedingly onerous because they are conducted on different planes of reasoning.

• DEMOGRAPHY — Modern demography is no mere compilation of population statistics. Figures on the density of population in a given area or comparisons of birth-death ratios by several countries tell only part of the story and, in themselves, constitute unreliable yardsticks for policy. They must be studied in conjunction with a nation's physical, economic, and political geography, its scientific level and industrial intelligence, its ethnic composition and psychological attitudes.

A country's density of population per square mile may be of political concern. Overpopulated areas tend to expand, to acquire more "living space." The former Axis powers' main rationale for their aggressive policies was the claim that they were vigorous, fast-growing nations, which required further growth. Not satisfied with the existing problem of an already overpopulated territory, they encouraged population increase in every way possible. All three powers had definite objectives: Germany sought an outlet toward eastern and southeastern Europe; Italy demanded adjacent territory across the Adriatic and attempted to revive the Roman Empire by controlling the Mediterranean; Japan desired control of the Pacific and domination of China.

There can be no doubt that these territories were crowded and that irresponsible leaders could easily exploit the slightest economic downward trend to stimulate a mood of near-frantic national claustrophobia. Yet they conveniently disregarded all diplomatic and scientific means to solve the problem. Despite epidemics and wars, Europe's population has increased approximately fivefold during the past three centuries. But it is an undeniable fact that during normal peacetime conditions, the living standard of contemporary Europeans is far higher than it was a century or two ago when the population was much less dense. Nor are the advantages of better living limited to certain social classes. However, the facilities to cope with a population explosion are limited and will become more so.

Look at the growth of population during the past three centuries: demographers estimate that the world's population around 1650 A.D. ranged somewhere between 450 and 550 million. Since 1650, "the rate of increase has risen far above what was estimated for any previous period."[11] This rise was caused by a decreasing death rate in conjunction with a fairly constant birth rate. Early in the twentieth century, a significant lowering of the birth rate brought concern to the governments of both Europe and the United States. But the threat of depopulation was averted by the birth-rate increase after World War II. Asia, Africa, and Latin America continue to experience both a decreasing death rate and a high birth rate.

Studies the United Nations and other official population experts submitted to the International Population Congress in Rome (1954) projected that the world population would increase from 2,400 million in 1950 to a minimum of 3,800 million in 1980; the medium estimate was 4,300 million; the high, 4,912 million. The question is whether or not our planet will be able to provide food, raw materials, and other essentials necessary to sustain an almost doubled population.

Much depends on the future political and economic organization of human society, and even more on the solution of technological problems (such as the harnessing of hydrogen power) which may bring into being entirely different living conditions. Barring nuclear war or a decisive change in the attitudes of influential governments toward birth control, the earth will probably become more crowded; privacy and individualism are bound to suffer, and Western civilization will undergo change due to the necessary regimentation inherent in a more tightly organized social structure.

[11] P. M. Hauser (ed.), *Population and World Politics* (Glencoe, Ill.: The Free Press, 1958), pp. 30–31.

At the present time, scientists disagree with regard to the earth's ability to sustain at a decent standard of living more than 2,500 million people. Some demographers question the UN experts' claim that "the world's food supply could be trebled by the end of this century" provided there exists a "single reservoir on which all can draw." W. S. Woytinsky states: "Under the most optimistic projections on the carrying capacity of the earth there remains the possibility that there will be vast areas of food deficit."[12]

How do governments react to such considerations? Population is, after all, a country's greatest asset. On the quality and quantity of its people depend a nation's manpower resource for industrial and agricultural labor, domestic trade expansion, and military potential. Realization of this fact caused the totalitarian powers to stimulate birth rate. Nazi Germany and Fascist Italy awarded medals and money to families which produced large baby crops. The Soviets used similar methods. After an initial period in which abortion was permitted, this policy was changed in the thirties when stringent laws prohibiting abortions were introduced. Subsequently, the enormous losses incurred during World War II were greatly compensated by a decrease in the death rate and a new upsurge in the birth rate which led the Soviet government in 1947 to reduce by half the bonus paid to parents of large families.[13] During the same period, Eastern European satellite populations increased except in Bulgaria and Romania. Their rate of growth appears to be demographically more healthy than Communist China's.

Peking apparently had trouble deciding whether to discourage or encourage the tremendous population increase. But after an interval in the mid-fifties in which it half-heartedly propagandized birth control, the Mao regime stopped the campaign, claiming Malthusianism to be un-Marxian. However, the economic catastrophes of the late fifties and early sixties have forced the Mao regime to reverse itself once more: birth control propaganda was reintroduced in 1962.

According to the United Nations Demographic Yearbook of 1965,

12 *Ibid.*, p. 67.
13 *Ibid.*, p. 225.

the estimated world population in that year was 3,285 million.[14] If we estimate the 1965 population of the Soviet Union at somewhat above 230 million, Communist China at approximately 700 million, and add the Eastern European and Far Eastern communist states, we must conclude that the communist-ruled countries hold sway over some one billion people. One need hardly point out that the population of the NATO powers totals only about 500 million people. The consequences of these facts raise grave problems almost as serious as those posed by the question of whether or not the earth can sustain a continuing population increase without creating pauperization and extinction of those values dear to Western civilization. Thus problems of demography loom large in the minds of policy-makers and influence the character of international relations and the status of national power positions. Obviously, the problem is one of long-range significance to foreign policy, since population fluctuations and concomitant trends in a country's power potential are among the more tangible indicators of its possible future developments.

The curve of proportional increase or decline in the population of the great powers has always influenced international relations. Depopulation is a particularly serious problem since it may lead to an upset of the power ratio. France's demographic developments, in comparison with those of Germany, offer a classic example. About two centuries ago, France was the most populous and most powerful country in Europe with the exception of Russia. It has fallen from first to fourth place at the present time. Meanwhile, the German population multiplied in inverse proportion to the French. Thus, in 1939, the Third Reich numbered 80 million subjects against continental France's 40 million. Up to World War II, France's weakening contributed to an imbalance of power in Europe, much to the detriment of the Western alliance and the struggle of Western civilization against Eastern communism.

This condition augurs a grim demographic future for Western Europe, since its nations cannot cope with the population increase in Eastern Europe, which will soon compensate for the USSR's alleged loss of 26 million people through death during World War II.

14 *United Nations Demographic Yearbook,* 1965, p. 103.

Population statistics of 1944 estimated that, by 1970, the Soviet Union would have more men of military age than its six largest European rivals combined.[15] Twenty years after the publication of this estimate, these figures had to be revised upward and there is little doubt that the USSR has made such economic and technological progress that it can easily feed, clothe, and house the 250 million inhabitants it may have by 1970. Even more staggering is Communist China's population growth. Estimated at 700 million in the mid-sixties, its population may jump to a billion by the end of the century, if unhindered.

• NATIONAL MINORITIES — Another demographic problem of internal and external significance is the ethnic question which requires appraisal of the character and attitude of national minorities. Few nations are homogeneous to the virtual exclusion of alien elements as are the Scandinavian states. Most countries have had minorities since they became nation–states. It will be remembered that most political boundaries were established without regard to ethnic leveling. Surprisingly few minorities have permitted themselves to be absorbed by their host nation; most of them have retained their "differences" in one way or another, keeping alive their original culture, traditions, and even language. Centuries of migration and continuous intermixture of heteronational elements have produced such minorities throughout Europe and to a lesser degree in Asia and Africa. Once established in national territories, these groups occasionally have grown to be majorities, or even nations. By far the greater number, however, was never absorbed and retained an identifiable culture.

It should be emphasized here that national or ethnic homogeneity is by no means a premise for the existence or preservation of a modern state. That national greatness bears no relation to homogeneity of population, or what the Nazis and other racists call "purity of race," is demonstrated by the "melting pots" of the United States and its antagonist, the Soviet Union. In both cases, one preponderant element — Anglo-Saxon in the United States, Great Russian in the

[15] D. Kirk, "Population Changes and the Post-war World," *American Sociological Review,* February 1944.

USSR — provided the national language and cultural unity. But both populations consist of a multitude of ethnic minorities, some of which have managed to preserve their ethnic character. The same is true of China, where the Han Chinese exert as much influence as the Great Russians in the USSR, but where many different ethnic components live.

While some minorities may differ with the national majority on a variety of issues, on the whole they have accepted their country's political and social organization and adjusted their cultural inheritance to their environment.

Where consequential national minorities exist, they have become subject to attention by the world community of states. Policy-makers, in particular, try to understand their aspirations and to gauge the extent of their influence upon the majority as well as the majority's attitude toward them. Such analysis is imperative not only for the study of national character but also for the detection of potential danger spots created by minorities which endeavor to remain apart, stubbornly isolating themselves and emphasizing their grievances. They are a possible source of trouble and often have been the cause of war. They have also served as a pretext for aggression. For example, Hitler used alleged grievances of German minorities in Czechoslovakia and Poland as a justification for attack. Ethnic groups have caused disturbances not only in Europe and the Chinese mainland, but also in the Middle East and South Asia. In the latter minorities live apart not only for ethnic but also religious reasons.

In view of their long-range objectives, the communist regimes in Eastern Europe and Asia would like to eradicate the political, social, and religious individualism of national minorities. It is perhaps too soon to tell whether or not the Kremlin will succeed in enforcing permanent ideological unity in those areas long torn by strife between national minorities. One cannot forget that communism's goal is the destruction of the nation–state and "bourgeois nationalist elements" which have no place in a "classless society." However, there is as yet no intention to destroy minority cultures provided their manifestations conform to communist requirements. The Kremlin has been careful to keep its russification efforts *sub rosa*; in true dialectic fashion, it has encouraged ethnic cultures while promoting

Great Russian culture and language. This is not necessarily a nationalistic policy but the result of the conviction that the October Revolution is predominantly the creation of the Russian people whose loyalty to the Soviet system is regarded as a better risk than that of other nationalities in the USSR. Communist China is far less cautious: it tolerates no minority rights. Exhorting the minorities to unite, it has imposed Han rule and the Mandarin Chinese language upon its entire territory so as to merge the many Chinese dialects into one single idiom and wipe out existing cultural differences which might lead to divided loyalties.

Some thought should be given to the religious aspects of national minorities. Throughout history, in Asia and Europe, the conflicts engendered by opposing religious beliefs have been numerous and catastrophic. Only recently, religion was the main cause for the division of the Asian subcontinent into India and the two Pakistans which, in turn, created new ethnic minorities in both states. To cite a classic European example, the Uniate Church of the Transylvanian minority in Romania was hotly attacked by the Greek Orthodox State Church. Even prior to communist rule, the Uniate Church was influential in promoting the differences between Transylvanians, Romanians, and Catholic Hungarians of that region. Other religious minorities are the Moslems in Yugoslavia and certain Soviet regions; Christians in Moslem countries; Christians and Moslems in China; Protestants in Catholic countries such as Italy and Spain; and, of course, Jews all over the world. Although nationals of the countries in which they live — if such privilege is granted — most of these minorities remain loyal to the creed of their forefathers.

If this has created difficulties and bloodshed in non-communist countries, it is considered intolerable in the "socialist camp." Since any religion would compete with the ruling ideology, anti-religious pressure is maintained by the USSR and the East European states. In China the problem is somewhat different. Buddhism and Taoism are weak, Islam restricted to tiny islands, and Confucianism, contrary to popular belief in the West, was virtually abandoned when the examination system was eliminated in 1905 and received the death knell by the May 4 Movement in 1919. It was not a religion but rather a moral system of social order under the rule of family patriarchs, the highest of whom was the emperor. In twentieth century China, it no longer has a reason for existence.

• TECHNOLOGY AND EDUCATION — It is universally recognized that the level of science and technology has become a decisive factor in world politics. It creates the deterrent to war, determines the relative power status in the East–West competition, modifies attitudes, topples obsolete approaches to social and international relations, and even attempts to change human behavior. As new inventions become part of our lives, new values are created and old ones discarded. Technology has always influenced the lives of nations and individuals. It has caused social and economic revolutions, enforced the re-evaluation of policies, and altered customs. In our century it has achieved more: it has raced ahead of the human capacity to grasp the meaning of scientific breakthroughs and consistently outdistanced the progress of conceptual comprehension. The communists have for some time used Marxist–Leninist principles to explain technological triumphs; it is hard to determine whether their efforts have satisfied the people. Western man is too sophisticated to be content with stereotyped formulae, but even he lacks genuine understanding of the philosophical ramifications of technology in the lives of individuals and nations yet to come.

It is useless to search history for analogies. Events such as England's Industrial Revolution will prove of little comparative value. For not only has contemporary technology progressed far beyond all previous achievements, but also it must be considered within the context of the East–West struggle. It is perhaps symbolic that the United States' release of atomic energy coincided with the Soviet Union's emergence as a world power.

The forward march of science has left no field of endeavor untouched. It has changed not only strategy but the entire concept of war and thereby forced political thinking into new channels. It was responsible for the spread of secular religions and made possible totalitarianism. It has modified the world view by exploring space and shrinking the distance which kept nations apart in the past. It has revolutionized economics and production both in industry and agriculture. It has affected public opinion through the mass media of communications. With the aid of cybernetics, it is trying to mold the human mind and to control it.

These facts leave little to the imagination. No segment of international relations remains unaffected. Physical and political geography must be re-evaluated, as must types and locations of natural resources. For, accompanying the epochal developments of nuclear power, which hold the double-edged promise of better living and swifter disintegration, are many other new techniques which promote rapid changes in national economies. Raw materials are being utilized more productively; new sources of natural wealth are being discovered; new substances (such as plastics) have been developed; transportation already is looking beyond the earth toward exploration of the universe.

Consequently, the policy-maker, forced to consider power in relative terms when formulating his program for action, can only attempt to ascertain the extent to which science may neutralize, if not devaluate, the geographic advantages of his nation. Decisions become all the more difficult since he is caught in a transitory period between recognition of still-valid concepts of international behavior and understanding of new techniques which, although progressively inactivating the old ones, have yet to evolve new thought patterns for controlling the ever-increasing technological forces.

The basis for future technological developments is, of course, the education of youth. Western statesmen and political analysts paid small heed to this vital fact until forced to realize that the Soviet Union's astounding technological progress, demonstrated by the successful launching of the first artificial earth satellite, the first moon rocket, and the first orbital flight by man could have resulted only from comprehensive and intensive technical training, combined with a tremendous concentration of national resources. Moreover, the Western countries, especially those more pragmatically oriented, have attributed too little weight to the high-pressure system of ideological indoctrination of the peoples in communist-ruled countries. One cannot emphasize too strongly that it is the combination of ideological training and scientific education which has engendered the rapid progress of Soviet and Chinese power and which clearly reflects the relentless drive toward communist conquest.

The educational program Khrushchev presented to the Twenty-first Congress of the CPSU, while essentially an intensification of one already in use, was geared to the Seven Year Plan adopted by this Congress. The difference between this and previous programs was the conscious and deliberate preparation for a fifteeen-year period during which giant strides were to be taken toward the Transition to Communism — as differentiated from Socialism. The Soviet leadership believed that the society they envisaged could be attained only by new generations of Soviet citizens fully indoctrinated in Marxist–Leninist principles, and skilled professionally or vocationally to the degree necessary to compete with the industrial accomplishments of the United States. There is no indication that Khrushchev's successors have altered this position.

Since the inception of the Soviet state, the educational system has undergone various modifications, most of them geared to the needs of a "socialist" society. It is evident that Soviet educational theories and practices succeeded. They made possible the emergence of Soviet industrial power and rapid technological progress; espionage alone could never have elevated Soviet science to its present status. One must remember that even under the Czars there were distinguished Russian scientists; such men as Pavlov and Kapitza were not products of the Soviet state. The Kremlin continued these traditions on a much magnified scale. It also directed Soviet science into usable channels, chiefly through the overall guidance of the powerful Academy of Sciences.

It must be added that this educational program is by no means limited to the study of science. In fact the students are overworked: in addition to their heavy academic requirements they are obliged to participate in "polytechnical" education[16] and indoctrination sessions, directed mainly by the youth organizations (the Young Pioneers and the Komsomols). Only through membership in these bodies can they attain Party membership and superior jobs.

[16] "Polytechnical" education means the combination of academic studies with actual production work in industry or agriculture. This Leninist concept desires to establish closer relations and better understanding between intellectual and manual labor. It aims at training the intelligentsia in the crafts, at least to the extent where the organization and effort of labor can be more readily appreciated.

This educational system, which is emulated by other communist countries, has a twofold objective: primarily, it must furnish the skilled manpower required by the state; secondarily, it strives to create the new "Soviet man" whose task will be preparing the communist goal of the revolution once transformation to a classless society becomes feasible. To the Soviet Communist Party, "Soviet man" is comparable to the Renaissance–Humanist vision of the "whole man." With a difference, however, since the status of "Soviet man" is to be attained by all men of the classless society, whereas previous ideals of educational universality necessarily were restricted to the upper classes, deepening rather than lessening the schism between the classes.

One need hardly mention that in Red China education and training also have high priority. But educational goals are much more difficult to achieve. In the first place, the Chinese language is extremely difficult, particularly in its written form, and the elimination of illiteracy, which still plagues a large part of the population, is therefore far more complex a problem and will take a much longer time than it did in the USSR. A simplification of often used ideographs has been completed; moreover, for some time linguists have experimented with a phonetic transliteration, using Latin (rather than Cyrillic) letters. These efforts seem to have been stalled. Secondly, while China had a good higher education system under the Kuomintang, primary education was inadequate and has so remained under the communists. The diversion of students to "productive" labor in agriculture and industry and pre-military training has slowed down education in high schools and universities. Thirdly, higher education has been geared to the needs of the regime's political purposes and must concern itself with interpretation of doctrine to the detriment of academic training. Basic technical research has not improved and the best scientists were trained abroad. Finally, the "cultural revolution" has completely disrupted the school system and it will take a long time to overcome the effects of Mao's destruction of schools and universities and introduce a reasonably efficient curriculum.

It would be a mistake to deduce that scientific development in Red China is bankrupt. Practicing scientists, many of whom were trained in the U.S.A., have proved their mettle in the rapid development of nuclear devices. But the new generations of potential scientists are greatly handicapped in their studies, a fact which will impede China's scientific and technological progress.

The communist system of education, training, and indoctrination cannot help but be of vital concern to free world governments: on its success may depend the continuity and future of the orbit. It is a barometer of sorts, indicating trends and prognoses of communism. Similarly, free world and, particularly, Western educational efforts should demonstrate to the communist leaders how purposefully non-communist education is pursued and what results may be expected of it.

• ECONOMIC GEOGRAPHY — Time was when statesmen examined a country's economic geography exclusively in terms of its natural resources, industrial capacity, agricultural production, transportation and communications systems, and manpower. By contrasting their findings with the state of their own economy they arrived at a reasonably sound estimate of the relative power status. This technique of analysis no longer suffices; it would in fact lead to wrong conclusions.

In a divided world, economic assets and liabilities must be studied in the context of the political concepts which created them. Since a nation's political philosophy engenders its economic principles, its success or failure in applying them determines its strength or weakness. A great variety of economic systems still exists. On the non-communist side, they range from evolutionary socialism to monopoly capitalism; the communists and their sympathizers in power control economies veering from a "moderate" to a more radical form of Marxism–Leninism. Only two extremes can be discounted: *laissez-faire* capitalism is obsolete and pure communism remains utopian.

A comparison of free world economies, despite their variations, still has some usefulness. But a comparison between non-communist and "socialist" economies is meaningless. This fact compounds the policy-makers' difficulties in reaching safe estimates. Western leaders are seldom economic determinists. But they are married to tradition not only in their concept of economic philosophy, but also in their judgment of economic endeavors abroad. Conversely, the communist leaders' preconceived view of capitalist economy is not only antiquated but also prejudiced in the extreme. Therefore, they too are bound to come to wrong conclusions, not only as a result of their basic misunderstanding of the workings of free economic systems, but also because doctrinal stereotypes have conditioned their thinking and determined their judgment concerning economic successes, failures, and future potentialities under "imperialism."

The problem is complicated by the combination of technological advances and Marxist–Leninist theses. Communist political economy is not a market economy in the Western sense. Specific tasks to be fulfilled are mapped out, partly by the Five Year Plans and partly by the gyrations of communist strategy and tactics. The Sino–Soviet leaders do not concern themselves with that shibboleth of the West — the balanced budget. Capital investment and spending depend entirely on political desiderata. The leadership determines the channeling of means and use of facilities, and its decisions are the direct outcome of long-range political planning.

The communists have great confidence in the correctness of their principles. Their belief in the veracity of their doctrine is clearly expressed in the following sentences:

> The social and economic system of Socialism is a new system which is developing and becoming stronger. The future belongs to it. Hence the future belongs likewise to relations of a new Socialist type in the sphere of international relations. The capitalist system is doomed, it has outlived its epoch, and the same is equally true of the corresponding type of international relations.
>
> "The essence of international relations under capitalism" said Lenin, "is the open plundering of the weak." (V. I. Lenin, Soch. t. 17, p. 16.) The predatory nature of capitalist international relations becomes particularly blatant in the epoch of imperialism. All the activities of the imperialist powers in the international arena, all their diplomacy, is in the ultimate analysis directed towards safeguarding the monopolies' opportunities for extracting super-profits acquired through the intensified exploitation of the workers in their own and other countries.[17]

[17] S. Sanakoyev, "The Basis of the Relations Between Socialist Countries," *International Affairs*, Moscow, July 1958. It is interesting to note that the same writer in an article entitled "The World Socialist System and the Future of Mankind," *International Affairs*, Moscow, October 1966, expands the above thesis by adding "anti-communism" as "the chief novel element in the foreign policy of modern imperialism, as compared with the exploiting states of the past."

No bridge of mutual understanding exists between this point of view and Western concepts of political economy. The Western mind reasons: trade with the East will add to Western prosperity; the bonds of fruitful exchange and international trade might contribute to conciliation and induce the Eastern revolutions to become evolutionary. The communist mind argues differently: let the capitalists make their profit and further exploit their workers so long as it helps to increase our strategic strength and raise our standard of living. We shall be credited with the results and, with less need to expend our capital and labor force on consumer goods, can direct all our economic might toward bolstering our "material-technical base" and overtaking the West economically. Thus we will demonstrate to the world in general and the neutral zone in particular what "socialism" can achieve.

The changes in world trade parallel those in international relations. The East–West schism has produced two separate zones of trade. That of the Soviet bloc functions within a closed circuit in accordance with numerous bilateral treaties and such multilateral planning as have been agreed upon by the Council of Mutual Economic Assistance (CEMA or COMECON). Soviet and East European trade with Western Europe has considerably increased, and the modicum of economic freedom of movement permitted the former satellites has spurred the West to promote commercial relations with Eastern European states, except East Germany and Albania. (There is, however, considerable trade between West and East Germany.) Since early 1967, the United States has made special efforts to "build bridges" to the East European states; Romania, unwilling to subordinate its economy to CEMA decisions, has made great efforts to stimulate commercial relations with the West.

Communist trade with non-aligned countries consists mainly of economic aid, barter rather than currency being the mode of payment. Since the intensification of the Sino–Soviet conflict, Red China, formerly represented in CEMA as an observer, has withdrawn and no longer is part of the Soviet–East European economic circuit. China's trade with the Soviet bloc has all but dried up.

The Western zone of trade is highly diversified but shows some signs of gradual integration. The Common Market "Six" and the "Outer Seven" may eventually cease to be competitors with opposing tariff policies. More difficult are trade relations between the NATO,

SEATO, and CENTO allies which are hampered by protectionist obstacles, problems of currency inconvertibility, and lack of dollar funds. As to the non-aligned, underdeveloped areas, vast international loans still are necessary to infuse strength into their economies. Trade with the new Afro-Asian countries is not a balanced commercial exchange but an attempt by the West to help establish sound economies capable of withstanding Sino–Soviet economic and political penetration. Also, certain non-communist trade areas discourage Western investments because of fear of "neo-colonialism" or outright pro-communist sentiments.

In contrast, and with the exception of Red China, the Soviet bloc's economic system is relatively well coordinated. The Soviet Union, after all, is a super power with an enormous economic potential and can provide Eastern Europe with strategic raw materials which it would be unable to obtain from the West. For Moscow, the potential of East European economy is important for strategic and political reasons. Thus most East European trade remains within the closed circuit. Lack of economic relations with Communist China has had little impact on the Soviet Union and its sphere of influence, while the loss of Soviet aid has seriously impaired and delayed the recovery of China's economic ills. Peking seeks to emulate Soviet practices by taking advantage of such free world trade as is available, which is not nearly sufficient to be of real help.

Lack of communist candor in publishing economic statistics makes it very difficult to estimate the true state of Eastern economics. However, certain basic premises which underlie economic estimates must be considered. For example, the more nearly balanced a country's economy, the stronger its position. Theoretically, in a balanced economy industrial and agricultural production are about equal and create national self-sufficiency in food, commodities, and raw materials. In peacetime, surplus production may be exported in exchange for imported luxuries or scarce materials; in crises, it may serve as barter for foreign currency or strategic goods. No country can produce all the raw materials and commodities it consumes. As a result, few relatively balanced economies exist. Even the United States must import certain raw materials, but its economy is well balanced as industrial and agricultural production are both high.

The USSR has the makings of a balanced economy and has made

great strides toward achieving a higher level of production, particularly since the end of the Stalin era. Its avowed purpose is to achieve a greater per capita production than the United States. Its agricultural productivity is relatively inferior to that of its industry. Thus, while the Soviet Union produces enough to feed its peoples, its economic balance will be impaired so long as agriculture cannot work more efficiently and industry cannot be diversified to serve the needs of all rather than be channeled into such priority projects as space exploration.

Most other countries, including those of political and strategic importance, do not have a balanced economy. As the former colonial powers lose their dependent territories, at best maintaining with them a union or commonwealth relationship, their balance of economy is impaired. They must import vital raw materials, even foodstuffs, to keep their industry humming and their population nourished.

An unbalanced economy can no longer be compensated by exploiting territorial possessions. Formerly, colonial empires would produce artificially a certain balance in the motherland (as for instance in the Netherlands or Belgium). But since World War II, many dependent territories have acquired self-rule and no longer need tolerate exploitation. There is evidence that colonialism may disappear before the century is over as new nations try to pursue an independent course of action, even to the extent of breaking away from such associations as the French Union or the British Commonwealth. Internationally sanctioned trusteeships have accomplished a considerable change in the status of colonies, as have world opinion, communist propaganda, and a growing consciousness of international morality on the part of the colonial powers. As a result, many dependent territories have lost their original value to the point of becoming liabilities, and the great empires of the past are disintegrating into cooperative groups of territories in which the motherland is at best a *primus inter pares*. So it was with the British Empire when it became the British Commonwealth of Nations. It is even debatable whether overseas possessions will prove to be of military value in any future war. Not only is the defense of communications costly, but also the political reliability of dependent peoples is open to doubt.

This brings us to the vital interest taken by political and military leaders in the natural resources of other countries. They must survey the deficiencies, surpluses, and accessibility of a nation's materials. They know that a country which lacks food or raw materials will attempt to insure their procurement abroad by establishing the cheapest, safest, and fastest routes of communication for its "life lines." Agreements concluded for this purpose cannot easily be enforced even by powerful nations. Experience proves they are best negotiated on the basis of mutual self-interest. Essentially, they are political and strategic measures to strengthen and balance defense potentials; their economic aspects are often secondary.

However, the scope of agreements became far more limited in the years following World War II. The two opposing camps traded with reservation, if at all. The West could not help but remember that whatever it exported to the socialist countries of the East might eventually be used against it. In the United States perhaps more than in Western Europe it was felt that, apart from strategic materials which could not be exported, even such items as consumer goods or foodstuffs would contribute to communist growth. However, in the sixties, considerable changes of policies by Western states took place. America's European allies increased trade with the East. The facts of economic geography, combined with a more moderate appearance of the Soviet bloc's political behavior, were irresistible. In the end, even the United States succumbed to the euphoria of détente and modified its position, particularly vis-à-vis Eastern Europe. President Johnson, in late 1966, pronounced the policy of "building bridges" to the East European states. Whether these bridges actually will be crossed from both sides and whether there will be any traffic to speak of remains to be seen. In any event, the Soviet bloc keeps trying to consolidate still further its economic position, having more or less overcome the era of deprivation resulting from rapid industrialization and agricultural mismanagement.

The neutralist zone, where East and West meet and compete economically, has become a target of lively solicitation. Regrettably, some of these countries have not yet developed the political sophistication to interpret the lures of communist trade and aid offers in terms of political and economic infiltration. In their eagerness to forge their own destinies, they have accepted economic assistance from, and signed trade agreements with, whichever power proffers the seemingly more advantageous deal. Communist offers frequently appear preferable because of their extremely low interest rate and acquiescence in projects regardless of merit. Furthermore, in the eyes of former colonial peoples, the communist states are untinged by imperialistic designs while the United States, although not a colonial power itself, is allied with proponents of colonialism. The specter of colonialism still haunts those territories which only recently have become sovereign states; this is often a determining factor in favor of trade agreements with the East.

Policy officials usually are highly sensitive to the nature and extent of economic stability or fluctuation in important nations: their prosperity or poverty is subject to political interpretation which may revise policy. In a community of states, sharp differences between living standards may cause deterioration of social relations and lead to general unrest. Policy formulation similarly is influenced by economic divergencies between the "haves" and "have-nots." A prosperous country is moderately safe from ideological penetration by extreme rightists or leftists, but a people forced to cope with want, unemployment, and hopelessness are especially susceptible to such "indirect aggression."

It is understandable why Soviet leaders follow US economic conditions with keen interest. They believe the "series of depressions" which they have predicted would virtually put the American people at their mercy and gravely imperil the Western alliance, whose economic backbone is the United States. Soviet economic developments receive corresponding attention from the free world leadership: should the USSR succeed in overtaking the highly developed Western economies, the neutralists would be enormously impressed. It might even lead to the adoption of Soviet methods, particularly in underdeveloped countries. Soviet failure, on the other hand, probably would have a sobering effect on uncommitted statesmen and might prevent their permitting too close an association with the communists.

China has always suffered from economic ills and, while natural catastrophes have contributed to famine, the insane policies of the Mao regime have vastly aggravated a situation which is almost innate in the physical, political, and economic geography of China mainland. The "great leap forward," the establishment of the "people's communes," and the "cultural revolution" have almost destroyed the effort of the communist leaders to develop a more viable economy. It has been estimated that the "great leap forward" has cost Communist China close to a decade of industrial growth.[18] But China has never had an easy life. The Chinese are hard workers and resourceful to boot; their manpower reservoir is virtually limitless and their stamina legendary, though misused by the Peking rulers. The development of nuclear devices, albeit with the help of American-trained Chinese scientists, has demonstrated that the Chinese potential in technological progress is considerable. If, after the death of Mao, a more rational regime comes to power, a slow and probably modest recovery could be achieved in the end — unless Maoist fanaticism survives its creator and once again disregards the facts of China's essentially unbalanced and undeveloped economy.

Within an association of states, each member's economic status is pertinent to the maintenance of its political influence. Statesmen often have been called upon to achieve political objectives through economic action. A case in point was the brilliantly conceived American plan to aid European recovery, which served as a most effective answer to communism. The Soviets have learned this lesson and imitate it in their own way; economic aid has become one of their strongest instruments of manipulation in the neutral areas. Due to the existing nuclear stalemate between East and West, problems of political economy and economic geography have become increasingly important. If there is to be no contest in war, economic competition and socio-ideological contests are deadly serious. Indeed they may become decisive.

Domestic Backgrounds of Conflict

Under totalitarian dictatorship, the nature and extent of domestic issues which influence foreign policy differ radically from those in a parliamentary democracy. In monolithically ruled countries, the one

[18.]See R. M. Field, "Chinese Communist Industrial Production," in *An Economic Profile of Mainland China*, Vol. 1, studies prepared for the Joint Economic Committee, Congress of the United States (Washington: U.S. Government Printing Office, 1967).

and only party is in charge, not of the state apparatus alone, but of society in its entirety.[19] Moreover, ideology not only permeates national life, it also shapes international relations. It is international as well as national; the dynamics of totalitarian dictatorship fizzle if it remains within the confines of its own country. Most "isms" strive for ultimate global conformity, and it is hard to say where domestic aspirations end and foreign policy objectives begin. For example, Nazi Germany's doctrine of racial superiority expressed itself in measures against excommunicated minorities at home and in the quest for supremacy of the "Aryan race" abroad. Discriminatory actions inside Germany were transposed into geopolitical designs for world rule. In turn, communist imperialism, which strives to expand not only for economic and strategic reasons but also in order to establish advanced ideological outposts, is based upon internal application of Marxism–Leninism. In order to achieve its ultimate objective, communism must be victorious throughout the world. Hence it is evident, though often camouflaged by soothing propaganda, that the established ideology has contributed to the shape of communist foreign policy to such a degree that it is difficult to determine whether foreign policy reflects domestic philosophy or global conditions have molded the political creed.

No such regime can exist without a rigidly determined dogma which disseminates a gospel of political, social, economic, and cultural principles and prescribes methods to achieve its objectives. Nor is such a system conceivable without the urge to convert the unbeliever at home and abroad. Since it is claimed that the doctrine is untouchable and the interpretation of its high priests infallible, criticism or doubt is heresy. Heretics and followers of other political religions, wherever they exist, are doomed to ultimate damnation. Offenders at home are excommunicated.

Totalitarian dynamics thrives on tension and revolutionary intrigue. With the obvious impediment of nuclear deterrence, its foreign policy is bound to be aggressive and to shun compromise if compromise affects its principles or objectives. Only when motivated by the need for a period of calm in which to consolidate political and economic

[19] Cf. C. J. Friedrich and Z. K. Brzezinski, *Totalitarian Dictatorship and Autocracy*, 2nd edition revised by C. J. Friedrich (Cambridge, Mass.: Harvard University Press, 1965).

gains does it relax tensions. Internal measures imposed to maintain a solvent economy, advance technology, and produce unflinching adherence to the secular religion — all are aimed at stockpiling power behind policy planning, with only marginal regard to the well-being of the citizenry.

In pursuing their tasks, policy-makers of dictatorships are rarely concerned with such domestic politics as confront statesmen in democracies. Whatever internal cleavages or pressures exist are not prominently evident. They can be suppressed by secret police and smoothed over by propaganda. Any revelation of factional strife is publicized by the victorious faction — after its opponents are purged. In any event, disputes existing within the ranks of an all-powerful party differ radically from the free interplay of factional opinion within parliamentary democracies. There may be power contests among leaders, but no evidence suggests that vested interests outside the party can effectively oppose the party's will.

The party dictates its will to the government executives who, in the majority of cases, are also party officials. Thus it is an error to believe, as do so many non-communists, that a change in personalities necessarily causes a change in policy. So long as the political religion persists, its priests — the party leaders — are but its instruments. For example, the ultimate political objective of the achievement of a communist world state remains immutable.[20] If this policy *appears* to change, it is a mere change of tactics toward its implementation. Tactics are reversed frequently, a fact which affords the communists initiative and creates confusion in the free world, where the study of communist strategy and methodology is still underdeveloped.[21]

---

[20] Cf. E. R. Goodman, *The Soviet Design for a World State* (New York: Columbia University Press, 1960).

[21] With growing frequency, since the early sixties, it has been pointed out by observers of the "socialist camp" that communism is in a state of erosion due to the process of modernization in the USSR and Eastern Europe and the disintegration of international communist organization. But the changes that have occurred in the Soviet bloc were overdue and have strengthened rather than weakened the regimes. They do not connote disintegration but consolidation. In this connection a study of the theses of the Central Committee of the CPSU of June 25, 1967 is recommended, entitled "On the 50th Anniversary of the Great October Socialist Revolution."

Conditions are quite different in parliamentary democracies. Whatever the constitutional law or the degree of state control over their economies, the formulation of foreign policy, and therefore the character of their concept of international relations, is subject to a variety of pressures brought to bear upon responsible government officials by three powerful forces: public opinion (which more often than not is generated by influential groups and individuals), vested interests of socio-economic groups, and political parties (which do not as a rule reflect the will of these groups accurately). Still, the constitution imposes limitations on these pressures.

The degree and nature of these pressures vary in accordance with the type of social and economic self-control. Group pressures and "lobbies" are stronger and more successful in the United States than in Great Britain; they were tremendous in pre-Gaullist France but weakened after the establishment of the Fifth Republic; they were weak but are becoming stronger in the West German Federal Republic; they have first lost but since gained ground in post-war Japan. As a rule, all liberal democracies grant free expression to their political and social pressure groups. The assumption is that no group or party except one opposed to basic democratic principles would be so foolish as to purposely endanger its country; this would endanger its own welfare along with that of its fellow citizens.

Since top policy-makers in the democracies are usually political appointees, they are duty-bound to carry out the voters' will, as is the rest of the administration. Although they may possess superior wisdom, they are not always free to formulate policies as they see fit. Somehow they must coordinate their own ideas with those of the parties or groups which brought them into power. If they recommend different policies without the consent of their constituents, they may be forced to resign. Rarely do they undertake the difficult task of persuading voters to accept new ideas.

The crises following World War II probably have produced more bipartisan and coalition international policies than ever before. Nevertheless, bipartisan approach to foreign policy in a democracy is the result of national necessity rather than preference. Even in an emergency, there persist genuine differences of opinion as to policies, methods of implementation, and choice of leaders. These differences range from disagreements on military preparedness and diplomatic recognition to high import tariffs and foreign economic aid. No foreign minister in a parliamentary democracy can recommend policies that clash with the wishes of the parliamentary majority and stay in office.

In a democracy it is unavoidable that deals will be made among various parties, party factions, pressure groups, and the government. If the people are not satisfied with the results, they may vote out the government by re-distributing power among the political parties. Democratic governments rule on sufferance of the majority's will; if they wish to remain in power, they cannot afford to refuse the advice of the majority's spokesman. Frequently, principles are traded; domestic concessions may lead to similar or related action in foreign affairs. Compromise is the nature of the democratic process. Its consequences are not always happy, but this is one of the prices we pay for freedom.

The manner in which parties or influential groups interpret freedom and democracy determines the lengths to which they will go to achieve popularity among their adherents by sacrificing, in the field of foreign affairs, principles of long-range benefit to the nation. Internal politics in traditional countries are, by their very nature, short-ranged. They attempt adaptation to prevailing conditions and accordingly appeal to the voters in terms of immediate objectives. The spoils of politics demand instant collection, and most voters are apt to be interested in the immediate rather than the distant future. The best foreign policy, however, is one of long-range value. Unless the electorate is well educated in international affairs, realizes its immense importance in the ideological struggle, and follows unselfish, far-sighted leaders, it may press for domestic concessions which sacrifice foreign policy principles.

Political, social, and economic groups, which heavily influence policy formulation, interpret their members' attitudes much in accordance with their own prejudices. Their ideas concerning imperialism, socialism, internationalism, isolationism, interventionism, pacifism, fiscal management, and personnel policy are bound to cause repercussions in their own foreign office and, as a consequence, in those of other countries. Their views on international relations usually are based upon friendliness toward those governments which they presume will further their own groups' interests, or upon fear or dislike of governments they regard as a menace to their groups' objectives. Philosophical and cultural affinities cannot but affect relations between nations, and it is the influence of the leaders of political and social groups which articulate such affinities.

Another issue is the nature of constitutional law, the impact of its tradition on usages and behavior, and its prevailing interpretation. The varied origin and development of constitutions in parliamentary democracies led to antagonisms which prevented cooperation and unity of purpose even in the face of rising communism. Only when this threat became acutely dangerous were traditional obstacles overcome, making possible mutual defense and economic cooperation alignments.

The communist states also have constitutions. The Soviet Constitution of 1936 is an outstanding example of a basic law which is all form and little content. Promulgated by Stalin, it codified the USSR's administrative formula, but constitutions are written not only to determine who has the power but how it shall be used. These are not the most important articles. The soul of a constitution, its very spirit, is the enduring and decisive element handed down from generation to generation. In the Soviet Constitution this element is missing. It could not be otherwise since it is doctrinally a temporary document, written for an allegedly transitory stage of a socialist society. It never influences Soviet strategy and tactics, but only forms the legal basis for the organs of the Soviet state and its constituent republics. No wonder that its tenuous philosophy is reflected in the *tours de force* of Soviet policies, both internal and external. The fundamentals of the Soviet state are contained in doctrinal principles, not in constitutional law. This is even more so in Communist China whose Constitution does not hide the role of the party and its revolutionary objectives.

The constitutions of the new Afro–Asian states have as yet left little impact on their policy and society; they are too recent and may yet be revised.

Clearly, then, the impact of constitutional philosophies and the way of life they engender show in domestic as well as foreign attitudes. A constitution, if it is more than a piece of paper, eventually will mold national character, attitudes, prejudices, and aspirations. Therefore, it forms an important part of the background of the country's political motivation and, in turn, of its views on international issues. It remains to be seen whether a new Soviet Constitution, if it is ever written, will reflect the actual state of Soviet affairs more realistically than did the Stalin Constitution of 1936, or whether it will be merely an expression of the post-Stalinist interpretation of Marxism–Leninism as applied to the USSR in "transition to communism."

Does constitutional philosophy influence public opinion and does that public opinion influence the policy-makers? Does the national mind, its social, economic, and political climate, produce a trend of thinking which eventually will impose itself upon foreign policy and thereby upon international relations? How articulate is it? Is it indeed the great oracle of democracy? Does it exist in totalitarian states?

In the democracies, public-opinion polls have developed highly scientific methods of sampling views. Leaving aside the element of imponderables, their findings seldom indicate an objective or informed approach by the "man in the street." Generally, public opinion on foreign affairs abounds in biased prejudices, subjective interpretation of news, and emotions. As pointed out earlier, the mass mind does not react rationally. Dependent as he is on newspapers, radio, television, and neighbors, the "man in the street" is likely to be influenced by his own personal involvements, if any, rather than on the reliable sources of information at his disposal.

Public opinion in foreign affairs rarely reacts without preconceived notions; for the most part, it is anchored in traditional concepts, outdated though these may be. It fears unconventional approaches abroad just as it fears them at home. Quick to reproach policy-makers either for being wrong or for having no policy at all, it cannot, by its very nature, offer constructive suggestions. The influence of mass communications media has increased but remains generally spotty; human nature tends to absorb or reject according to its tastes. Tolerance and objectivity are individual attributes; the mass mind may well be enlightened and no doubt its existence in democratic nations is part of the necessary checks and balances, but in international relations it usually lacks the cool, realistic, objective reasoning for which trained specialists strive.

No way has yet been devised to produce a public opinion on specific foreign policy issues that could inspire an official policy. It is even questionable whether prevailing trends can be ascertained with reasonable certainty. In nearly all cases, public opinion declares itself for or against policies with insufficient knowledge of the background and reasons for such policies. It can rarely contribute to the solution of international problems. Analysis of foreign relations requires not only specialized training but also creative intelligence and years of practical experience, domestic and foreign. Policy recommendations from anyone lacking these qualifications are almost certain to be unusable. No layman would dare to diagnose an illness: that is the trained physicians' business. Similarly, no person lacking the necessary background and education can bring into play his full critical faculties however he may excel in hindsight.[22]

Since World War II, the number of citizens who try to obtain a clearer picture of the world issues at stake has increased. Prejudice and misinformation have not been eliminated, but the more serious-minded media of mass information have done much pioneering work, and the communication between heads of state and the people has qualitatively and quantitatively improved. Cordell Hull's ideal that "the people, who are sovereign, must not only educate their servants but must be willing to be educated by them"[23] is perhaps nearer to realization than ever before.

One reason for this may be that modern democratic policy-makers prefer to share their heavy responsibilities with their fellow citizens. The recent trend is for heads of state to utilize radio and television to put the issues before the people and ask support for their policies. In so doing, they demonstrate their desire for popular participation in decisions which affect the well-being of everyone. Generally, officials and parliamentary leaders responsible for foreign relations appreciate communications from the public; they are receptive to such democratic techniques as petitions, letters to the editor, and statements of

[22] Cf. T. A. Bailey's excellent study on the impact of public opinion on foreign policy, *The Man in the Street* (New York: The Macmillan Company, 1948).
[23] Department of State Bulletin, April 15, 1944, p. 340.

organizations created to articulate the voice of the people. They approve of debates and commentaries on radio and television or in the press — provided they are moderately conducted. But they also realize that public opinion at best no more than reveals the thinking of the electorate. They are aware that public advice cannot be based upon the best and latest information, much of which is confidential and limited to official use.

How much and what type of information should be disseminated to the public? In a democracy, and particularly in the United States, freedom of information is a strongly developed concept. Mass communications media go very far in printing or broadcasting news the publication of which frequently is not in the best interest of the national security. If news is withheld for security reasons, there is a general outcry: the public has the "right to know." Do such views contribute to a better understanding of the problems? There is serious doubt that they do. On the contrary, they may even add to the confusion; security news items have a way of being half-true, since full information cannot be divulged. Certainly, in a democracy there should be free access to information. But limitations are necessary in matters of national security and foreign relations. To better educate public opinion, more effort should be undertaken to disseminate basic information through government-sponsored offices. Britain and France do, to mention only a few; the US has never done it, except in wartime. Congress is extremely wary of what it calls domestic propaganda. Yet, through the polls, the people's influence on the choice of foreign policy officials is great. In order to choose discerningly one must possess intelligent views on international relations. Even one who votes for internal reasons cannot escape the fact that there no longer is a separation between domestic and foreign issues. All these considerations add up to the conclusion that the impact of public opinion on foreign affairs, so far, has been inconsequential.[24]

The picture is vastly different in totalitarian countries, where great efforts are being made to produce a uniform public opinion which in reality conforms to that of the ruling party. Whatever genuinely

---

[24] Cf. *The Mid-Century Challenge to U.S. Foreign Policy,* The Rockefeller Panel Report (New York: Doubleday, 1959), p. 64.

individualistic views exist are shackled by censors. Support for the policies of the regime in power is enforced. No qualifications are tolerated. There is no diversity in public statements: the lines established in Moscow or Peking must be followed explicitly. Arguments would invoke the crimes of "dogmatism," "revisionism," rightist or leftist "deviationism," "hooliganism," or "anti-party activities."

The communist agitation and propaganda apparatus is set up to prepare the mass mind for receptivity to regime policies. Great precaution is taken to prevent publication of foreign news except when it serves the party's purposes. Furthermore, many news items are doctored by omissions or quoting out of context. The isolation of the Soviet people is not so stringent as during the Stalin era but the vast majority of citizens still is exposed to completely one-sided information and their view of the world is thoroughly colored by the party's and government's lopsided reporting and interpretation. Even the Eastern European states, while not quite as isolated, are still very far from the wide open societies of the West. Red China, of course, has cut itself off completely from the rest of the world, including other components of the "socialist camp."

Combined with this isolation and a steady stream of indoctrination (replacing information) is an educational curriculum which, under party supervision, is conceived to train the child in the official doctrine from infancy through adulthood. Relations between "socialist" and "imperialist" states must of necessity be part of the overall curriculum. Thus public opinion is carefully shaped at an early age — one might say brainwashed — into a standard mold. Versatility of thought processes and broad understanding of other political systems are not considered desirable. What matters to the communist leaders is the acceptance of a one-sided world concept and faithful, if not enthusiastic, compliance with their orders. Only in this sense do they recognize the existence of a public opinion.

It is true that even in totalitarian countries, the regimes desire the voluntary support of the masses. But if it is not forthcoming, it is stimulated by persuasion or coercion. Thus, in the Western sense, there is no public opinion in communist-ruled states, for it is not freely arrived at and the issues of foreign affairs are exclusively a matter of party decision and government implementation.

••••4••

Cold War Economics

Political Economy — Bipolar

The principles of domestic economy necessarily reflect the conduct of external affairs. Political and economic policies flow from the same source. Changes in economic systems lead to changes in foreign relations just as political considerations modify economic philosophies. There is, consequently, a close interconnection between the political (ideological) and economic behavior of a nation. The revolutionary upheavals which affected world politics during the first half of the twentieth century not only have caused a profoundly transformed national economic system; they also have left their mark on international commerce, making economic warfare a part of the bipolar struggle between socialist, capitalist, and mixed systems. The communist countries are by no means the only ones affected although their break with tradition is far more drastic than were the modifications of the remnants of the mercantilist and *laissez-faire* schools which characterized nineteenth-century economies. But the revolutionists forced the traditionalists to revise their economic principles.

In contrast to the economic views and organization of the communist-ruled states which preach public ownership and planned economy, the non-communist world presents an almost chaotic picture of economic individualism. Its principles defend a wide range of private, semi-private, and semi-state-controlled economies, none of which has been able to maintain complete freedom of economic action. Even the free enterprise systems in the United States and Western Europe have become increasingly subjected to rules dictated by political necessities and national security precautions. These diverse Western economic philosophies are the result of defense measures rather than an attempt to "balance" power; all are reflected in prevailing political principles and are more or less determined by national self-interest, although they may have agreed, *nolens volens,* to accept U.S. leadership and assistance. This has been difficult for some countries, particularly Great Britain, whose pound sterling dominated the world markets before the dollar took precedence. Nor was the shift of economic influence from London's "City" to New York's Wall Street a source of unmitigated happiness for the United States. In a world of destitution and poverty, a rich nation's responsibilities are heavy indeed. The citizens of such a nation, who must help carry the burden in form of taxes, may well wonder if their sacrifice is warranted when they receive little gratitude and considerable abuse from some recipients of their aid.

Yet the Western states had little choice. The Afro–Asian neutralists were in a better position: they could accept aid from both the West and the East, claiming that their non-commitment policy forbade them to show favoritism — the favor being the acceptance of aid. As a result, there has been keen competition in establishing aid monopolies in the "zone of peace." Naturally, the West is concerned lest the invisible strings attached to communist aid cause economic infiltration and create a dependence upon military assistance. The Moscow–Peking leaders want to eliminate Western and specifically American influence from those countries which are greatly indebted to the U.S. foreign aid program. Although the economic philosophy of the uncommitted countries tends toward state control, many of them are further from Marxist economic principles than from the freer ways of the West. But since they wish to develop their own ideas, they tend to reject Western individualism as well as Eastern collectivism. This means there is a strongly competitive economic struggle between the contending super powers, reflecting the political-ideological chasm between them. It also means that economic conditions in the United States are of overpowering importance to the survival of the free world.

Let us recall that the rift between the two opposing camps is due mainly to a fundamental ideological cleavage. But political philosophies, as previously pointed out, go hand in hand with economic concepts. The United States has always believed that economic liberalism guarantees its citizens political freedom. It has ever wanted to maintain a state of economic individualism — free enterprise — with as few governmental controls as possible. More than their Western allies, the American people are suspicious of planned economy, although cooperatives find much favor in some regions, and such federal projects as the TVA generally are not regarded as government "interference" in a free economy. Compared with its status half a century ago, capitalism has become restricted. The antitrust laws, the growing power of labor unions, heavy progressive taxation and control over the export of strategic materials to politically suspect buyers, together with certain precautionary statutes of the New Deal, have braked irresponsible actions which might harm national economic strength. Thus, most restrictions must be regarded as safeguards rather than obstacles to free enterprise, which admittedly can be impeded by monopolistic capitalism as well as by socialism.

Whatever limitations of United States overseas trade exist are sanctioned by a Congress whose determination to preserve free enterprise is well known. These limitations protect economic security which may be threatened by inflation, scarcity of exportable goods, or the probability that exported material might eventually be used against the United States. Such restrictions may indicate a slow change in economic concepts but essentially are regarded only as emergency measures.

The West European allies of the United States have a liberal economic policy as well, but it is one with considerably broader state control. This may be attributed, in part, to a post-World War II tendency to veer toward a more planned economy. Unquestionably, this trend was stimulated by the belief that reconstruction could be tackled only with state aid, that individuals should not profit from a national emergency, and that the political demands of growing elements left of center must be met. Moreover, the commitments toward economic cooperation among West European states required a greater degree of national planning. Besides, certain aspects of most European economies have usually been controlled by the state, e.g., currency and foreign buying, transportation, and utilities. Thus, the American quest for free and equal trade opportunities will not necessarily be wholly subscribed to by formerly war-ravaged nations. Even after their economy has achieved a new stability, and provided a compromise has been reached between the political moderates and radicals at home, the tendency is away from, rather than toward too much, economic liberalism. It remains to be seen whether such a compromise can be achieved or whether an increasing trend toward socialist forms of economy will create a breach between American and non-totalitarian planned (and partially nationalized) economies. However, the unbridgeable abyss between such mild forms of Western socialism and the Marxian economies in the East may tend to keep West European — and for that matter, Asian — versions of economic socialism rather close to American free economy.

The communist rulers believe in the Marxian principle of liquidating private enterprise because, in their opinion, capitalists cannot help but exploit those without capital; capitalism creates wars and prevents international cooperation, its bourgeois value system is obsolete and doomed to die by the laws of dialectical and historical materialism. Thus, the communist governments, under orders from their parties, have taken over all means of production, all land, and all natural resources. They control the use of the labor force; their trade unions merely furnish their governments with additional control organizations and have no bargaining power. Without attempting to equalize incomes during the period of "socialist transition" (to communism), under the "temporary" dictatorship of the proletariat, the Soviet bloc, in contrast to Red China, has left some incentives for higher earnings but has totally eliminated private capital investments. Soviet "capitalists" may buy government bonds but have not necessarily the right to sell at will or at maturity of the bonds. They may acquire the extra conveniences of luxury goods, if available, but they can own no producing industry, farm, real estate (summer cottages, "datchas," are built on government-owned land), or sizable trade establishment.

The USSR has set up export and import monopolies that operate under the supervision of the State Planning Committee, Gosplan, which is responsible for the Five and Seven Year Plans. Foreign trade activities are directed by the State Committee of Foreign Economic Relations, spearheading the Ministry of Foreign Trade. Foreign buying and selling are thus strictly regulated and subordinated to overall planning.

Such planning is no longer restricted to the Soviet Union. The

Kremlin has attempted to create, through CEMA, an integrated East European economic organization which would assign its members specific tasks in accordance with their economic assets and know-how. Although CEMA still is an influential body and has, in fact, grown stronger during the sixties, Moscow has been unable to succeed more than partially. CEMA members, particularly Romania, were unwilling to sacrifice their economic sovereignty but in view of their dependence on Soviet trade, most of them had to make concessions.

Prior to the escalation of the Sino–Soviet conflict, Peking was represented at CEMA as an observer. The Mao regime inferred that China's economy differed from that of Eastern Europe but that, by keeping informed, it could gauge the assets and requirements of the "fraternal" countries and adjust its own economy accordingly. No longer being "fraternal," Peking is not now represented in CEMA and trade between Red China and the Soviet bloc has virtually come to an end. Thus the communist orbit can no longer be looked upon as a more or less coordinated economic system.

Clearly, the two opposing economic philosophies are separated by beliefs and principles which neither group intends to compromise. These principles are reflected in the domestic systems which symbolize the ideas of the two super powers. Thus, the economic order of battle is identical with the political order of battle, and the protagonists intend to defend their ideas to the bitter end.

Foreign Aid

During World War II, the United States was the "Arsenal of Democracy." It mobilized its armed might and marshaled its economic forces to fight against totalitarian tyranny and to bring about an enduring peace with economic well-being. To stem the Axis tide, the United States initiated the Lend-Lease program; it became the principal contributor to the United Nations Relief and Rehabilitation Administration (UNRRA).

Immediately after the war, when the Soviet Union was following a program of economic isolation into which it dragged those states that became its satellites, the United States began to implement a program of active assistance to war-torn nations. It did not wait for the organization of the International Bank for Reconstruction and Development and the International Monetary Fund. After having assisted many members of the United Nations under Lend-Lease legislation and contributing most of the funds necessary for UNRRA, it began to make credits available through the Export–Import Bank (founded in 1939). It later subscribed a major part of the capital for the International Bank and the Monetary Fund. Also, through special bilateral agreements, individual loans were granted to Great Britain, France, Greece, and Turkey.

Already in December 1945, the United States Government had announced proposals for the expansion of world trade and employment. In accordance with overall policy, they favored free trade, opposed governmental restrictions, and denounced restrictive business practices (such as cartels or price fixing) that would impede full employment. This policy has been adopted by the International Trade Organization (ITO), set up by the Economic and Social Council of the United Nations (ECOSOC). Its specific duty is to deal with these problems on an international scale. ECOSOC hopes that the member states of the UN will be induced to conclude agreements which will reduce tariffs, limit the activities of international cartels, eliminate preferential rates discriminating between the products of different nations, and outlaw export subsidies or dumping. (Unfortunately, ITO has been unable to fully implement this program.)

In June 1947, the United States Government announced the creation of the European Recovery Program (ERP) or Marshall Plan to assist those countries which needed American help to overcome the destructive effects of Axis crimes. ERP was designed to "help suffering countries to help themselves" and, in so doing, to arrest the political radicalism which thrives on economic deterioration. In effect, the Marshall Plan was established to prevent a new totalitarianism from replacing the old one. Tyranny, the United States Government felt, grows out of despondency and desperation and, once established, endangers peoples far and wide.

Finally, the so-called Point Four Program of technical assistance to underdeveloped countries was established.[1] In some ways, it had a greater psychological effect than the Marshall Plan itself, even though expenditures were only a fraction of the latter's outlay.

Foreign aid is a practical demonstration of a policy which is both political and economic. Inasmuch as huge expenditures are involved, the execution of this policy depends upon the consent of Congress, which must annually pass appropriations. Even though the principle of foreign aid involves long-range policy planning which pertains to the security of the United States in particular and the West in general, Congress until recently has refused to make long-range appropriations, insisting on yearly examinations of the aid programs. Only in 1961, did it accept, in principle, President Kennedy's recommendation to permit five-year planning to the extent of 1½ billion dollars annually, to be reviewed and approved *ex post facto*.[2] In this connection it is noteworthy that those foreign policies which depend upon economic efforts require more parliamentary supervision than those purely political policies in which no immediate expenditures are involved. In parliamentary democracies, the people's representatives hold the nation's purse strings. Strictly political issues are subject to occasional investigation, especially those pertaining to national security, but the conduct of foreign affairs is generally left to the "technicians." And yet, economic policies reflect the political principles underlying a nation's behavior pattern.

The powerful impact of ERP and its unquestionable benefit to Western stabilization have caused the Soviet Union to imitate and convert the Plan for its own particular purposes. Soviet economic aid has, in fact, become a well-entrenched feature of what is called "peaceful competition." Communist China, weak as its economy still is, has entered the field competing with Moscow for influence in the third world. It is necessary to examine the nature of this communist economic warfare weapon more closely.

The Soviet Union imitated the American principle of economic aid which it did not fully employ until after the death of Stalin when

---

[1] Announced by President Truman in his inaugural address of January 20, 1949.
[2] See Public Law 87–195, 87th Congress, S. 1983 of September 4, 1961, entitled "Act for International Development of 1961."

prevalent conditions permitted application of the aid tactic as a proper instrument of the cold war. The violence unchained by Stalin after World War II to speed revolution in Western Europe had come to naught. It was evident to the new Soviet leaders that they could go no further without running the risk of war — which they were unwilling to do. It is true that violence had achieved its objective in Asia, where Chinese communism conquered the mainland with surprising speed. Nor could the Korean aggression be forgotten. Nevertheless, the centers of opposing powers in America and Europe had remained inviolable.

Communist leaders are no dreamers. Nor do they pay much heed to the "shame" of retreat. The "operational code" of the Kremlin[3] provides sufficient reasons for retreating when advantages thus far secured are endangered by holding untenable positions. Therefore, new strategies and tactics — the word policies is advisedly not used — had to be developed. There is to be "peaceful coexistence" with capitalist powers which is only a holding operation against the West. A policy of economic aid and assistance is held applicable to the non-aligned areas which have thrown off the shackles of "colonialism" and appear to be steering clear of the East–West conflict. These countries, intensely proud of their new independence, would have been antagonistic to Soviet domination in any form. The Kremlin, appreciating this fact, played upon the surging nationalism, sought to stimulate it further, and exploited it against the former colonial powers. The Communist Chinese, also vitally interested in the non-aligned countries, proceeded along similar lines, with the advantage in Africa and Asia of not being a white people. The former colonial areas paid scant attention to the historical fact that Russia had subjugated Central Asian peoples and subsequently tried to russify them under Soviet rule, though it must be admitted that these minorities became Soviet citizens and their countries parts of the USSR. Red China followed the Han tradition of suppressing minorities even while exhorting them to unite for the sake of communist objectives and China's reconstruction. In contrast, Western European nations are

---

[3] N. Leites, *The Operational Code of the Politbureau* (New York: McGraw–Hill Book Co., 1951), *passim*.

the archetypes of colonizers, and the United States, whose colonial undertakings were minor and short-lived, was made co-responsible for the sins of colonialism. Communist propaganda saw to it that the West's voluntary liberation of most of these countries was acknowledged not as an act of mature statesmanship but as "neo-colonialism," at least while economic connections still existed.

Since Khrushchev, attempts to influence neutralist nations through communist parties, legal and illegal, were held to a minimum. Instead, the USSR assumed the position of a great benevolent power offering help by extending low-interest credits, mainly for the construction of industries and the development of natural resources. "The Soviet leaders may have felt that they had little choice but to get into the aid business, if they wanted to exercise continuing influence in the course of events in the underdeveloped countries."[4] These countries are in Africa, Asia, the Middle East, and Latin America; in Europe, only Iceland and Yugoslavia obtained economic credits. It is interesting to note that Soviet aid generally supports the governments in power even if they are not "socialist." Red China's aid is predominantly extended for purposes of propaganda, subversion, and infiltration. Beneficiaries are individuals friendly to Peking and radical groups (such as trade unions) and native communist or socialist parties. While no exact statistics exist, it is generally believed that the Soviet Union contributed about 70 per cent, the Eastern European satellites approximately 20 per cent, and Communist China the rest toward economic aid. Needless to say, this combined outlay is considerably less than the aid extended by the United States during the same period.

One would imagine that the tremendous American exertions would produce a strong and lasting impact on the underdeveloped areas, despite the fact that Western monies are given only upon receipt of a satisfactory explanation of their intended use while the Soviets ask no questions. One would also expect that the many American grants, outright gifts, would impress recipients enough for them to be satisfied to pay the higher interest rates required on Western loans. Not

---

[4] J. S. Berliner, *Soviet Economic Aid* (New York: F. A. Praeger, Inc., 1958), p. 17.

so. Moscow always knew how to win a "favorable image in the eyes of many people in the underdeveloped countries who are not communists."[5] Red China during the first decade of its existence also received preferential treatment by popular opinion in these countries but its glamour steadily faded after the Tibetan persecution, the catastrophe of its "big leap," its massive foreign policy failures, and the "cultural revolution." The United States, on the other hand, has never lost its taint of "imperialism," despite all the help it has extended to these areas, and the war in Vietnam has been well used by the communists to further denigrate US humanitarian efforts.

It is uncertain whether these areas will ever tip the scales of balance between the bipolar groups. They do, however, constitute a potential source of trouble to the West which could be activated by the communists. These is also opportunity for Soviet infiltration through technical advisers and other personnel connected with the aid program. These emissaries are responsible for "selling the USSR to the leaders and people of their target area." Since they also are obliged to collect intelligence data, as is every Soviet citizen abroad on official business, they serve as spies as well as propagandists. They combine the impression of their selfless sympathy for the "zone of peace" with attacks against the Western powers as colonialist exploiters. In comparison with Western credits, theirs are small, but they offer a low interest rate and may disregard losses if political advantages can be achieved. They give aid "with no questions asked" and permit repayments in local currency or such available commodities as their leaders are willing to accept in lieu of money. Finally, there is the professed policy of granting credits without "strings attached." They appear genuine because offers of aid have been made to such countries as Iran, Turkey, and Pakistan, which cannot be accused of being overly favorable to communist states. The United Arab Republic (Egypt) is an interesting case in point: the Nasser regime has no sympathy for indigenous communists and treats them roughly but the Kremlin, eager to stir up trouble in the Middle Eastern power vacuum, has provided it not only with weapons but

[5] R. L. Allen, *Soviet Economic Warfare* (Washington, D. C.: Public Affairs Press, 1960), pp. 132–133.

has financed the gigantic Aswan Dam. But for the unfortunate policy of the late US Secretary of State John Foster Dulles, this could have been avoided and the Arab–Israeli war of June 1967 might not have occurred.

The student of East–West tension is aware that no communist aid offer is extended without calculated political reasons. In the first place, an atmosphere of good will toward communist-ruled states is to be created, possibly in conjunction with ill will toward the USA and the West. Secondly, opportunities are to be sought for political and ideological infiltration under the protective cover of supporting national aspirations. Finally, dependence on Soviet bloc or Chinese assistance and trade is to be established while dependence upon the West is gradually minimized. If the "socialist camp" succeeds in achieving these objectives, its interests in influencing local politics can be expressed freely, indigenous communist parties can help to secure a foothold for encroachment, and the West can be denied access to economic resources or trade within the dominated areas.

It has often been asked how it is possible for the uneven and partially weak economies of the East to undertake such a costly program as economic aid. The answer to this question is twofold.

First, as stated above, communist economy is shaped by political and ideological decisions. It is not a profit economy even though some trends such as Liebermanism may give such an impression. (Indeed, even Peking has accused the USSR as "neo-capitalistic.") Its development is strictly state-controlled; its resources can be channelled according to political goals which, in turn, are strategic stages to be reached under well-defined conditions. It cannot be compared with free Western economy, which is controlled only to the extent necessary to protect free enterprise from economic libertinism rather than to gain political power for the state.

Second, the long-prevailing impression that communist economy is necessarily poor needs qualification. If the strength of a national economy is gauged in accordance with the power of the state, Soviet economy is strong now and promises to become even stronger. If an economy is judged weak because of insufficient production of consumer goods to improve the living standard of its citizens, then indeed Soviet economy is weak and Chinese economy calamitous.

Unfortunately, in the struggle between totalitarianism and democracy, state-party power is decisive.

It would be disastrous if the clarity of Western economic analysis were permitted to be blurred by political animosity. Since its creation, the Soviet Union has succeeded in pulling its economy out of a quagmire of backwardness. A modern industrial establishment was created and, since the death of Stalin, living standards have slowly but steadily improved. Disregarding the lack of consumer goods industries and the continued weakness of agriculture, the recent Soviet Gross National Product (GNP) is equal to that of the United States. Economic gaps may be considerable yet they do not really affect the Soviet power position.

The other communist giant, Red China, came into being when the Soviet experience was already more than three decades old. Its problems are greater both in quality and quantity than were those of the young Bolshevik state in the twenties and many of them are of its own making. The inordinate impatience of its leaders which led to the "great leap forward" turned out to be a major blunder, and the establishment of the People's Communes, anti-human as they were, further aggravated conditions. Natural catastrophes, both floods and droughts, all but ruined agriculture, and the industrial goals had to be sharply decreased to release manpower for salvaging the sources of food. When the retrenchment from the "big leap" and the de-emphasis on the communes had helped the economy to recover somewhat from these political and natural calamities, the "cultural revolution" disrupted it again, and the consequences may well be so disastrous that one can hardly calculate how many years it will take to make up for the loss in industrial production and agricultural neglect.[6] On top of this, the Moscow–Peking conflict dried up Soviet aid.

Communist China is in a precarious situation and presumably will remain so for some years. But it would be an unforgivable mistake on

---

[6] Cf. Field, "Chinese Communist Industrial Production," in *An Economic Profile of Mainland China*, Vol. *1*, studies prepared for the Joint Economic Committee, Congress of the United States (Washington: U.S. Government Printing Office, 1967).

the part of Western observers to repeat the miscalculations of the thirties, when the Soviet Union was virtually given up for dead. China has gone through many times of trouble; its potential will in the end assert itself. The Chinese are tough, frugal, and enormously industrious; although their problems will be with them for decades to come, it would be senseless to forget that they are a great and populous power hostile toward the West and apparently devoted to the communist doctrine as interpreted by Mao Tse-tung.

To sum up — what do these considerations mean in terms of international relations and the formulation of foreign economic policies?

In a time when world views on economic theories and practices were similar, governments could more easily agree on mutual objectives and map out plans for international convalescence. But in a world split between free and controlled economies, with some nations trying to combine features of both, agreements are difficult, sometimes impossible, to reach. Day-to-day political opportunism may permit short-range accommodations as communist tactics recommend; long-range understanding cannot be expected. Even within the framework of the United Nations the Soviet bloc refused to cooperate in economic measures designed to implement the Bretton Woods proposals for postwar reconstruction.

To be sure, business is still being transacted on a limited scale between the Soviet bloc and the West. The Soviet Union will buy or sell so long as its interests are served. Controlled socialist economy would not strengthen capitalist economy by buying the latter's products unless it needed goods badly. Communist clamor for free trade is nothing but a method to mislead public opinion. This is perfectly natural in the Leninist view. After all, the economic principles of the communist states are determined by Marxism–Leninism as reinterpreted from time to time by Soviet leaders.

The organizing of state trading agencies is no political concession to countries in which such agencies are located but a temporary expedient to maintain trade until such time as the Soviet bloc no longer needs to trade with capitalist powers. Soviet successes in economic development have brought the USSR nearer to its goal, but its enormous capital investment in weapons development and such specialized projects as space exploration have deprived it of progress in other areas of economy; agriculture still has not lived up to Khrushchev's promises which surely was one of the reasons for his ouster.

Red China's efforts, after having shown some results of its frantic efforts for the first eight years of its existence, have temporarily collapsed as a result of natural calamities and self-induced catastrophes such as the "big leap forward" and the "cultural revolution." But the Chinese are only down, not out. It cannot be foreseen how long the country will need to stand on its feet again; much will depend on its relations with the USSR and the East European states and a revision of its principles. Mao probably will not concede the error of his ways, but his successors may adopt more realistic measures. China will remain a power to be reckoned with, as demonstrated by the surprisingly rapid development of its nuclear arsenal.

To Have and to Hold: Problems of Security

Our investigation of national power has shown that its significance and extent have been greatly modified by the progress of technology. In the period of transition from the electronic to the nuclear era, some traditional yardsticks of evaluation have survived, but in terms of national security, they have lost much of their former meaning. As social and technological revolutions render increasingly obsolete former notions of foreign affairs, lack of precedent makes it extremely difficult to devise a reasonably stable security system.

The traditional West finds this situation more arduous to cope with than does the revolutionary East. Our approach is conditioned by the heritage of Western thought. Yet there is urgent need for adjustment to the fact that our traditions are opposed by iconoclastic revolutionists. Our own methods do not suffice to contain the danger; to adopt the enemy's is to sin against our very nature. The revolutionists can more easily shed the conventions of traditional ethics. Having severed their links with the past, they are not bound by pre-revolutionary concepts. Consciously, at least, they feel free of guilt. They seek security to protect what they have and to fortify the bridgehead of revolution. In the democracies, the citizenry has hardly begun to evaluate its position and to understand the need for sacrifice to meet the challenge to its philosophy of life.

The non-communist allies in Europe and Asia have warned their peoples of this threat in conventional terms, but failed to put the successes and intentions of the communists into the proper ideological and technological context. Our approach, on the whole, has remained negative and defensive. Imprisoned by old-fashioned reasoning and the sometimes desperate attempt to superimpose obsolete thinking upon contemporary requirements, we have lacked imagination. This is humanly understandable but politically indefensible.

Since World War II, communist regimes have extended rule or influence over an additional 700 million people and thus are in position to hold sway, directly or indirectly, over almost one third of the earth's population. Their territorial spheres of influence have expanded by about 25 million square miles. They have succeeded in harming Western interests throughout much of the uncommitted world and have never ceased to attempt penetration of Western spheres of influence in Asia, Africa, and Latin America. They have leveled an incessant barrage of "anti-imperialist" propaganda against the West, particularly the United States. They have not permitted the world to enjoy a genuine peace since the end of World War II and desire no such peace except on their own terms. To the communists, "coexistence" is merely a continuation of the ideological and economic struggle without open hostilities.

Under such circumstances, how can the security of the Western world be assured? Is the search for an effective stalemate the only means to prevent the communists from swallowing the other two thirds of the earth's population? Can security be achieved by isolation? By participation in collective security pacts? By regional arrangements of mutual defense and economic cooperation? Or is international organization a solution?

Security from the danger of foreign aggression is the rock-bottom requirement of every government's internal and external policies. The endeavor to safeguard this security has bedeviled statesmen for centuries. Several methods have been used to implement security requirements: isolation, autarky, and neutralism; balance of power; collective security; arms control and disarmament; protective alliances; and international organization.

• ISOLATION, AUTARKY, AND NEUTRALISM — *Isolation,* however "splendid," is now archaic. Prior to the advent of modern state and communications systems, a country could remain neutral in the face of conflict involving nearby powers. A favorable geographic position helped; for example, the United States was blessed with protective bodies of water which, before the post-World War II technological revolution, remained formidable obstacles to predatory aggressors. After the war, only super powers could afford the luxury of nation individualism and that within strict limits. Modern communication techniques and the consequent vulnerability of all nations to intercontinental aircraft and missiles have rendered isolation obsolete.

Autarky is not necessarily identical with isolation. It may possibly exist, to a degree and for a limited time, in large countries possessing great natural wealth and industrial facilities. But interchange of goods is as important as interchange of ideas; they cannot be blocked indefinitely.

Neutralism is a hidden form of isolation. It differs somewhat from *neutrality*, which in international law has been defined as a recognized abstention from involvement in war between other nations. (The Hague Convention of 1907 codified the rights and duties of neutrals.) Not always was such legal status accepted by belligerents. The case of Switzerland is exceptional and due to that country's favorable topography and relative smallness. This is not to say that a neutral state cannot be more favorably inclined to one side than to the other provided it forbears demonstrating such sentiments by violation of neutrality. Austria is a case in point.

Neutralism is a far more opportunistic position. One might say it is a strategy, employed predominantly by the new and uncommitted Afro–Asian countries, not only to steer clear of the struggle between the opposing super powers, but also to obtain from both of them as much aid as possible. Small wonder the powers which determine the character of international relations, in seeking to fortify their political and economic positions, try to prevent these countries from falling under the adversary's influence. Thus, the wooing of neutralists has been steadily intensified. As a result, they have left the side lines to become passive participants in the bipolar wrestling for predominance, whether they like it or not.

The communists, blocked by the nuclear deterrent, encourage neutralism in order to prevent uncommitted countries from having close relations with the West and to keep them open for their own manipulations. The West's basic apprehension about neutralism is not the fear that a country will become genuinely neutral, but that by infiltration the communists will gradually bring it into their fold.

With all their belligerent noises, the men of Peking, weak as they are, have difficulties remaining logical in reconciling doctrine with the realities of their situation. They are violent in language but cautious in action. Unless they throw all reason aside and are bent on producing a *Götterdämmerung* Chinese style, they will be wary of an armed conflict which may become too big for them to handle. They would conduct a "war of liberation" — but only without too much risk. Moreover, Soviet policy of "peaceful coexistence" — not to mention their economic calamities — puts a damper on their belligerency, no matter how vigorously they might argue against the principle of coexisting with the "imperialists." Undoubtedly, this position has influenced both Moscow's and Peking's attitudes in the Vietnam war.

If the West, in case of local conflict, stands firm and demonstrates its determination to prevent further communist encroachments, the result may be neutralization of a contested territory by mutual consent of the super powers. This concept of enforced neutralization could become a pattern whenever conflicts are fomented by infiltrating communist-supported forces and could determine the future of Vietnam. In the course of the years, one could envision a number of Afro–Asian countries being subjected to such enforcement.

One cannot assume, however, that after neutralization of an area, the major communist powers would continue to recognize this state of affairs indefinitely. Efforts would be made to obtain the sympathy of the governments and the peoples. The goal is to induce neutralist countries to join the "socialist commonwealth" on their own account. In such an event, there is little, if anything, the free world can do without negating its own principle of self-determination.

• BALANCE OF POWER — The traditional concept of the balance of power has fascinated generations of political savants, whose interpretations of it vary. For the purpose of this examination, let it be defined as the quest for equilibrium between nation–states, designed to prevent any one of the group of nations from gaining ascendancy over the others.

An objective analysis of the concept yields little in its favor. Though justifiable during certain periods of history, since the beginning of the twentieth century it must be regarded as obsolete. Indeed, it was perhaps already obsolete in the very century which enshrined it as the guiding philosophy of international relations because it did not — and could not — succeed in maintaining power relations such as those established by the Holy Alliance. Old powers faded as new ones appeared; new interests created new alliances; and conditions outside Europe gained increasing influence on the power constellations of nations and alliances. These constellations, not only in Europe but throughout the world, have changed radically because of the ideological schism between the traditional and revolutionary powers. Such bipolarity is one of the main factors that have destroyed the classic balance of power system. An additional phenomenon is the disappearance of a balancing power such as Great Britain or the Austro–Hungarian empire prior to World War I.

Essentially, the rigidity of bipolar power *matching* ("coexistence" in communist terms) differs from the flexible maneuvering of the nineteenth-century power *balancing* mainly in the diminishing opportunity to change the pattern of balance and the resultant stiffening of ideological incompatibility. Even more important is the fact that *war, in the nuclear era, can no longer be looked upon as a practicable instrument of foreign policy.* (See Chapter 6.)

Once it was, as Clausewitz wrote, the continuation of foreign policy "by other means." The possibility of its use affected a nation's policy. War was like a ghost which could be materialized at will: hence the tendency to balance war-making potential. But the nuclear deterrence created a balance of terror which virtually precluded maneuvering and made the specter of nuclear war sufficiently visible for the governments to shrink from inviting its presence. Despite the Kremlin's occasional "rattling" of the Bomb, the policy of "peaceful coexistence" indicates Soviet recognition that its objectives must be reached by means short of war. One protagonist's edge in technological progress could not end this stalemate because even a few retaliatory nuclear weapons would suffice to cause the attacker untold harm. The Mao regime, which has successfully produced nuclear prototypes, officially rejects this reasoning but almost certainly must be aware of its correctness.

The scientific race between the USA and the USSR in which Red China now participates indicates a recognition that deterrence can never become a *status quo* and, further, proclaims the intensity of the struggle for influence on world opinion. Moreover, there is military, political, and economic competition. The USSR proposes to gain ascendancy over the United States by ideological impact, economic expansion, superior scientific training, and the intended creation of that paragon, the *homo sovieticus*, who is prepared to enter the realm of communism, content with only his needs and without desire for his deserts.

These efforts are made not only for security but to unbalance the "imperialists" by means less risky than nuclear warfare. They are made in the belief that, according to the unshakable law of historical materialism, "imperialism" must inevitably fall into decay, and that "peaceful competition" may hasten the day. In other words, the "socialist camp" seeks more than mere security, namely, undisturbed time to create the "material-technical base" for communism. The struggle between the two protagonists is irreconcilable. It cannot be explained simply in terms of conventional power politics, where adjustments and concessions are feasible. It is a battle for prevailing philosophies of life.

The sought-after uncommitted countries would bring additional strength to whichever camp they chose, merely by being benevolent while ostensibly remaining neutralist. But they have neither the power nor the cohesion to decide the issue. It is unlikely that all or most of them would throw in their lot with either Moscow or Peking. Meanwhile the nuclear arsenal remains the great "balancer." "Peaceful competition" can be a decisive unbalancing factor only if the Western alliance neglects to play its part.

We can see that the scales which weigh the balance of power are frozen by the socio-political doctrine and the nuclear arsenal of the chief antagonists. Is there a way out of the deadlock? Can collective security succeed where balance of power has failed?

• COLLECTIVE SECURITY — Collective security is a system of alliances which is built neither to match power nor to balance it. The participating states pledge to regard an attack against one member as an attack against all. Collective security, which was attempted by the League of Nations Covenant (Articles 10–16), was most clearly the object of the Treaty of Locarno of 1925 because that Pact did not specify a particular adversary. The Pact sought to establish a guarantee of peace from Germany, Belgium, France, Italy, and the United Kingdom. The former enemy promised to accept arbitration of unsettled issues with Belgium, France, Poland, and Czechoslovakia. The Pact raised extraordinarily high hopes throughout Europe and the world; rarely had an international agreement so caught the public fancy. It remained for Hitler to break it in 1936 when he marched into the demilitarized Rhineland.

Unquestionably, the Pact's intention was sound. Had the world been spared the rise of totalitarianism with its ruthless disregard of treaties, the idea of collective security, in possible conjunction with the League of Nations, could have generated a long period of peace. Unfortunately, the development of ideological and technological revolutions has since rendered collective security obsolete as a universal concept.

Among politicians, the concept of collective security has enjoyed little popularity. It received support neither from nationalists, who put sovereignty above all considerations, nor from Marxists, who fear it may obstruct socialist expansion. As an abstract ideal, collective security advanced the European "concert" to one of international scope. But the inevitable consequences of a divided world rendered the ideal unattainable. Could international organization be regarded as an alternative? The League of Nations had tried and failed; the United Nations met with some success but was unable to enforce genuine world-wide cooperation among its members. In a sense, international organization is collective security at its best; if it failed in its simpler stage, how could its most sophisticated form be expected to work?

The difficulties spring neither from jealousies among free world nations nor attempts at power balancing acts within the Western alliance, nor even the influx of new inexperienced states whose representatives wish to be regarded as the equals of experienced statesmen of long diplomatic tradition. Rather, it is the built-in intransigence of the communist states, which look upon stability as incompatible with their goal of revolution. As members of the UN, possessing through the Soviet Union the right of veto in the Security Council, they can prevent the organization from opposing communist-organized aggression. Moreover, even the free world nations are reluctant to oppose such aggression; when the UN did undertake active measures against the communist invasion of South Korea, most members contributed only token forces and left the United States to bear the brunt of the burden.

Collective security cannot function if it embraces only "friendly" nations. The very term implies that antagonistic states become part of it and be given opportunities to assuage their antagonism through participation in a community of states whose goal is to ensure peace. Such was the objective of the Treaty of Locarno. Based upon concepts of Western civilization, it presupposed acceptance of recognized ethics and international law. No need to point out that the "isms" do not recognize the very concepts they tend to destroy.

• ARMS CONTROL AND DISARMAMENT — Perhaps the heart of the problem of how to ensure national security is the arms race between East and West. It would have been natural, after the exertion of a terrible war, to follow the road to disarmament. The United States, having almost eagerly wrecked its enormous fighting machine, relied on the atomic bomb and the United Nations. Stalin willed it differently, and his initiative stimulated rearmament and the nuclear race. When the USSR acquired the nuclear weapon, the United States, naturally though reluctantly, had to enter the race again if only to maintain a balance of terror. But the danger of political or military miscalculation must have been recognized by Moscow as it had been by Washington and its allies. The Kremlin's elevation of "peaceful coexistence" from a tactic to a policy almost certainly testified to the Soviet leaders' realization that the risk of conflagration was too great to be accepted and that Leninist doctrine had to be changed to meet the new situation. Only Peking was reluctant to accept "peaceful coexistence" as more than a brief, temporary stratagem. The Chinese communist leaders still were so deeply immersed in Mao's version of Marxism–Leninism and so new in the experience of power that the more cautious Soviet attitude appeared to them as a violation of revolutionary principles — a position that became very clear after the Sino–Soviet conflict came into the open in April 1960.

For years, representatives of the opposing nation groups have tried to negotiate a stop to the arms race either by controlling arms production, including nuclear weapons, or by complete disarmament of nuclear and conventional types of weapons. Both political and technical proposals have been made. The Rapacki Plan (1958) proposed a de-nuclearized zone across Central Europe. Similar schemes were suggested for Asia and Latin America. The creation of an international machinery to control production and tests of nuclear weapons has been negotiated unsuccessfully; even if scientists should find a way to conduct a meaningful inspection, the political implications of an army of inspectors "invading" communist territory has thus far presented unconquerable obstacles to agreement. However, some progress has been made through the test ban treaty of 1963 and the agreement prohibiting the use of nuclear weapons in outer space (1966). As of this time, neither treaty has been signed by either France or Red China. Efforts are underway to negotiate a nuclear non-proliferation treaty but its prospects will depend in particular on the attitude of non-nuclear powers on the question of uses of nuclear energy and the perennial problem of inspection. A special case is the development of an anti-ballistic missile system (ABM) which the USSR has begun to install and which the USA will have to create unless both parties come to an agreement which would save billions of dollars. But if the price the Soviets ask is the elimination of the superiority of America's nuclear stockpile, the road to agreement will be full of obstacles.

This is not the place to discuss in detail negotiations and agreements regarding arms control or disarmament but merely to point them up. As Kissinger emphasized, the idea that "the best method of achieving stable peace was to remove the causes of political conflict"[1] has changed due to technological volatility: "A major cause of instability is the very rate of technological change."[2] But stability cannot be achieved on technological grounds alone. Unless the basic ideological cleavage between communists and non-communists can be

[1] H. A. Kissinger, *The Necessity for Choice* (New York: Harper and Brothers, 1960/61), p. 210.
[2] *Ibid.*

bridged or adjusted, disarmament negotiations will be conducted mainly for the sake of world public opinion. For the communist leaders, the search for "peaceful coexistence" by arms control or disarmament serves both propaganda and strategy: they glorify themselves as champions of peace while trying to slacken the vigilance of the free world. Moreover, they believe that disarmament, by engendering economic upheaval in capitalistic countries, would enhance their position vis-à-vis the neutral nations by exemplifying their own prosperity. Realizing this, the West is not overly impressed with Eastern protestations for peace and disarmament, certainly not until effective control over arms production can be set up. Without it, the race for superior weapons systems remains a grave danger. One cannot rely on honest intentions; honesty in international relations is rare and not characteristic of the "socialist camp." While it would be naive to assume that the world is divided into angels and devils, still, it is fair to state that the ethical concepts which determine the actions of traditional states do not sanction the thoroughly unscrupulous policies of revolutionary governments which shy away from nothing which might help to achieve their ends. Quite likely the communists have similar reservations toward the "imperialists." The diametrically opposed political philosophies of the two camps are not conducive to mutual trust.[3]

Moreover, there is evidence for those who care to look beyond the veneer of détente that the long-range goal of communist parties remains fundamentally aggressive and aims at eliminating capitalism and "imperialism" in order to establish a socialist and eventually communist world system. In contrast, and perhaps as a result of this communist stance, Western strategy is essentially defensive, and there

---

[3] However, as Professor Ralph K. White pointed out to the writer, there is a "danger that an unduly simple black-and-white picture may develop, which oversimplified reality by picturing 'the enemy' as wholly diabolical and one's own nation as wholly moral, with rationalization of every morally questionable thing that one's own nation does in its struggle against the forces of evil. In recent years psychologists have given increased attention to this black-and-white picture and to its origins." White mentions two contributions in particular: F. Heider, *The Psychology of Interpersonal Relations* (New York: Wiley, 1958), and L. Festinger, *A Theory of Cognitive Dissonance* (New York: Harper and Brothers, 1957).

is no policy goal which would infringe on either the political or the economic sovereignty of any country. (The unique exception of Portugal does not alter the overall picture and must be regarded as a passing phenomenon.)

While some aspects of arms control may be attainable (without eliminating the arms race), disarmament unfortunately remains as yet a platonic concept: for the time being, it is unlikely to materialize and guarantee national security. Furthermore, collective security and international organization exert little influence over would-be aggressors, and the basic causes of the protracted crisis remain unresolved. Where does this leave the world as we approach the seventh decade of our century?

It stands confused and uncertain amidst overlapping and insufficient security concepts, primarily because the schism between the revolutionary and traditional groups of states has made impossible an integral mutual security arrangement. To protect itself against the danger implicit in this situation, the West has tried to hold the line with conventional means. Its governmental machinery, being subject to democratic checks and balances, cannot make the quick decisions of a dictator. Its pursuit of prosperity and the good life have led to a reluctance to sacrifice. It is confronted with the dilemma of how to retain a peacetime economy in the face of heavy outlays required to maintain a strong defense establishment as well as a sound social and economic life. Its attempts to negotiate controversial issues out of existence are frustrated because the communists do not cooperate: they calculate that time is on their side and so is their growing power.

In the face of an obstinate opponent, the West strives to bolster its power with collective security treaties, active participation in international organization, and stockpiling of nuclear and conventional weapons. In doing so for the legitimate reason of defending its philosophy of life against communist encroachment, it is inevitably involved in matching the opponent's deterrent power. There is no room today for the flexible balancing of the "international hierarchy" of the "Concert of Europe."

From the point of view of Western security, the division of the world into conflicting political systems is an appalling phenomenon. It renders useless the established norms of political conduct. Traditional considerations have given way to a bewildering conglomeration of approaches and techniques which must be met by a totally new concept of security. There once existed a "kind of communal constitutionalism" of the state system which promoted "restraining interplay and proper equilibration of military-political and socio-economic as well as purely institutional factors."[4] To some extent, the West still practices such interplay, but the neutralists have not absorbed the idea and the communists disdain it.

The communists' security problem has its complexities, too. The USSR was once recognized as the most powerful and influential component of the "world socialist system" and while it still holds that position in Eastern Europe, actually it has lost much of its hegemonial position. With the exception of Yugoslavia and Albania, the ostensibly independent Eastern European states remain under the dominating influence of Moscow, especially in all issues of foreign and military policy; even Romania which has assumed the most independent stance, remains economically and militarily subject to Soviet restraint. Communist China is going its own disastrous way and may well constitute a special security problem for Moscow. The parties around the world are no longer under the Soviet *diktat*; however, most of them tend to support Soviet policies while leaving themselves polycentric freedom of dissent.

Nevertheless, world communism continues to concentrate its technological and economic potential into predetermined channels so as to surpass the West, often at the cost of deprivation of its peoples. It need not justify its action before public opinion which it creates at will, for there is no border line between policy and propaganda. Having at its disposal a gigantic political and military apparatus, all communications media, a highly developed technology, and a growing economy, it can probe for a power vacuum and try to fill it wherever it occurs. Unwilling to risk nuclear war, and relying on the same unwillingness in the free world, it pursues its aim to demonstrate the "superiority" of the "socialist camp" by which it expects to

---

[4] G. Liska, *International Equilibrium, A Theoretical Essay on the Politics and Organization of Security* (Cambridge, Mass.: Harvard University Press, 1957), p. 23 ff.

win a bloodless victory, particularly over those nations which may be induced to believe that communism is the "wave of the future."

The security problem of the West is an entirely different matter: it is as complex as democratic processes and as difficult as achieving unity of thought and action among the individualistic governments of individualistic nations. Within its own "camp," the United States, often called the leading power of the West, does not, by its very nature, exercise influence comparable with that of the Soviets in their orbit.

Western society is pluralistic and individualistic; strategy and tactics must be negotiated one by one. This awkward and time-consuming process does not always lead to full agreement, coordination, and implementation. Similarly, the Western security system is multifaceted, consisting of a variety of measures which, combined with nuclear deterrence, constitutes a sort of balance of power opposite the East. However, it should be re-emphasized that the use of the term "balance" does not connote maneuverability. Within the Western group of nations, there is room to maneuver; in the Eastern camp, where it would be interpreted as an indication of weakness, there is none or, at best, as little as the USSR — or Red China — will expediently permit. The East's Marxist–Leninist rationale by definition is impervious to concession, except in minor issues. Communist flexibility is tactical only; its basic principles remain untouchable. There is no common platform for a *permanent* settlement between East and West without a convergence of the opposing political philosophies. Nevertheless, negotiations must be carried on to maintain a working relationship which is indispensable on this shrinking planet.[5]

• PROTECTIVE ALLIANCES — Security has two aspects: one is physical, the other intellectual and spiritual. The "isms" and modern technology have merged them. Security can be threatened by infil-

---

[5] In this connection, the behavior of Soviet Premier Alexei Kosygin during his visit to the United Nations General Assembly session on the Arab–Israeli conflict (June 1967) is of interest. Soviet strategic involvement in the Middle East rejected both concessions and compromise; Soviet diplomatic tactics permitted a meeting with the President of the United States which contributed nothing to a solution, but created a favorable image of a Soviet leader among the American people.

tration of ideas as well as by missiles with nuclear warheads. Nevertheless, the contestants' armed strength still is a predominant factor; its extent may determine the intensity with which intellectual and spiritual values are attacked or defended.

Primitive men, when attacked or threatened by danger, banded together. Sophisticated modern governments tended to do the same. In many cases it turned out not to be a satisfactory arrangement, and the line-up of alliances changed. But after the experience of World War II, there was much less room for maneuvering. Besides, governments became increasingly wary of alliances lest they commit themselves to an unalterable course of action. This was no sudden development: between the wars, Nazi Germany began to destroy the multilateral system of international organization and regional alliance by unilateral aggression; Fascist Italy and militarist Japan also disdained it. In the absence of the United States, Britain and France were unwilling to commit their resources to a collective security system. The Soviets joined the League of Nations very late in a desperate attempt to increase their own security. The West united against the Axis threat and the USSR became a *de facto* member of the alliance when Germany attacked Soviet territory. (Prior to this attack, the Soviets had called the war "imperialist," now it became a "just" war in defense of the "motherland.") The collaboration between the West and the USSR was a common-law marriage, dictated by necessity; at that time, Nazi aggression constituted a greater immediate menace to the West than did Soviet communism; first things had to be dealt with first. But there never was a formal treaty of alliance between the West and the USSR, nor was the Soviet leadership ever willing to consult as closely with the West as did the Allies among themselves.

The war over, Stalin almost immediately reverted to his hard, anti-"imperialist" line and implemented it by a series of aggressive acts: threats to Iran and Turkey; support of the Greek communist guerrillas; seizure of the Central–Eastern countries including Czechoslovakia, former bastion of democracy in that area; the Berlin blockade; harassments by the Cominform; and stimulation of serious unrest in France and Italy. Such menacing policies, initiated so soon after one of the most destructive of all wars, generated actions designed to prevent a repetition of 1939 when, in a more or less unprepared state, the West

European democracies had been forced into war against Nazi Germany. The first action was taken by Great Britain and France who signed a fifty-year Treaty of Alliance and Mutual Assistance in March 1947 (The Dunkirk Treaty). This nucleus of future Western regional arrangements, carefully designed to conform to the United Nations Charter, was greatly strengthened in April 1948 by the enactment of the Marshall Plan which has since become a global institution reaching far beyond Western Europe.

Another regional arrangement consonant with the UN Charter was the Rio de Janeiro Treaty of 1947 in which all American states except Canada, Nicaragua, and Ecuador, signed a mutual defense agreement, and the Bogotá Conference of 1948 in which the Charter of the Organization of American States (OAS) was adopted. On March 17, 1948, a Treaty of Economic, Social, and Cultural Collaboration and Collective Self-Defense was signed in Brussels by France, the United Kingdom, and the Benelux countries. It was amended in October, 1954, and renamed Western European Union (WEU). This Treaty, like that of Dunkirk, was to remain in force for fifty years. The Consultative Council of the Brussels powers, established to carry out its objectives, may be regarded as precursor to the North Atlantic Council of the North Atlantic Treaty Organization (NATO).

The Council first met on April 17, 1948. On June 11, 1948, the "Vandenberg Resolution" was passed by the United States Senate, proclaiming American determination "to exercise the right of individual or collective self-defense in accordance with Article 51 of the UN Charter." This important proclamation, setting forth US policy in favor of collective security, cleared the way for the signing of the North Atlantic Treaty on April 4, 1949, after only two months of negotiations, by Belgium, Canada, Denmark, France, Iceland, Italy, Luxemburg, the Netherlands, Norway, Portugal, the United Kingdom, and the United States. Greece and Turkey acquired membership in 1952, and were joined in 1955 by the Federal Republic of Germany.

The Treaty carefully pays homage to the obligations of the signatories to the United Nations (Article 7) and states that the objectives of NATO are not only military defense but also social and economic cooperation (Article 2). Its essence, however, is Article 5: "The Parties agree that an armed attack against one or more of them in Europe or North America shall be considered an attack against all . . ."[6] Economic rivalries, so prominent among the European powers in pre-war times, are to be minimized, by the encouragement of economic collaboration and the elimination of "conflict in their international economic policies." In other words, "peace is not merely the absence of war: its maintenance requires continuous cooperation by governments in the economic, social and cultural as well as in the military field."[7]

NATO was created as a concerted effort to prevent Soviet aggression. Its original strategic concept called for readiness to repel an attack, or, at least, slow it down until a retaliatory counteroffensive could be mounted. Since NATO has two great bases, one in Europe and one in America, the impairment of one would not prevent the other from striking back. The underlying theory was to prevent the aggressor from achieving a quick victory so that the diversified resources of the NATO member countries could eventually outproduce and wear him down.

The USSR's possession of thermonuclear weapons and its successes in heavy-thrust missiles have forced NATO to reconsider its policy and strategy. Among the adjustments to the new technological developments have been the inclusion of NATO in the "nuclear club" and the strengthening of its conventional forces despite concepts of push-button warfare. NATO's non-military tasks have remained in the sphere of good intentions; economic cooperation came under the establishment of the Common Market and the Outer Seven rather than NATO itself. As a protective shield for Western European social and economic development and as a deterrent against Soviet aggression NATO has unquestionably played its part well.

---

[6] Note that Article 5 leaves it to each party to decide for itself whether and what assistance should be rendered to an assaulted member state.

[7] Lord H. L. Ismay, *NATO, The First Five Years, 1949–1954.* See also Alastair Buchan, *NATO in the 1960's: The Implications of Interdependence* (rev. ed.; New York: F. A. Praeger, 1963); K. H. Cerny and H. W. Briefs (eds.), *NATO in Quest of Cohesion* (New York: published for The Hoover Institution on War, Revolution, and Peace by F. A. Praeger, 1965).

However, the attitude of France, which has been problematic from the outset, has diminished the NATO power aggregate. While other participating powers are not averse to sacrificing some prerogatives of sovereignty, the Fifth Republic has been advocating a "Europe of fatherlands" none of which would be ready to cede any sovereign rights. It would be a Europe of nineteenth-century character with the difference that the center of power was then located in Central and Western Europe, while today it is dispersed between the super states, the USA and the USSR, with Europe in the middle and the Asian powers on the side lines.

President de Gaulle, being a nineteenth-century man, does not appreciate the meaning of the ideological schism; for him the conflict between the Eastern and Western blocs is and remains an old-fashioned power struggle and the Soviet Union just a nation–state. Therefore, his approach to contemporary world politics cannot help being antiquated. The General also appears to discount the changes in France's relative power position: trying to revive the ancient glory of France prior to the nineteenth century, he wants the impossible because France was then one of the leading and most populous countries in Europe. But after the end of the Napoleonic era, her position in the "concert" of European powers gradually slid and the preponderance of power shifted to Britain and imperial Germany. The enormously destructive wars of this century further — and decisively — contributed to France's diminution in status, and his proliferation of nuclear power through a *force de frappe* does not change this fact. In a time when reasonable statesmen have come to the conclusion that cooperative communities of states may be the solution in both defense and socio-economic affairs, General de Gaulle has turned back the clock.

NATO can function effectively only if military integration of its components can be achieved. This de Gaulle has vetoed; first, by designating French forces as distinct units which must remain under French command, and, later, by ordering NATO forces to quit their French bases. While asserting that France would remain a member of NATO, he continued to oppose an effective collective defense effort against possible Soviet aggression which, he insists, will not occur. NATO headquarters consequently has been relocated in

Belgium but it would be self-deception to assume that such an arrangement does not weaken Western defense against the East.

Although de Gaulle and his spokesmen frequently have inferred that a future defense organization of associated European states would replace NATO, even within the Continent's political framework France is "going it alone." While developing its own nuclear force, like Communist China, it has refused to sign the nuclear test ban treaty. De Gaulle's primary concern has been to remove the United States as a political factor from Europe even though he is convinced that, in the event of emergency, the United States could not afford to see Western Europe fall to the communists and therefore would come to the rescue anyway. It is generally believed that de Gaulle's anti-American — and anti-"Anglo-Saxon" — policy is strongly influenced by his resentment of the treatment President Roosevelt and Prime Minister Churchill meted out to him during World War II. Thus an ambitious man's hurt ego has wrought havoc in an organization which contained Soviet communism, has once again unchained the dangerous forces of European nationalism and has interrupted the trend toward a politically and economically united Europe.

Since there is no evidence that the Soviet Union has changed from a communist to a traditional nation–state — although the Kremlin's tactics have become more moderate — nothing could be more dangerous than Gaullist France's virtual abandonment of NATO. A united military organization cannot remain effective without political unity. De Gaulle counts on United States' protection but denies his American allies a political voice. And when he speaks of Europe, he does not necessarily include Great Britain: the "Anglo-Saxons," to him, are suspect of collusion and this is one of the reasons why Britain's entry into the Common Market would not be to his liking.

During the first years of its existence, with all its difficulties and internal squabbles, NATO was a relatively effective organization and was instrumental in containing the communist advance on Western Europe. When de Gaulle came to power in 1958, Stalinism had lost much of its force and a more pragmatic type of communism was developed by Khrushchev. This led de Gaulle to believe, as did so many of his contemporaries, that the ideological impact of Marxism–

Leninism had spent itself and that the Soviet Union could now be regarded as a non-revolutionary power. This no doubt strengthened his determination to "reform" NATO. Since the first step toward this "reform" was to expel allied forces from French bases, other ways and means must be found to maintain a shielding force against sudden Soviet aggression. A cooperative protection of Western Europe is possible through the combination of a new NATO plus the nuclear deterrent. After all, the Soviet policy of "peaceful coexistence" is the result not only of Stalin's denigration but even more of NATO's existence as a nuclear power combination.

The security pacts in the Pacific area, also born out of the spirit of united free world defense against communist aggression, are different in origin and organization. Three events led to these arrangements: the Chinese Communists' conquest of the Chinese mainland in 1949, the outbreak of the Korean War in 1950, and the Indochina conflict which ended in 1954.

Already in March 1949, Philippine President Quirino had called for a Pacific security pact along the lines of the proposed North Atlantic Treaty. At first, his efforts had little success. A conference held at Baguio in May 1950 was attended by delegates from Australia, Ceylon, India, Indonesia, Pakistan, Thailand, and the Philippines. Its results were negligible, due largely to India's and Indonesia's determination to avoid commitments. The conference ended with pious resolutions, but without acceptance of the Philippine demand for a regional security pact.

However, the United States and the Philippines reached a number of agreements when they signed the Mutual Defense Treaty on August 30, 1951. Two days later, the ANZUS pact was concluded, a Mutual Defense Treaty between the United States, Australia, and New Zealand. On September 8, a security treaty was signed by the United States and Japan as part of the peace settlement. Yet, the communist danger in the Pacific was so acute to the West and the Western-allied states, especially after the Indochina settlement, that serious preparations were initiated to build a defense organization to provide protection against communist encroachments. On September 6, 1954, the constituting meeting was held at Manila, attended by representatives of Australia, France, Great Britain, New Zealand, Pakistan, the Philippines, Thailand, and the United States. The conclusions of the negotiations and the signing of the Southeast Asia Treaty Organization (SEATO) took place on September 8, 1954, indicating that details must have been worked out well in advance.

This Manila Treaty contains a "Pacific Charter," drafted at the suggestion of Philippine President Magsaysay, which proclaims the unselfish intentions of the SEATO powers. In view of the Asian peoples' strong suspicion about colonialism and the communists' successful propaganda against Western "imperialism," it was considered necessary to state at the outset that the Treaty was designed to maintain "peace and security in Southeast Asia and the Southwest Pacific." Accordingly, the Charter binds the Treaty partners to the principles of the United Nations (equal rights and self-determination of peoples) and promises cooperation in the "economic, social, and cultural fields in order to promote higher living standards, economic progress and social well-being in this region."

The SEATO Treaty concerning mutual assistance differs considerably from that of NATO. Unlike the latter it has no international commands or forces behind it. The Treaty provisions contain no reference to the phrase that an attack against one of the partners will be regarded as an attack against all. It merely states in paragraph IV. 1, that armed aggression in the designated area will be regarded as a threat to safety and measures will be taken by the Treaty partners in accordance with their "constitutional processes." An addendum called "Understanding of the United States of America" states that the term aggression applies only to communist aggression, and that aggressions of different nature will result only in consultation as projected in paragraph IV. 2, in order to "agree on the measures which should be taken for the common defense."

The SEATO Treaty reiterates portions of previous regional agreements (US–Philippines, ANZUS). Nor are the economic paragraphs new: the intention to promote economic welfare in the Treaty area was already "expressed for South and Southeast Asia in the Colombo Plan as well as for the world at large in the United Nations Technical Assistance and the United States Point Four programs."[8] But of the countries located in the area covered by the Treaty, only the

---

[8] *Collective Defense of South East Asia, The Manila Treaty and Its Implications* (London and New York: Royal Institute of International Affairs, 1956), p. 9.

Philippines and Thailand signed; Indonesia and Burma were absent, and Indochina's participation was not possible even though the Treaty contains a Protocol designating the states of Laos, Cambodia, and the "free territory under the jurisdiction of the State of Vietnam" as unilateral beneficiaries of SEATO. Since the majority of signatories were non-Asian states, it is not surprising that the SEATO Treaty was criticized in the Philippines as having insufficient Asian substance.

The leaders of those Asian states which refused to sign the SEATO agreement probably remembered that their countries were once within the Chinese Empire's sphere of influence, if not outright satellites of imperial Peking (Korea, Vietnam, Laos, Cambodia, Siam, Burma, Tibet, Nepal, Malaya, and parts of Indonesia). But this relationship depended on the political and economic strength of the imperial position and varied in intensity throughout the history of Asia. The Chinese Communists will hardly remain satisfied with a voluntaristic policy on the part of Asian countries and may well aspire to create an Asian satellite system comparable to that of Eastern Europe.

Unquestionably, SEATO is a much weaker defense organization than NATO. One reason is the limited commitment of the United States. Another reason is that the Asian states are not united against the communist threat, the nature of which is far from being appreciated partly because it appears in the guise of anti-colonialism. The Western powers are pilloried as protagonists of the colonialism which Asia is trying to overcome. Undoubtedly, the Asian states are aware of their strategic and economic importance to the West. They want to use these assets advantageously because they need help to develop as viable states. Peking's obvious designs on South and Southeast Asia will sooner or later force the non-aligned states to determine which road to take.[9]

As to the Central Treaty Organization (CENTO), offspring of the former Baghdad Pact, it is more a demonstration than an effective

[9] India's strict non-alignment policy has become a little less strict since the Chinese aggression in 1962. Accepting arms and other help, mostly from the United States and to a much lesser degree from the USSR, indicates a "hidden" alignment which India needs to withstand possible future Chinese encroachment.

defense pact against Soviet encroachment. Even before the Revolution, Czarist Russia's interest and interference in Middle Eastern affairs repeatedly created unrest or uneasiness in that region. The Soviet regime did not forswear Russian aspirations. In fact, World War II and its aftermath increased Soviet activities in the Middle East. To gain a freer hand, the USSR renounced its non-aggression treaty with Turkey, signed twenty years earlier, and tried to subvert Iranian Azerbaijan, where Soviet troops had been stationed since 1941 to prevent Nazi entrenchment. Failing in this, and in view of Stalin's concentration on revolutionary activities in Western Europe between 1945 and 1950, the Soviets had to limit their Middle East plans to the usual communist tactics. But when it became apparent that the West firmly withstood communist maneuvers in Western Europe and when the Middle Eastern states developed an increasingly militant nationalism directed chiefly against the "colonialist" West, the Kremlin again reactivated its Middle Eastern expansionism.

Confronted with the threat of Soviet power, some Moslem nations originally sought to protect themselves by regional alliances. In April, 1954, Turkey and Pakistan allied themselves for the purposes of mutual defense and cooperation. A few months later, Iraq suggested to Egypt that the collective security arrangements of the Arab League be broadened to meet the requirements of Article 51 of the United Nations Charter and to enable the United States and Great Britain to join such a regional pact, provided solutions could be found for the problems of Suez and Palestine. Iraq made similar overtures to Turkey which received them more favorably than Egypt, with the result that in early 1955, the former decided to strengthen their relations along the lines of a defensive alliance. The treaty of mutual cooperation accordingly concluded on February 24, 1955, became known as the Baghdad Pact.

The first Western power to join was Great Britain (April 5, 1955), which stated that its express purpose was to "protect the right flank of NATO."[10] Hand in hand with this British decision went an adjusted Anglo–Iraqi agreement. In September, 1955, Pakistan officially joined, and Iranian adherence was formally announced in November, 1955.

---

[10] Statement of the British Foreign Office of April 4, 1955.

The attitude of the United States remained sympathetic but essentially non-committal until Washington announced in November, 1956, that "a threat to the territorial integrity or political independence of the members would be viewed by the United States with the utmost gravity."[11] However, at the Karachi meeting of the Pact Council, the United States accepted the invitation to become a member of the Military Committee. Thus, while the United States attended the Council meetings only as an observer, it participated as an active member in matters of military defense.[12]

Significantly, no other Arab state joined. Jordan at first was inclined to accede, but the Amman government ran into serious opposition, accompanied by riots, and finally was compelled to promise support for Arab unity. This meant submission to pressure from Egypt, Syria, and Saudi Arabia and resulted in Jordan's refusal of military and financial help from the Pact powers. Thus the Baghdad Pact was supported only by one Arab state, Iraq, and more specifically by one man, Iraq's Prime Minister, Nuri Pasha. Consequently, the life of the Pact was precarious.

The Iraq revolution of July 1958, and the subsequent overthrow of the monarchy and the Nuri Pasha government, broke down the original concept of constructing a "northern tier" as a *cordon sanitaire* against the USSR. The growing communist influence in Iraq rendered questionable its membership in the Pact carrying the name of its capital. The revolutionary regime could hardly support a policy which was defended by its archfoe Nuri. The renunciation of its membership even before the end of the prescribed five-year period in 1959 was not surprising.

In August 1959, the other members reconstituted themselves into the Central Treaty Organization (CENTO) with headquarters in Ankara, Turkey. The United States still did not become a full-fledged member, but did sign bilateral defense agreements with the remaining members: Turkey, Iran, and Pakistan. Nevertheless, the

11 "The Baghdad Pact," Central Office of Information, Reference Division, London, June 1958.
12 The United State also became a member of the Counter-Subversion and Economic Committees.

elimination of Iraq from the northern tier posed serious strategic problems, primarily because "more important than Iraq's military contribution was Iraq's geographical contribution as the main junction of communication linking Iran to Turkey and NATO."[13] Moreover, "Iraq's departure . . . erased the last vestiges of our dream that the alliance would attract Arab states."[14]

It is doubtful that CENTO, as constituted in 1959, can fulfill the functions for which the Baghdad Pact was conceived. It is not even a demonstration because the moment the Soviet Union seeks a détente, as it now does with Turkey and Iran, and promises economic and military aid, these countries — however anti-communist they may be — will think twice before rejecting the offer. Pakistan has become very cool toward its former American ally and friendlier toward Red China than would have been expected, mainly because Peking supported it in the Kashmir conflict and the US exerted pressure on both India and Pakistan to end the war of 1965. Indeed, it is doubtful that Pakistan can still be regarded as a *bona fide* member of CENTO. Thus CENTO was a good try but it has deteriorated to the extent that it is more a historic than a contemporary political phenomenon.

Does the concept of security treaties and organization remain a Western peculiarity? In a sense it does; one cannot actually compare the communist security system with that of the West or elsewhere in the free world. The differences are significant in that they show the character of intra-communist bloc relations and reveal a great deal of the communist view of the world. They point to some of the underlying reasons for the permanent world crisis.

When the Soviet Union was the only socialist country in the world, it sought to further its security through manipulation of the other communist parties. But only after World War II, when it could impose its puppet regimes upon the Central–Eastern European states, did it develop security arrangements with these countries as well as with those states elsewhere which fell prey to communist conquest.

Subjection of countries formerly allied with the Axis powers was

[13] C. L. Sulzberger, "The Danger of the Missing Link," *New York Times,* October 3, 1959.
[14] *Ibid.*

easy and pretexts abounded. Nor was it difficult to gain hold over Czechoslovakia, the only state whose popular vote favored communists and fellow-traveling socialists. The "liberalization" of Poland was somewhat more problematic. Nevertheless, the imposition of a regime loyal to the Kremlin was achieved, and the wartime Polish government-in-exile was ignored — as were Western protests. Moscow had strongly supported Tito's partisan regime; in turn, the Yugoslav communists helped the Albanian communists come into power. In the Soviet Zone of Germany, a puppet regime was installed consisting of long-standing rabid Stalinists. Moreover, Moscow destroyed national independence in the three Baltic states, Latvia, Estonia, and Lithuania, incorporating them into the Soviet Union.

In preparation for these developments, the Kremlin had signed treaties with the Czechoslovak government-in-exile in 1943. Early in 1945, pacts were concluded with Poland and Yugoslavia. Successively, treaties were signed with the other Soviet satellites. Since the Kremlin has always insisted on providing a "legal" basis for its schemes, its satellite empire was bound closely by a net of political, economic, and military treaties which became the legal basis for the creation of a *cordon sanitaire*, extending from the Baltic to the Adriatic. Similarly, immediately following the Chinese Communist seizure of power in 1949, a Sino–Soviet treaty of military and economic assistance firmed up relations between the two powers in 1950.

The Communist Information Bureau (Cominform), established in Belgrade in 1947, cannot strictly be termed a protective alliance. It was an attempt to organize and coordinate an aggressive policy of antagonism and violence against the West. But all efforts to subvert and penetrate the Western democracies failed. Not only did Stalin's arbitrary methods alienate Yugoslavia and cause it to leave the Cominform in 1948, these methods also shocked the West into the precautionary action of setting up NATO. Having caused communism more harm than good, the Cominform was conveniently dissolved in 1956, when Khrushchev sought to re-enroll Yugoslavia in the "socialist camp"; but Tito maintained his freedom of action and refused to recognize Soviet hegemony in the communist world.

Apart from the treaty net linking the USSR, its Eastern European satellites, and Communist China,[15] two arrangements were concluded which could be called regional. The first, signed in 1949, is the Council of Mutual Economic Assistance. Primarily economic and concerned with organizing Eastern European division of labor in industry and agriculture, it was probably designed to counter the Marshall Plan. The second, the "Warsaw Pact of Friendship, Cooperation and Mutual Assistance" of 1955, is essentially a treaty of military coordination directed against NATO and the Western European Union.

CEMA originally emphasized bilateral cooperation in matters of foreign trade and the exchange of technical and economic experience. The first plenum in Moscow apparently established a Secretariat; the second plenum in Sofia seems to have promoted creation of joint technical information exchange committees between bloc nations. It is not known whether the recommendation was ever carried out.

Between 1950 and 1954, no plenary meetings were held. During this passive period, changes in CEMA's objectives may have evolved. Since 1955, its main interest has appeared to be the organization of coordinated economic planning in the Soviet orbit. Communist publications have emphasized that the bloc's economic goal is to be improved by a division of labor, i.e., by assigning to individual states such tasks as they can best accomplish according to their particular economic assets. For example, quotas in heavy industry, shipbuilding, or chemical products can best be filled by East Germany; agricultural products by Bulgaria and Romania; weapons and light machinery by Czechoslovakia; coal by Poland. The development of this system would, of course, take time, but, if perfected, would aid the Soviet bloc, although it might render the "specialized" nations even more dependent upon import for goods no longer sufficiently produced.

Judging from the increasing frequency of news reports on CEMA meetings since 1954, especially since the new Soviet Seven Year Plan was announced at the Twenty-first Congress of the Communist Party

---

[15] The 1950 Sino–Soviet Treaty of Mutual Assistance has not been cancelled although it may be considered suspended during the conflict between the Soviet and Chinese parties.

of the Soviet Union (CPSU), this organization, after a very slow and reluctant start, appears to have gained momentum and probably is already implementing Soviet economic policies. To make the system more palatable, the USSR seems to have decreased its exploitation of satellite economies by contributing to an improvement of living standards through a counterpart of the European Payments Union. At the same time, reversing its original position, CEMA presumably eschews bilateral agreements and compels its members to deal with each other collectively. Surpluses and deficits occurring in USSR–satellite trade may now be balanced. Communist statements also have indicated that CEMA is ready to deal with non-communist countries but objects to both the Common Market and EURATOM as "obstructive foreign trade." Indeed, the progress of the Common Market and its envisaged combination with Great Britain and possibly the other members of the "Outer Seven" have increasingly worried Soviet leaders. As communist economies have shown signs of weakness, "doomed" Western capitalism appears to have become stronger. The urgent convocation of a top-level CEMA meeting in June 1962 was a demonstration of the Kremlin's concern over these developments.

As has already been mentioned, CEMA's charter members were the Soviet Union and the Eastern European states. Yugoslavia, denied membership in 1949, became an observer in 1956. With the exception of Outer Mongolia, which became a full member in 1962 after first having been an observer, the Asian communist regimes have been reluctant to become full members; they have confined themselves to the role of observers. China, once an observer, no longer participates but undoubtedly will be reinstated if, after Mao's demise, a rapprochement between Moscow and Peking is achieved. The possibility of North Korea and North Vietnam becoming full CEMA members cannot be excluded but would pre-suppose closer association between Soviet and Red Chinese economies.

On May 14, 1955, the Soviet Union and its East European satellites signed a twenty-year mutual defense treaty, the Warsaw Pact. A unified military command under Soviet leadership was agreed upon. A Political Consultative Committee was created and military headquarters set up in Moscow. Although not a signatory, Communist China pledged its support. Its delegate declared in the founding session that "Communist China will fight alongside the USSR and its allies if war should break out in Europe." East Germany, also not a signatory, participated in the first conference of the Political Consultative Committee to consider major problems.

In January 1956, the East German People's Chamber adopted a bill forming a "People's Army." At the meeting of the Consultative Committee in Prague, the member nations decided to incorporate the East German armed forces into the Pact's combined armies, establish a Foreign Policy Commission, and set up a permanent Secretariat. The problems of coordinating the policies and tactics of all communist nations were also discussed at this meeting and the prospects of a future central communist roof organization probably were aired.

Admittedly, the Warsaw Pact is a countermove against NATO and the Western European Union Treaty, signed in Paris in 1954. It was forecast at a Moscow meeting five weeks later when the Kremlin warned that ratification of the WEU Treaty would lead automatically to the establishment of an "Eastern NATO." WEU was ratified on May 5, 1955; ten days later, the Warsaw Pact was signed. However, the Pact provides for its own abolition in the event an all-European security system is created.

While originally the Warsaw Pact probably was designed as an organization for Soviet political control over the satellites, this has changed due to the development of polycentric communism. However, especially since the early sixties, its military importance has increased. Coordination of military efforts and combined maneuvers are particularly noticeable in the areas of the "northern tier," Poland, East Germany, Czechoslovakia, and, to some degree, Hungary. While much of this increase of military strength and activity is directed against West Germany, it may also be politically motivated by the thought of possible negotiations with the West in the event of a *quid pro quo* with NATO.

There are superficial similarities between the "Eastern NATO" and the Western European organizations. But NATO and WEU are voluntary regional arrangements, freely arrived at by sovereign states; the Warsaw Pact merely extends "legal" status to an already extant situation. Because the East European states are regarded by the Kremlin as within its security sphere, any conflict threatening this *cordon sanitaire* would mobilize the USSR and its East European vassals into united action under the Soviet High Command. The Warsaw Pact, therefore, is not a genuine regional arrangement. Rather, it is a stratagem to tighten Soviet control while propagating Soviet bloc unity throughout the world.

Far beyond the concept of mere security are those measures designed to project the unity of the "socialist camp." The communists view regional arrangements as temporary milestones along the road to a world state. National security will be replaced by bloc security — ensuring the inviolability of the "socialist commonwealth." The tendency toward integralism is a natural Marxist–Leninist phenomenon. It remains to be seen whether the Sino–Soviet controversy on methods to achieve this goal will in the end further or lessen its chances.

There are, clearly, two different approaches toward communist association. One, tactical and regional, aims to obtain certain objectives of political, military, and propagandistic nature. The other, strategic, seeks to transform the "socialist camp" into a "socialist commonwealth," a loose association of like-minded Marxist–Leninist states whose real bond is based not on written agreement, but on ideological similarities and a community of interests opposite the "imperialists."[16]

Although the USSR would not dominate such an association, its power and prestige within the communist movement would unquestionably mark it the leading state of the "socialist commonwealth," co-equal with Communist China, but more influential in creating policy and interpreting doctrine. The impact of Soviet presence in the East is still great, greater than that of the United States in the West. Easily the most powerful nation of the free world, the US may try to influence or persuade its partners to agree with certain policies, but it does not and cannot impose its will.

Here, again, we see the great conceptual difference between the

---

[16] K. London, "The Socialist Commonwealth of Nations," *Orbis*, Vol. 3, No. 4, Winter 1960, *passim*. See also K. Grzybowski, *The Socialist Commonwealth of Nations: Organizations and Institutions* (New Haven: Yale University Press, 1964), *passim*.

two antagonists in the field of foreign relations. This being so, the question arises as to how the communist states can reconcile their attitude with an international organization such as the United Nations, to which most of them belong.

• INTERNATIONAL ORGANIZATION — Efforts to preserve peace and security by means of international organization are of recent origin. To be sure, attempts at multilateral association were made in Europe, Asia, and the Middle East. Their rationale was protection and prosperity. But all endeavors, from ancient times until the beginning of the twentieth century, remained uncoordinated. World War I brought about the first genuine international organization in the League of Nations. Although it failed in the end, it inaugurated an era of collective security agreements prior to World War II, notably the Pact of Locarno in 1925.

With the demise of these pacts and the League itself, the idea of international organization did not die. A new organization had been planned even before Allied victory was secured. One might say that the history of the United Nations began with the promulgation of the Atlantic Charter on August 14, 1941, by President Roosevelt and Prime Minister Churchill. The Charter was an idealistic document, enumerating principles reminiscent of President Wilson's Fourteen Points. It was designed to raise Allied morale and keep burning the flame of hope among oppressed peoples. Yet it was more than a declaration of principles: it became part of the Declaration of the United Nations of January 1, 1942.

The United Nations was established formally in San Francisco on June 26, 1945. Its Charter was signed by fifty nations. After ratification by the sponsoring powers, it came into force on October 24, 1945. Since then, its membership has more than doubled. Unfortunately, this growth is not commensurate with the organization's success. As an instrument of international security it has faltered; it kept some conflicts from threatening peace, but could not prevent such a major catastrophe as the Korean War. The UN has been hamstrung from the outset by the division of its membership into bipolar groups. As time went on, it has been further hampered by the activities of those new members who have achieved independence but not nationhood and who have had neither the time nor the opportunity to learn the mores of international relations.

Provisions were made in Chapter VIII of the UN Charter to allow for regional arrangements or agencies to maintain international peace and security. (Articles 52–54.) The significance of these stipulations is great. Scarcely a regional arrangement exists which does not state expressly that it considers itself to be under the auspices of the United Nations and that the treaty has been concluded within the stipulations of the UN Charter whose Chapter VIII provides the contractual framework. It is obvious that the founding fathers of the Charter, although progressing beyond the League, did not conceive of the UN as a universal organization which could decide world political issues by fiat. Rather, they seemed to envision a roof organization, an international "holding company," under which sovereign nations could continue to associate in the interests of mutual security and peaceful arbitration.

This demonstrates, first, a confirmation of the sovereign rights of member nations to ally themselves with any other nation regardless of whether or not the policies inherent in their agreements are to the liking of members outside the pact. Secondly, it admits implicitly that the power and influence of the UN, although considerable in many respects, still are not great enough to maintain universal peace without relying on the encouragement of regional pacts. Thirdly, it anticipates the ideological schism between East and West, but tries to maintain flexibility so as to remain maneuverable in administering world peace.

Thus, Chapter VIII was obviously a compromise. On the one hand, the authors of the Charter probably foresaw that regional arrangements might hamper the Security Council. On the other hand, the nations of the world were not yet ready, World War II notwithstanding, to sacrifice more than token sovereignty so long as the schism between communism and capitalism continued to frustrate the One World concept. In addition, the framers of the Charter found themselves confronted by regional arrangements already in existence: the Inter-American Pact of Chapultepec had just been signed, the Arab

League had been formed during the war, and the development of Western European political and economic pacts had begun.

The question of whether regional security pacts can be forged which are compatible with the Charter but outside the Security Council's control has not been conclusively answered. A genuine test case has not yet arisen. At least, such mutual security treaties as NATO or the Warsaw Pact have not been found inconsistent with Chapter VIII. The problem is unsolved and probably will remain so.

The more complex question of how the UN can deal with the political and ideological chasm between the "commonwealth of socialist nations" and the free world is even further from solution. The development of two antagonistic groups of states, led by super powers, can hardly be classified as regional arrangements. The Western group was created to defend itself against communist encroachment, the Eastern to consolidate communism in order to establish eventually a communist world state.

As a result, the United Nations is, metaphorically, a rump organization. The communist members are boldly present, but their spirit is missing. They exploit their membership in this international body for their own purposes. They are unwilling to contribute to the guiding principle "to practice tolerance"; by their attitude they have neither reaffirmed "the dignity and worth of the human person," nor "the equal rights of . . . nations large and small"; nor have they collaborated with the "center for harmonizing the actions of nations. . . ."[17] Thus the contributions of Soviet bloc members have been generally negative, and the maintenance of world peace depends not so much on the United Nations as on the existence of the nuclear stalemate and the desire of the Soviet leaders to peacefully "coexist" lest the outbreak of hostilities destroy their efforts for peaceful conquest.

The tenor of the past four Congresses of the Soviet Communist Party in 1956, 1959, 1961, and 1966 makes it perfectly clear that the political and economic successes of the Soviet bloc have strengthened

[17] Cf. Preamble and Article 1 of the UN Charter.

communist confidence in ultimate bloodless victory through the West's default. Convinced of the inevitable demise of the "bourgeois system" and desirous of hastening its end (without undue risks), the communists pursue "united front tactics," which means they associate and organize with non-communist sympathizers and, by dint of superior discipline, gain control of an organization. In a broader sense, this tactic of apparent cooperation may be used in national parliaments and international forums. Even if controlling influence seems impossible to attain, the communists permit no slackening of interest and effort but try to derive all possible advantages from an adverse situation. Inasmuch as they have succeeded in blocking Security Council action unacceptable to them and have utilized the veto as an instrument to perpetuate their obstinacy, they can focus their activities on the obstructionist tactics they have developed to a fine art since the time of Lenin.[18]

It would be fallacious to consider the United Nations as a failure. Nor can the impact of its moral stature be overlooked. In the social, economic, and cultural spheres, it achievements have been impressive, though limited by the recalcitrance of the communist members. Also, it has succeeded in marginal fields of endeavor. But major political issues have remained unresolved primarily due to studied communist obstructionism. Moreover, the Soviet leaders have consistently tried to conclude agreements outside the international organization, thereby compelling the Western powers to adopt the same tactic.

With such a handicap in mind, how can we adjudge the accomplishments of the United Nations in assuaging international conflicts since the end of World War II?

Soviet intransigence caused the first such conflict in Iran when Stalin stalled in the northern province of Azerbaijan where Soviet troops had been stationed during the war as a result of Allied agreement. Moreover, the Kremlin engineered local rebellion designed to make Azerbaijan an independent territory. Iran complained to the Security Council and when the matter came to discussion, the Soviet

[18] An essential element for the enforcement of UN Charter provisions is an international military force. The communist members of the UN have steadfastly blocked agreement on this vital matter.

delegates stalked out. The case finally was resolved by an Iranian withdrawal of the charges under heavy Soviet pressure and the evacuation of Soviet troops.

The 1946 communist uprising in Greece was ostensibly supported by Yugoslavia, Bulgaria, and Albania. In 1947, United Nations investigators ascertained that the three communist satellites — Yugoslavia at that time was still within the Soviet orbit — were indeed prolonging the civil war. The USSR vetoed the Greek Government's complaint to the Security Council. The General Assembly then took over, appointing another investigating commission which reported that conditions were unchanged. The UN remained paralyzed. The rebels' defeat was due primarily to Tito's break with Stalin which caused Yugoslavia to withdraw its support, and also to the considerable American and British aid to the legitimate Greek Government. The rebels had kidnapped many Greek children, but the UN never secured their repatriation.

In the case of the Soviet-staged Berlin blockade, UN arbitration efforts failed. Final agreements were negotiated between Washington and Moscow directly at the UN but not through UN machinery.

Insofar as the Korean War is concerned, the Security Council's decision to battle the communist aggressor with a composite UN force was reached only after the Soviet walkout. Nevertheless, the legality of the decision remains doubtful. Article 27 of the Charter states in paragraph 3: "Decisions on all other matters [i.e., non-procedural] shall be made by an affirmative vote of seven members including the concurring votes of the permanent members; provided that, in decisions under Chapter VI, and under paragraph 3 of Article 52, a party to a dispute shall abstain from voting." Although obviously involved in the Korean aggression, the Soviet Union legally was not a party to this dispute. It has therefore been claimed by some international lawyers that the failure of a permanent member to cast a vote in a non-procedural matter would have the practical effect of a veto. Be that as it may, the Soviet delegation, after having returned to the Council's session, consistently blocked its efforts. The General Assembly's condemnation of aggression in Korea, which brought about an arms embargo, had a moral rather than actual effect. Without the eventual direct negotiations between the two super powers, the conflict might have continued. But it is significant that the Soviets did use the United Nations forum to initiate these negotiations: the Soviet chief delegate made a speech in which he implied that the end of the conflict should be negotiated and that the USSR was willing to offer its good offices to that effect.

There have been instances in which the UN was able to prevent the spreading of conflicts in areas marginal to the centers of the cold war struggle. For example, it helped to prevent the civil war in Cyprus to involve both Greece and Turkey. It played a beneficial, though much maligned, part in the Congo unrest. Although sharply attacked by the communists and some uncommitted states, it did succeed in upholding the legal government, maintaining a modicum of pacification, and stopping trends which could have developed into civil war and a complete political vacuum. For almost a decade the UN barrier in the Gaza strip between the United Arab Republic and Israel prevented major flare-ups; a UN patrol along the Syrian–Israeli border was less successful. But the UN Secretary General hastily obeyed the Egyptian President's demand to withdraw the UN contingents from the Gaza strip, thereby opening the door to the outbreak of hostilities between Israel and the Arab states in June 1967.

Regrettably, the United Nations now functions as a fractionalized organization in that the anti-communist members work to contain communism, the non-committed states more often than not remain on the fence or attack the Western "colonialists," and the communist bloc systematically obstructs the establishment of integral, universal security. This is not to deny the potential blessing of an international organization such as the UN and the actual advantages achieved in non-political fields. But the UN has not become an instrument of international security; it would be dangerous to base national policies on a contrary assumption. So long as the two world power centers and their associated groups remain as deeply and irreconcilably divided as they are, the UN can only try to mobilize world opinion to exert restraining pressure on the opponents. The UN would be effective if its membership were not rent by ideological schisms, could establish a strong international police force, and control nuclear weapons. We cannot expect this to happen in the near future.

..6....

War and Peace in the Nuclear Age

The history of the world is primarily a history of wars. Innumerable attempts to abolish war have failed. From the beginning of time, violent solutions to arguments between clans, tribes, dynasties, and nations were considered a matter of course. Indeed, some scholars have pointed out that major progress of human civilization is unthinkable without war: "War has been the method actually used for achieving the major political changes of the modern world, the building of nation states, the expansion of modern civilization throughout the world, and the changing of the dominant interests of that civilization";[1] or "War . . . has been used to achieve liberty, to secure democracy, and to attempt to make it secure against the menace of its use by other hands."[2]

The ancient Romans said: *Si vis pacem, para bellum."* (If you wish peace, prepare for war.) A modern social scientist put it this way: "If we expect war, we may create an atmosphere favorable to a so-called 'preventive war.' If we do not expect war, we invite aggression."[3] In a world shaken by ideological contests, in an era that has produced two of the world's bloodiest wars within the lifetime of one generation, no government can risk relying on the good intentions of other governments. International bodies have not been successful in preparing the way for alleviating mutual suspicions. A realistic statesman is bound to recognize that a foreign policy is only as strong as the defense potential behind it.

[1] Q. Wright, *A Study of War,* Vol. 1 (Chicago: University of Chicago Press, 1942), p. 250.

[2] J. T. Shotwell, *War as an Instrument of National Policy* (New York: Harcourt, Brace and Company, 1929), p. 15.

[3] H. D. Lasswell, *World Politics Faces Economics* (New York: McGraw–Hill Book Company, Inc., 1945), p. 8.

121

We mentioned above such elements as topographical and demographic conditions which necessarily determine the limit of a nation's aspirations and thereby establish the fundamentals of national foreign policy. Such limitations are indicated by the relative strength of armed forces (actual and potential), the capacity of industry and agriculture, the natural resources and stockpiles available, the quality of transportation and communication systems, and the geographic location. These traditional yardsticks of national power were applicable for centuries. But the splitting of the atom has changed the picture radically. To be sure, the production of nuclear weapons still requires a large industrial and technological establishment which, for the time being, small and underdeveloped nations can ill afford. The time may come when even they will be able to manufacture The Bomb, which is the reason for attempts to prevent nuclear proliferation by law. In the meantime, only those nations with major resources can develop and manufacture nuclear weapons.

The possession of such weapons is not, in itself, sufficient. They must also be deliverable. Even in its advanced state, the airplane may no longer be the most feasible carrier. Rocket-powered missiles have been developed which can deliver nuclear warheads anywhere in the world at a speed which will allow the target area little or no time for interception and protection. Existing differences between the nuclear and missile capabilities of the USA and USSR probably cannot tip the power scales of terror.[4] Only major technological breakthroughs (such as an effective anti-ballistic missile system) or neglect on the part of either side would alter this balance sufficiently to eliminate the nuclear stalemate or deterrence.

It has been argued that deterrence is not automatic and may be harder to maintain as time progresses, that it demands "hard, continuing, intelligent work, but can be achieved"; that it should by no means be regarded as "the whole of a military, much less a foreign policy . . ."[5] One can agree with the proposition that the maintenance

[4] Red China has succeeded in developing a thermonuclear device but as yet has no efficient delivery system. France's *force de frappe* is likely to remain of limited dimensions as compared with those of the super powers.

[5] A. Wohlstetter, "The Delicate Balance of Terror," *Foreign Affairs,* January 1959, pp. 212, 221, 234.

of deterrent power makes it impossible for any contestant to rest on his laurels, a fact appreciated in the West as well as in the East, and that, consequently, a substantial portion of a nation's resources will be channeled into technological research and development. But, in the age of atoms, rockets, and conquest of space, it is difficult to envision any military strategy or foreign policy which would not be dominated by the specter of nuclear conflagration.

To appreciate the great difference between the war factor in international relations prior to and after the advent of nuclear power, it is necessary to realize the change in the concept of war produced by the new technology.

History shows that the fear of the use of force to attain policy objectives was always an element of decisive importance in the behavior of nations and in the motivation of national policy. Not only was foreign policy formulated with an eye to possible military actions or reactions by other powers, but domestic politics, too, were influenced by the war-making potential of foreign nations and the inclination of their leaders to use it. No responsible government could chart its course without considering the possibility of war. Governments were correspondingly cautious, especially toward powerful nations. Policy objectives had to be limited, and their implementation by peaceful means was designed to prevent a violent solution. At the same time, no government could assume that its own peaceful intentions were necessarily reciprocated by other powers, whose intentions might be aggressive and expansive. This state of affairs led to the creation of a balance of power by establishing groupings of nations with similar interests as supposedly the best insurance against the hazards of conflagration. The threat of military action or the consciousness of a strong defensive position was at the bottom of most policy formulations and determined which methods would be used to implement these policies.

But, since mid-twentieth century, for the first time since the beginning of civilized history, international relations are being conducted with the restraining influence of the threat of a major war considerably strengthened. As the result of the availability of nuclear weapons and the missiles to deliver them anywhere, the leading atomic powers cannot but conclude that clear-cut victory is impossible and large-scale destruction of their territories a certainty. Nonetheless, a danger of miscalculation exists which is recognized and constantly kept in mind. A surprise attack could be extremely risky since the attacked power might have at its disposal retaliatory weapons which would neutralize the initial advantages of the attacker. On the other hand, localized conventional warfare could deteriorate into nuclear action which in turn might easily provoke general war. In brief, in the nuclear age, war no longer is a "continuation of policy by other means," no longer offers decisive solutions.

The consequences of this extraordinary turn of events are baffling. They require a new outlook in international relations. They would have been confusing enough to statesmen or strategists functioning in a period of traditional maneuvering among nation–states. But, coinciding as they do with the ideological struggle between communist and anti-communist forces, they must be analyzed as part and parcel of the bipolar stalemate in both the ideological and technological fields; they have led to and forced us to cope with a permanent crisis.

The Soviet drive for "peaceful" and "competitive" coexistence remains well within the confines of the traditional communist doctrine. But, in view of the nuclear deterrence, it assumes new significance. It took the Kremlin some time to digest the meaning of the atom bomb. If Stalin had a plausible Marxist–Leninist interpretation, he did not announce it. Nor have his successors been able to more than half-heartedly explain that nuclear war would destroy capitalism but not communism. This thesis was prominently stated at the Twentieth Congress of the CPSU by Khrushchev, Mikoyan, and others. But, two months later, in a speech at the Soviet Embassy in London, Khrushchev said: "Today, as a result of the development of technique, war would be a benefit neither to one side nor to the other. It can only bring colossal destruction."[6] He frequently repeated this statement, and a growing Soviet literature on the hazards of war in the nuclear age has elaborated this point of view. A leading Soviet strategist put it bluntly:

[6] April 19, 1959.

The development of the technique of exterminating people has resulted in a situation that makes it impossible to resort to war as a means of solving political disputes as was done throughout the age-long history of mankind . . . A rocket and nuclear war is extremely dangerous not only for the side subject to attack, but is at the same time suicidal for the aggressor. It is our opinion that in terms of military technology, war as an instrument of policy is outliving itself.[7]

As a good communist, the author qualified his statement by concluding that the absence of war is based not so much on weaponry as on a change in "social and political conditions which have emerged in the world."

Whether or not Khrushchev's successors believe that their social and economic fabric has greater resilience than that of the United States, they seem to realize the extreme hazards of nuclear war. But they also want the world to believe that they equal the West in nuclear power and that they are able and determined to retaliate with destruction, should destruction come to them. This is no idle boast, as their 1961 and 1962 test series demonstrated. Yet when confronted with the specter of nuclear war, the Soviet leaders are just as reluctant to go over the brink as is the US Government. The Cuban missile crisis in 1963 is a case in point. The prompt removal of Soviet missiles from Cuban soil as a result of what might be termed a US ultimatum now is history and so is President Kennedy's refusal to risk his country's security. The reckless Chinese leaders accused the Kremlin of cowardice, and Khrushchev's caution probably was noted with dismay by some other communist parties. But the nuclear balance of terror helped reason to triumph.

Lenin warned that "imperialism, the highest stage of capitalism," would *inevitably* lead to war. Stalin basically confirmed this view. Neither could have foreseen the coming of the nuclear age, and Stalin, who lived to see it, apparently did not grasp its meaning. However, realizing that hydrogen bombs had no ideological preferences, Khrushchev caused the Twentieth Congress of the CPSU to

[7] Major General N. Talensky, "On the Character of Modern Warfare," *International Affairs,* Moscow, October 1960.

create the concept of "non-inevitability" of war. This principle was re-affirmed at subsequent Congresses as well as in numerous statements made by Soviet leaders and in official Soviet communications media. Hence, so long as the strength of the "imperialist" powers matches or surpasses that of the "socialist camp," the Leninist–Stalinist concept of war no longer applies. No wonder then that the authoritative Soviet Communist Party magazine *Kommunist* realistically called for an epoch of prolonged coexistence and economic competition between the two systems and emphasized the profound conviction of communists that the question of further paths of development of communism will be decided in the final analysis not by means of war but by various kinds of peaceful competition.

The Soviet success with rocketry since the launching of the first *sputnik* produced a more cocky language on the part of the Khrushchev regime, accentuated by considerable missile-rattling whose loudness was gauged to the alleged lack of American rocket development. Nevertheless, his own attitude and that of his successors toward war has remained generally cautious, and the quest for "peaceful coexistence" continues. It must be added that Soviet aversion to war is based not only upon recognition that local wars could lead to general conflagration and large-scale war to nuclear devastation. The Kremlin also reasons that the power of the "socialist camp" has grown tremendously and continues to grow; that in contrast the capitalist countries are losing their political and economic grip and are bound to decline; and that consequently "peaceful" efforts by the "world socialist system" will be sufficient to cause the downfall of imperialism without resort to open hostilities.

The Peking leaders do not see it this way. In the first place, their fear of nuclear war appears to be less intense than that of the Kremlin although it would be a mistake to believe that they would throw all caution to the winds at a time when their hands are full with China's precarious economy and internal political pressures. Secondly, they are not so convinced as the Soviets that bloodless victory of communism is possible. Thus they display a more aggressive attitude which they summed up in the famous articles on Leninism, on the occasion of Lenin's ninetieth birthday, in one of their official party organs, *Red Flag*, in April, 1960, which led to serious repercussions in

Moscow–Peking relations. Discussions during the Romanian Communist Party Congress in Bucharest, summer 1960, were unsuccessful. Finally, in November–December 1960, more than eighty Communist Party representatives met in Moscow, at the Conference of Communist and Workers Parties. After acrimonious arguments and a final week of secret negotiations between Moscow and Peking leaders, a Statement was published, indicating that a compromise had been reached in which the Kremlin's "peaceful coexistence" policy was accepted by the Communist Chinese. At the same time, it was reiterated that war is "not fatally inevitable," that the principles of "Panch Shila"[8] still applied, and that "peace is the true ally of socialism, for time is working for socialism and against capitalism." However, as the Sino–Soviet conflict grew in intensity, Peking reduced "peaceful coexistence" from a strategy to a mere tactical ruse of brief duration.

This is not the place to discuss the tortuous arguments between Moscow and Peking which came to a head at the Twenty-second Soviet Communist Party Congress where the Chinese delegation walked out of the convention and Albania associated itself with China. There is a mounting literature on the subject.[9] After all, Sino–Soviet relations are crucial to the communists as well as the free world and a genuine break between the two communist giants may tear asunder the "socialist camp."

Within the context of this chapter it is important to keep in mind that Peking did not share Moscow's conclusion on the nature of

---

[8] The Bandung principles were advanced jointly by the Chinese Communists, the Indians, and other Asian nations, at Bandung, 1955. They went further than mere "peaceful coexistence."

[9] Among recent studies of the Sino–Soviet conflict are: G. F. Hudson, R. Lowenthal, and R. MacFarquhar, *The Sino–Soviet Dispute* (New York: Praeger, 1961); K. London (ed.), *Unity and Contradiction: Major Aspects of Sino–Soviet Relations* (New York: Praeger, 1962); W. E. Griffith, *The Sino–Soviet Rift* (Cambridge, Mass.: MIT Press, 1964); K. Mehnert, *Peking and Moscow* (New York: Mentor, 1964); D. S. Zagoria, *The Sino–Soviet Conflict, 1956–61* (New York: Atheneum, 1964); D. J. Doolin, *Predatorial Claims in the Sino–Soviet Conflict* (Stanford, Calif.: The Hoover Institution, 1965); K. London, "The Sino–Soviet Conflict," *Current History* (October, 1966); W. E. Griffith, *Sino–Soviet Relations, 1964–65* (Cambridge, Mass.: The MIT Press, 1967).

nuclear war and the necessity for "peaceful coexistence." To keep the record straight, peaceful coexistence is a "line of mobilization of the masses"; it does not imply a rejection of the class war: "coexistence between states of differing social systems is a form of class struggle between socialism and capitalism." But, although both general and local wars are discouraged, wars for the "liberation" of "national democracies" (newly independent former colonial or semi-colonial territories) are still defended as "just." Thus, according to Moscow, so long as imperialism continues, the sources of aggression will remain and therefore "complete disarmament" is in the interest of maintaining peaceful coexistence.

If we accept the premise that both East and West realize the extreme hazards of armed conflict and that the neutralist states are *eo ipso* against war, it might be concluded that the prospect of general war has receded. Although it obviously cannot be excluded from the security planning of the bipolar nation groups, due to its mutually destructive potential, it is no longer a decisive instrument of foreign policy. Paradoxically, the utility of the war threat as a weapon of propaganda has increased as demonstrated by statements of the Soviet and Chinese leaders warning the United States on the escalation of the Vietnam war.

This situation has exacerbated and perpetuated the cold war which in the case of the USSR has outwardly softened its character and therefore led many people and some governments to believe that it no longer is a reality. The communist struggle for universal victory continues. But the Soviet leaders of international communism have modified their strategy for attaining the ultimate goal. As a result, they have employed new tactics to fulfill their strategic norms. They no longer rely on violence, nor do they maintain their former rigidity in international relations. Instead, they are increasing, accelerating, and broadening all "peaceful" means of political and economic combat. Since the risks of military retaliation appear to be much reduced, they feel freer to infiltrate, subvert, and "persuade" on a large scale while maintaining their armed forces in a high state of efficiency. Confident of the nuclear stalemate, backed by a strong military establishment, trusting in the impending doom of capitalism as predicted by historical materialism, the communist leaders now are trying to fill the political vacua wherever they exist in the third world. They are being helped by underdeveloped states which are eager to obtain political and economic bargains expeditiously, have banked for some time on the reluctance of former imperial powers to use "gunboat diplomacy," and are not sufficiently aware of twentieth century America's aversion to colonialism. Realizing Western unwillingness to think in terms of military solutions, they have indulged in much harder, sometimes irresponsible, bargaining.

This unique situation has created a paradox to puzzle the policy-makers. On the one hand, it is possible to believe that the advent of the nuclear age may have initiated the era of peace devoutly hoped for by uncounted generations but never before attained. On the other hand, it may be just this situation that will stimulate a more subtle but hardly less vicious and dangerous struggle by the communists for man's spiritual and economic dependence. Against Western determination to preserve cherished traditions and ways of life will be set Eastern determination to destroy these ideals and replace them with some version of Marxism–Leninism, using "non-violent" methods of combat.

The West is not well equipped for this type of conflict. Dictators can more easily manipulate funds and direct trends in political warfare. For them flexibility and integration of media are a matter of course. Conversely, democracy is efficient in time of war or emergency, but much less so when there is "business as usual." Furthermore, democratic society may be unwilling to make sufficient sacrifices in a period of so-called peace. There are as yet limited facilities to deal with the non-violent tools of revolution. Western governments, the Iberian peninsula excepted, must cope with freely elected parliaments and therefore are reluctant to antagonize public opinion by demanding more contributions not only to maintain costly military forces and weapons development, but also to organize a comprehensive, integrated counter-offensive against the new communist moves. We are therefore confronted with the fact that there exist as yet no real safeguards against international lawlessness nor sufficient means to counter non-violent combat. Such means are not easy to devise. The most imaginative thinking and the finest brains are required to invent and develop them. In effect, one may suggest that in this era of cold war, brain power has become the most essential prerequisite for coping with unconventional conflict.

It need hardly be emphasized that national defense, in whatever form, has not become an outdated concept. But it has changed character. The ideological schism compels the maintenance of opposing armed camps; technological developments tend to hold the camps at bay. This dilemma plagues policy-makers in the West where the maintenance of peacetime economy is rendered increasingly difficult if military readiness is to be advocated. This is one of the most difficult problems plaguing the Johnson administration in its attempt to conduct the Vietnam war while at the same time trying not to sacrifice the "Great Society" program. There is no such dilemma in the East, for the communist movement has always been both militant and military in concept; "socialist" economy can be manipulated to suit the Party's political demands.

Under communist regimes, the armed forces are merely an arm of the Party. High-ranking military leaders are first and foremost members of the Party; if they become too popular, they are removed from the public eye. The treatment accorded to Marshal Zhukov, under both Stalin and Khrushchev, is a telling example of what can happen to a famous general who becomes too ambitious. Communist policy is formulated by the Party leadership and executed by the appropriate government offices; the armed forces are expected to support the Party internally and externally, but their influence on policy is generally restricted to purely technical advice.

Democracies have safeguards against overly strong influence by military leaders. Constitutionally, military establishments cannot make foreign policy even though they can influence political decisions. In the nuclear age, this influence has narrowed down to technical advice which must be supplemented by technological estimates, economic analysis, and political judgment. As a result, there has occurred in the United States and other Western countries a virtual merger of policy-makers, military strategists, and scientists in the high councils of government. The conduct of foreign relations remains the responsibility of the foreign offices, but overall problems of national security are determined by coordinated efforts of interdepartmental committees. This development results from the fact that general war, while still possible, is no longer probable; that it cannot be excluded from security consideration but is no longer a genuine part of foreign policy; and that bipolarity has engendered a twilight existence of world politics wherein there is neither general war nor genuine peace. Limited wars, as we know from Korea and Vietnam, are still possible but the adversaries are careful to avoid miscalculations lest the struggle get out of hand.

It is true that, in the nuclear era, whatever military actions have occurred remained localized and were fought with conventional weapons. But it would be foolhardy to build political and military policy on the premise that local wars will automatically stay limited. Being prepared for both conventional and nuclear conflict is admittedly expensive, yet no nation can afford to neglect this two-pronged protection if it wishes to remain free. Indeed, nuclear deterrence may lose its meaning as a war-blocking agent unless the free world can "create a military capability which can translate our technological advantage into local superiority."[10]

In any event, it cannot be emphasized too strongly that the technological deterrent is not static. To maintain it one has to invest ingenuity, work, and money, for an indefinite period. An imbalance of deterrent power means almost certain defeat for the weaker side.

[10] H. A. Kissinger, *Nuclear Weapons and Foreign Policy*, p. 155.

••••7••

The Makers of Foreign Policy

Who Has the Power in the West?

In the foregoing chapters we have discussed the consequences of the unprecedented events which changed the nature of international relations. Having established the conceptual premises for the permanent crisis, we will now observe the effect of these innovations on the practical work of policy-making and diplomacy on both sides of the Iron and Bamboo Curtains. It should be revealing to ascertain whether the men responsible for the conduct of foreign affairs have adjusted to conditions resulting from these ideological and technological developments.

Constitutional laws governing the administration and techniques of international relations vary somewhat among non-communist states, but show great divergencies with the concepts and methods of the communists. These differences are fundamental in that they concern the prime policy objectives of the communist-ruled countries as contrasted with the aspirations of the Western or neutral countries. In democratic societies, the constitutions comprise the basic laws of the land, embodying not only administrative concepts but also national philosophies. In communist-ruled nations, constitutions are legal pretense; the basic approach to all problems is determined by Marxism–Leninism in either Soviet or Chinese interpretation, not necessarily in great detail, but certainly in spirit.

The chief distinctions between the world's foreign offices are the nature and extent to which they exert influence over foreign policy and their constitutionally defined relations with the executive and legislative branches of their governments. For example, under a proletarian dictatorship, a foreign office can be no more than an advisory, administrative department which supervises the correct implementation of ordered policies and fulfills technical functions. We shall see later that foreign policy in such states originates in an authoritative body composed of a few key party leaders who may or may not be leading government officials. Almost invariably, the final decision is made by the one man who happens to be the dominating personality. Little or no regard is paid to public opinion which can be manipulated by the media of the propaganda monopoly.

In the democracies, the conduct and control of foreign policy are circumscribed not only by the constitution, but also by parliamentary or popular reactions. But it is only fair to state that final decisions, even in the democracies, quite often depend upon one man. The history of United States foreign relations has frequently demonstrated that legally unassailable actions are undertaken by the President without prior consultation of Congress and the Department of State. Similarly, the British Prime Minister who is only the head of the government and not, as is the American President, the head of state, has a decisive and final voice in vital decisions. In the Fifth French Republic, President de Gaulle exercises a virtually authoritarian power. Many other examples from parliamentary democracies confirm that at the pinnacle of the state or government the power of decision narrows down to one personality. The difference between East and West lies in the accountability: the democratic decision-maker is responsible to his parliament, i.e., the people as a whole; the totalitarian dictator is allegedly responsible to his ruling party, but since he leads the party, he is responsible only to himself. But, as the fall of Khrushchev demonstrated, even he may be finally accountable to the party.

Under no political system is a foreign minister endowed with exclusive powers. He is subordinate to his head of state, parliamentary body, and/or political party. In fact, ever since the "summit" conferences, which began in the wake of World War I and increased in volume during and after World War II, the stature of foreign ministers has declined. The chiefs of state or government frequently have assumed responsibility for top level negotiation and final decision of supreme issues in foreign relations. The foreign ministers, conferring with their opposite numbers, can expound their country's adopted policy line but can make no decision involving a departure from this line. In this respect, there is little difference between democratic and totalitarian foreign ministers except perhaps that the Western states- men have somewhat more maneuverability in minor matters. Under communist rule, they are little more than technical advisers and glorified messengers, subject to strict and specified orders of the party leadership. In non-communist countries, they conduct the business of international relations under the control of their chiefs of state or government, in conjunction with heads of interested ministerial departments and leaders of the political parties. A thumbnail sketch comparing the sources of policy-making power in both West and East will help to put into clear focus some of the important reasons for policy clashes.

• United states — The Constitution of the United States did not expressly delegate authority for the conduct of foreign affairs to any specified agency. However, it was inferred from the beginning and long since has been accepted by constitutional lawyers, that initiative for the formulation of principal foreign policies remains in the hands of the President. The Department of State, established by law in 1789, is the legal organ of communication between the President and other countries. Therefore, the Secretary of State, the Department's administrative head, becomes official spokesman for the President and government of the United States vis-à-vis foreign governments.

The Constitution provides that the President inform Congress concerning the "State of the Union." Article II grants him the power to nominate United States envoys to foreign countries "with the advice and consent of the Senate," receive foreign ambassadors and other "public ministers and consuls," and play a dominating role in exercising the two most important prerogatives of all: the treaty- making power and the war-making power.

These powers are, however, limited by Congress. "The President shall have power," says the Constitution, "by and with the advice of the Senate to make Treaties, provided that two thirds of the Senators present concur." The Senate may also accept the President's pro- posals conditionally, that is, it may wish to modify treaties without rejecting their substance. But it is the President who finally ratifies such treaties by signing them. Only thus can they become law.

Declarations of war must be passed by Congress, usually at presidential instigation. In practice, however, the President, as chief executive with power to conduct foreign relations, and as commander in chief of the armed forces, can order military action before or without declaration of war by Congress. This is particularly important in an era of undeclared or gradually escalating hostilities without formal declarations of war (Korea, Vietnam) or in the event of sudden attack by long-range missiles. In such cases, the constitutional authority of Congress to declare war amounts to official and legal recognition of already existing conditions. In theory, Congress might not sympathize with the measures of the President and affect the continuation of armed conflict by refusing to provide funds for the conduct of war or even by impeaching the President. The Constitution is silent about ending a state of war. By practice and decision of the Supreme Court, it is now established that war may be ended by treaty — in which case only the Senate would be involved in ratification — or by joint resolution of Congress, repealing authorization of hostilities.

Information concerning international problems may be requested of the President by both houses of Congress. But the increasing complexity of international relations and the concurrently heavier responsibilities for policy decisions have caused American presidents in recent times to seek close cooperation with the advisory bodies of the Congress, notably the Foreign Relations Committee of the Senate and the Foreign Affairs Committee of the House of Representatives. Constitutionally, the Senate holds a stronger position than the House in determining foreign policy since it is regarded as an advisory body to the President in matters concerning foreign affairs. However, the House can exert strong influence through its control of the purse strings of the United States Treasury. It can pass, cut down, or deny requests for money appropriations. In this way, it can cause organizational modifications and even personnel changes in both the Department of State and the Defense Establishment, thereby exerting considerable influence on relations between the United States and the world. While it is sometimes held that the power to rule by appropriation is against the spirit of the Constitution which provides for separation of the legislative from the executive branch of government, there seems to be no indication that the founding fathers wanted to prevent such a possibility. The House of Representatives, like the Senate, may also express its views on foreign policy by passing, modifying, or rejecting proposed laws which have a bearing on foreign affairs, such as tariffs, subsidies, and price support. It may pass resolutions stating its views concerning any foreign policy, extant or proposed. The Congress may also question the Secretary of State regarding policies and, in fact, has done so frequently. It cannot officially question the President; his delegate in charge of foreign policy must defend his position.

To avoid strenuous policy disagreements between the executive and the legislative branches, and the pitfalls of appropriation cuts, the President must remain in constant touch with both houses of Congress and confer personally with party leaders when decisions of great importance are forthcoming. Since World War II, there has been an increasingly bipartisan approach to problems of foreign policy. However, this by no means precludes outspoken criticism from the "loyal opposition" and even from the President's own party as has been demonstrated in the case of the Vietnam War.

Despite his subjection to constitutional strictures, the President can postpone or circumvent congressional participation in treaty actions by negotiating "executive agreements." This has been done by many presidents of the United States, including George Washington. The vast majority of these agreements were approved retroactively by the Senate, but others were amended, turned down, or never acted upon at all, without necessarily losing their international validity. It should be added that executive agreements may concern not only the initiation of treaties but also the termination of existing treaties. During the war, executive agreements were concluded between the United States and the Soviet Union.

It is clear that the President has not exactly a free hand in conducting foreign relations. As a political leader, he is subject to party criticism. As the leader of the executive branch of the government, he must cope with the whims and wishes of the legislative branch. He must abide by the laws of the land lest he become entangled with the judiciary branch. He also will have to consult the barometer of public opinion, uneducated as it sometimes may be. And yet, he is regarded as the supreme arbiter of American foreign policy and, by inference, is the most important man of the Western alliance, if not the free world, when it comes to determining foreign policy.

If the President is the supreme arbiter of American foreign policy, what is the position of his Secretary of State? He is a political appointee, subject to Senate confirmation. While his activities may be criticized and his policies disapproved by Congress, he may be removed from office only by the President. His term ends only with that of the President, unless the latter requests his resignation. However, should the President be re-elected, the Secretary must submit his resignation and the President either accepts his resignation or reappoints him. He is the ranking member of the Cabinet but, since 1947, no longer second to the Vice-President in succession to the presidency. Although the foreign affairs spokesman for the President and the United States Government, he is not the center around which relations with foreign countries revolve. The President himself is the pivot.

The Secretary's position as the presidential adviser contains a unique aspect: he is both accountable and not accountable for policy. The President retains full responsibility and has the choice of supporting or repudiating his Secretary. If the Secretary has presidential confidence, he is sacrosanct. The only measure Congress can take against him is denial or curtailment of money appropriations. Since this would jeopardize the security of the country, even budgetary reprisals can hardly be taken promiscuously. On the other hand, the person of the Secretary is certainly not inviolable. He must be prepared to spend unconscionable time being questioned by the Congress — a questioning which more often than not amounts to a cross-examination.

• GREAT BRITAIN — In Great Britain control of foreign policy legally rests with the Crown and is exercised by the Cabinet. The Cabinet is led by the Prime Minister who makes all appointments to ministerial positions. The Secretary of State for Foreign Affairs (Foreign Secretary) ranks among the principal members of the Cabinet. He heads the Foreign Office and is assisted by the Permanent Under Secretary and three or four Ministers of State.

The Prime Minister is the most powerful official in the British Government. Like the American President, he selects his Cabinet members or causes them to resign. If he wishes he can reshuffle them to avoid dissolution of the entire Cabinet and the loss of desirable men. He retains power so long as his is the majority party in the House of Commons and it continues to sustain him. But "unlike the President of the United States, who determines the extent to which he will consult with members of his executive family, the Prime Minister is the leader but not the master of the group, and he is bound to observe the rights of those who jointly share responsibility with him."[1] He is in fact, though not in law, the working head of the State, endowed with more power than most constitutional rulers. This power can be broken only by a defeat at the polls or a parliamentary vote of non-confidence, indicating defection from the majority party and thus causing fall of the Cabinet.

Like all ministers the Foreign Secretary is individually responsible to Parliament for the conduct of his office. He answers questions in the chamber in which he sits, and he explains and defends the Government's external policies. Parliamentary dissatisfaction with these policies may be expressed in party meetings or by formal motions of censure, but as long as the Foreign Secretary has the support of the Prime Minister, party discipline is almost certain to rally a majority in his favor. Should defections or abstentions on critical votes involving foreign policy indicate considerable dissent within the majority party, the Prime Minister may seek to mollify the critics by policy shifts or a Cabinet reorganization to bring in a new Foreign Secretary. He may also use the threat of a dissolution of Parliament and an appeal to the electorate.

The British Foreign Secretary has relatively more freedom of decision than his American counterpart. He decides many important questions on his own authority and confers with the Prime Minister only on major issues. If conditions force him to consider a departure from traditionally established policies that might affect the fate of the country, he consults with the entire Cabinet. He relies heavily on

[1] H. M. Stout, *British Government* (New York: Oxford University Press, 1955), p. 57.

the expert advice of the Foreign Office staff of permanent officials, a highly select group of experienced civil servants, comparatively well paid, secure from parliamentary attacks, and protected from extreme budgetary fluctuations.

Like most ministers of foreign affairs, the Foreign Secretary is a coordinator rather than a creator. His burden of work and responsibilities are so heavy that he frequently must delegate power among subordinates. Contrary to American practice, his duties are not confined exclusively to administering Britain's international affairs. As an important member of a highly integrated and mutually responsible cabinet, he must attend to national as well as international politics; as a prominent member of the majority party, he must be ready to appear before Commons and defend Her Majesty's Government's policies. He has formal duties toward the Crown. He will have to convince members of the Commonwealth of his policies' justification, for British foreign policy vitally affects the foreign policies of these countries and the status of the remaining Crown colonies. He is responsible for presenting his party's policies, and particularly its concept of world politics, in a form acceptable to the voting public.

The British Foreign Office is relatively more powerful than the US Department of State. In the United States, as we have seen, the treaty-making power rests with the President who is advised by the Secretary of State, but is controlled directly by the Senate and indirectly by the House. In Britain, this power, nominally in the hands of the sovereign, is actually wielded by the Prime Minister, the Foreign Secretary, and, in important issues, the Cabinet. This constellation does not vary even in the event of a declaration of war. If the Cabinet must exercise the sovereign's war-making power, it needs only her assent. Parliamentary ratification is no legal necessity and the House may object only by a vote of non-confidence or a refusal to pass money appropriations. In practice, however, the Cabinet refrains from using its war-making power without advance parliamentary agreement.[2]

• FRANCE — The power in the France of the Fifth Republic rests

[2] See *Britain, An Official Handbook* (London: Central Office of Information, 1966), Chapters 2 and 4.

basically with the President — and with the President alone. Although the legal responsibility for the conduct of foreign affairs was shifted to the Premier, the years following the acceptance of the new Constitution on September 28, 1958, have demonstrated clearly that the President is in a quasi-dictatorial position to determine internal and external policy.

On the books, France is a democracy. Under Charles de Gaulle, this is a misnomer. The term "guided democracy," coined by the former Indonesian President Sukarno, would better apply. It is no longer the parties which decide the nation's course, but the government. The government, however, is a creature of the President: his word is law. He appoints the Premier, and the Premier's choice of the cabinet members depends upon the President's nod.[3]

Since the Foreign Minister will have to carry out the President's policies, his relationship to either the Premier or the President bears little resemblance to that set forth in the 1946 Constitution and far less to that of the British Foreign Secretary to his Prime Minister. Nor can it compare with the line of command which exists between the American Secretary of State and his President. In fact, the position of the French Foreign Minister wields less genuine influence than that of any foreign minister in the West.

Like his American and British colleagues, the Foreign Minister is a political appointee. But, since the Premier chooses him, obviously with Presidential advice and consent, it is doubtful that under the Fifth Republic any Foreign Minister will be appointed who has only political and no substantive qualifications. On the other hand, his influence has diminished considerably in comparison with his postwar position. His responsibility toward the Parliament is practically non-existent; the Premier is responsible. His policies must withstand the probing of both the Premier and the President. On issues of particular importance, he functions as adviser rather than policy maker.

Unquestionably, the President is decisive in French foreign policy. In the new Constitution, his position has been tailored to fit General de Gaulle. If future presidents are able to maintain his standards,

---

[3] See J. Chatelain, *La Nouvelle Constitution et la Régime Politique de France* (Paris: Editions Berger-Levrault, 1959).

the constitutional provisions concerning foreign affairs will remain effective. If not, the entire edifice of the 1958 Constitution may be shaken, for it is founded on the personality of one man. Should a future President abdicate certain powers to the Premier, the Parliament might become correspondingly stronger and make its weight felt, possibly by disrupting political life and international relations — thereby defeating the purpose of the new Constitution: stabilization of France's polity.

• WEST GERMANY — The position of the Federal Republic of Germany and the circumstances under which its Basic Law came into being are as unusual as those of post-war Japan. Germany was still under Allied occupation when this Basic Law was promulgated on May 23, 1949, with the concurrence of the occupying powers, United States, Great Britain, and France (but not the USSR). The Law became effective as the West German Constitution on March 15, 1955, when West Germany's status as an occupied country ended. From that date, the continuation of Allied troop garrisons was a matter of free agreement between sovereign states. Gradually the Federal Republic became a strong partner of the West in the political struggle against the East, a member of NATO and of the Common Market; it was allowed, in fact encouraged, to build up its military forces so as to play its role in the Western defense organization.

The Basic Law determines administrative and substantive responsibility for relations with other countries. It assigns to the Federal President duties which are exclusively symbolic and representative. The real power is invested in the Federal Chancellor and the Administration; i.e., the Federal Ministers. Elected by the *Bundestag* (West German parliament), the Chancellor is the leading member of the majority party. Officially he must be appointed by the President, a mere formality; he can also be dismissed by the President, a most unlikely event. The Chancellor proposes ministerial appointments to the President, which is a euphemistic gesture. The "proposal" is tantamount to a selection already made, and the President could hardly decline to follow the Chancellor's "suggestion."

The Basic Law states that "the Federal Chancellor shall determine and assume responsibility for general policy. Within the limits of this general policy, each Federal Minister shall direct his department individually and on his own responsibility. The Federal Government shall decide on differences of opinion between the Federal Ministers." In practice, the term Federal Government is interchangeable with that of the Chancellor; if he is as strong a personality as Konrad Adenauer, he *is* the government; if he is weak, the government is weak and subject to intramural power struggles.

No specific reference to foreign relations is made in that part of the Basic Law which outlines the functions of the *Bundestag*. Similarly, the position of Federal Chancellor may be likened to that of British Prime Minister. The Federal President, however, exerts less influence than the reigning British monarch, who is a unifying symbol throughout the British Commonwealth and whose legal and personal standing in the United Kingdom is powerful, if somewhat intangible. The Chancellor wields all the power and the President remains a figurehead. This leaves the determination of foreign and security policy *de facto* in his hands, reducing the Foreign Minister's status to that of an advisor-assistant.

As an occupied country without sovereignty, Germany had no relations with other nations and could develop no foreign policies. Whatever connections it had with the outside world were handled through the occupation authorities. But once sovereignty was in sight, the West German Government, with the blessings of the allied authorities, began to build a new Foreign Office (*Auswärtiges Amt*). It quickly grew into an efficient organization but, due to its expanding responsibilities, attained its final shape only during a reorganization in 1958–59.[4] Its continuity is safeguarded because the Foreign Minister is the only political appointee; all other personnel belong to one of the three layers of civil service. The principle of personnel interchangeability has been established; the second highest official of the Foreign Office, the Secretary of State, like the British Permanent Undersecretary is actually in charge of the *Amt*: "From the point of view of the Federal Minister, the State Secretary is the head

---

4 Cf. H. Krueger, "German Diplomacy," in S. D. Kertesz and M. A. Fitzsimmons (eds.), *Diplomacy in a Changing World* (South Bend, Ind.: University of Notre Dame Press, 1959).

of the Foreign Office's hierarchical organization and is entrusted with the responsibility to submit comments or reports to the Minister in coordinated and finalized forms."[5]

The position of the Minister for Foreign Affairs is similar to that of the British Foreign Secretary, as is their relationship with their respective chiefs. Still, one might speculate that the British Foreign Secretary has somewhat more freedom of action than has his German colleague, especially after the retirement of Chancellor Adenauer whose influence on foreign affairs was overwhelming.

• JAPAN[6] — The New Constitution of Japan was promulgated on November 3, 1946. It was written under the influence of American democratic philosophy; Japan was then still an occupied country and the US Supreme Commander, General Douglas MacArthur, the factual ruler of the island empire. When the occupation status ended with the 1952 peace treaty, those American military forces which remained in Japan were charged with helping to protect a defenseless country against communist encroachment. A special treaty with the Japanese Government (February 28, 1952) permitted them to stay under a clearly defined statute. A revised form of this treaty was signed in 1960 despite violent leftist opposition.

According to the preamble of the Constitution, the "sovereign power resides with the people." The Emperor, formerly the god–king, is now merely the symbol of the state and derives "his position from the will of the people." His duties are strictly ceremonial; the monarchy is constitutional in the democratic tradition. He appoints the Prime Minister, but it is the Diet, the Japanese parliament, which designates the appointee.

The Diet "shall be the highest organ of state power" and the executive power "shall be vested in the Cabinet." The Prime Minister heads the Cabinet, which is collectively responsible to the Diet. The Cabinet, in addition to other functions, shall "manage foreign affairs" and "conclude treaties," seeking prior or subsequent approval of the

[5] See Bulletin of the Federal Press and Information Service, Bonn, March 28, 1959.

[6] While Japan is not a Western power, its political organization is modelled along the lines of Western democracy and it is an ally of the United States.

Diet "depending on the circumstances." Therefore, "it can actually be said that in the management of foreign affairs, the Prime Minister proposes and the Diet disposes."[7] In other words, the Prime Minister, like his British counterpart, has the decisive voice in directing relations with other nations; the Foreign Minister, who heads the Ministry of Foreign Affairs (*Gaimusho*), is his principal adviser. As in Britain, the Prime Minister and his Cabinet are necessarily members of the majority party. But his stand against the opposition is more difficult than that of his British counterpart, whose opposition is "loyal"; in Japan, it is hostile. A conservative government must face the socialists, who are Marxist-oriented and whose left wing is close to the communists.

The extent to which the Foreign Minister retains the initiative in international affairs depends on the personality of the Prime Minister, just as it does in Britain. But, even under the best of circumstances, the Foreign Minister works for the Prime Minister. Nevertheless, his standing in the Cabinet is high. The Prime Minister, being a member of the majority party, indirectly controls the Diet so long as he and his party agree. The strength of his position, naturally, affects that of the Foreign Minister.

However, despite the supreme constitutional power vested in the Diet, its "chief function . . . so far as foreign policy is concerned is consultative."[8] In this field, the exchange between the Prime Minister and the Diet is quite lively. But on the whole, the influence of the Japanese Diet is limited despite its high constitutional stature; the cabinets in power since the promulgation of the Constitution have taken the initiative and led the Diet rather than been led by it. A few issues have caused serious debate, one of them being the status of the treaty with the United States regarding American military forces stationed in Japan. But in all cases, the government has prevailed.

The reasons for this lack of effective opposition to the government's foreign policy — excluding the perennial opposition of the Marxists — may be lack of experience and a "strong tendency to regard foreign

[7] Ch. Yanaga, *Japanese People and Politics* (New York: John Wiley and Sons, Inc., 1956), p. 369.

[8] *Ibid.*, p. 373.

policy as the special preserve of the government experts who endeavor so far as possible to keep it out of reach of parliamentary debates."[9] These are obvious remnants of the long period during which the Diet was completely under the thumb of the Japanese militarists and became a rubber-stamp parliament. Moreover, the electorate is not too well informed about the intricacies of international relations. The only issues with which they are apt to confront their representatives are the maintenance of peace and the opening of new trade avenues.

Who Has the Power in the East?

• THE USSR — Soviet foreign policy and its controlling factors are no longer, in Churchill's words, a "riddle wrapped in a mystery inside an enigma." For students of Soviet government and politics and of the international communist movement not much of a riddle is involved. The question of who actually controls Soviet foreign relations can be answered as unequivocally as in the case of democratic or fascist systems. Of the many factors which determine the shaping and implementation of Soviet foreign policy, the Ministry of Foreign Affairs is of minor importance.

Constitutionally, the Supreme Soviet, as the highest legislative body of the USSR, possesses treaty, war, and peace making powers. But the Constitution of 1936 is, politically and administratively, a cruel deception. Major provisions have never been implemented. Significantly, the dominating position of the Party is not even mentioned. If it is ever rewritten, it may be more realistic and the position of the Party may be constitutionally determined.

The Supreme Soviet, the "parliament" of the USSR, is equally deceptive. Its functions are carried on by a Presidium while the Soviet is not in session — which is most of the time.[10] It is constitutionally responsible for ratifications of international treaties and can even proclaim "a state of war in the event of armed attack on the

---

[9] *Ibid.,* p. 374.

[10] The Chairman of the Presidium of the Supreme Soviet is the nominal head of the USSR, popularly known as "President" outside the USSR, but his functions are purely ceremonial.

USSR . . ." but obviously would be unable to make such a decision without order or sanction of the Party Politbureau which tells the Presidium of the Supreme Soviet what to do.

Experience has demonstrated again and again that the Plenum of the Supreme Soviet is nothing but a sounding board for the Soviet leaders. It is a rubber-stamp parliament, pure and simple. Since there is not, cannot be, any opposition to the legislative proposals submitted to it, it does not assume the functions of a parliamentary body. The measures of its Presidium and the handling of foreign affairs by the Kremlin are scarcely affected by possible divergent opinions in its plenary sessions. Thus, in a government that allegedly represents the people, popular control of international relations is eliminated; any which appears to exist is purely academic veneer.

The Presidium of the Supreme Soviet itself is only a weak reflection of the greatest power in the USSR, the Communist Party. *The Party rules the country.* It has assumed a "guiding and directing role" in all Soviet government agencies, not only by its sheer power and prestige, but also by a party organization which parallels that of the government. In other words, the official executive organs of the Soviet Government are duplicated by smaller party offices, located inside and outside of government agencies. This does not necessarily mean that communist party members within the Soviet Ministry of Foreign Affairs (in the Russian abbreviation, *Minindel*) wield much influence over policy. Party members are not always identical with Party delegates assigned to do special jobs. Just as in other Soviet government agencies, such party delegates work in the *Minindel* (and in all Soviet embassies) and have organized a so-called "Activ," which is permitted to submit "suggestions" concerning foreign affairs and the efficiency and loyalty of employees. It is doubtful, however, that their recommendations ever carry any appreciable weight in policy determination.

The Party, interpreting prevailing conditions and apparent political opportunities in terms of communist ideology — which does not exclude extreme realism in tactics — issues overall directives known as "Party Lines." These orders are followed as the law of the land, and Soviet policy and diplomacy are oriented accordingly. The *Minindel* receives these directives for implementation. It probably contributes to their creation only by furnishing background studies and professional analyses and estimates.

The Party's power is vested in its Central Committee which, in turn, is steered by the Politbureau. The Secretary General of the Party (there are several Secretaries) is Chairman of the Politbureau.[11] In the executive branch of the Soviet Government the highest group of officials is the Council of Ministers of the USSR. It "exercises general guidance in the sphere of relations with foreign states." The chairman of the Council roughly corresponds to the position of Prime Minister. The Party Politbureau and the Council of Ministers of the USSR appear to be corresponding bodies, but in reality they are not. Party and government are theoretically distinct, but for the most important purposes they are identical. The executive is simply an arm of the Party. Some top party leaders are also top government officials. For example, after having become the Party's First Secretary and Chairman of the Central Committee's Presidium, Nikita Khrushchev became Chairman of the Council of Ministers, holding both jobs simultaneously. Other members of the Politbureau have held jobs either in the Council of Ministers of the USSR, the Presidium of the Supreme Soviet, or one of the major Union Republics. Of these, the Party position is by far the more important. This may be the reason why the policy of holding dual jobs has become somewhat more limited in recent years. The Party does not want a strong executive; even the heads of the more important ministries are rarely chosen for Politbureau membership and must be content with their status as purely substantive or technical administrators. Since it is a prerequisite, the fact that ministers are Party members does not necessarily grant them access to the high Party councils.

It is no secret that foreign policies are formulated, not by the *Minindel*, but by the Politbureau, in the name of the Party. The members of the Politbureau probably listen to the views of the Council of Ministers and the Foreign Minister. They also consider the opinion of such high party and government officials as they may

[11] In 1952, the Nineteenth Party Congress changed the name of the Politbureau to Presidium and that of the Secretary General to First Secretary. CPSU Chairman Brezhnev reverted to the original nomenclature in 1966.

care to summon, but the Politbureau, with the support of the Central Committee of the Party, remains the only decision-making body and issues its orders to the implementing agencies. Until Stalin's death, little was known about the manner in which the Politbureau reached its decisions. Since then, the more relaxed attitude of the Soviet leaders has made it possible to learn somewhat more about the decision-making process through their occasional remarks to newspaper correspondents and casual conversations with diplomats. During the period of the so-called "collective leadership," discussions in the Politbureau and the Central Committee seem to have been quite lively and differences of opinion were openly stated. There probably is more give-and-take in the meetings; the post-Stalinist rulers, having become more subtle in their approaches and methods, will want to be briefed realistically. Decisions are influenced not only by facts but also by their ideological interpretations. The Politbureau, it must be remembered, is supreme guardian of doctrine, and its thought processes therefore differ from those of Western pragmatists.

It must again be emphasized that the USSR's position in the world is shaped, in communist eyes, by Marxism–Leninism. Since Trotsky's doctrine of "permanent revolution" — a permanent state of revolutionary war against non-Marxist powers — was discarded in favor of consolidating the USSR and creating "socialism in one country," the non-Soviet world has been led to believe that "peaceful coexistence" between the socialist and capitalist camps was possible. Indeed, the World War II cooperation between the Soviet Union and the Western allies seemed to demonstrate such a possibility. This collaboration was expected to continue in postwar years, particularly through the United Nations.[12] Alas, it never materialized.

The position of the Foreign Minister is not predicated on his being a Communist Party member and chief of the *Minindel* but depends upon his standing in the hierarchy of the Party. Relatively few Soviet Foreign Ministers have had so high a standing as Molotov, who was not only a senior member of the former Politbureau, but also Vice-Chairman of the Council of Ministers of the USSR. Due

---

[12] K. London, *Backgrounds of Conflict* (New York: The Macmillan Co., 1945/1947), p. 245 ff.

to his high Party position, he exerted a much greater influence upon the formulation of foreign policy than such men as Litvinov or Gromyko. The former, for all his astuteness and diplomatic talents, was never influential in the Party and was even looked upon with suspicion; the latter is regarded as a loyal and literal implementor of Soviet policies but not as a power in the high councils of the Kremlin.

Within the *Minindel,* the Minister is supported by the unique institution of the *Collegium.* Its members are said to be designated by the Council of Ministers and to enjoy certain prerogatives. Consisting of Deputy Ministers and *Minindel* Division heads, its probable function is substantive support of the Minister. The *Collegium* may appeal to the Council of Ministers if its recommendations are rejected by the Minister, but it is unlikely that this contingency has arisen often, if at all. Moreover, to a considerable extent the argument is academic: the Party makes the final decision, voiding or accepting either the Minister's or the *Collegium's* view, or both.[13]

It is noteworthy that the Soviet authorities are very flexible in assigning qualified personnel. Any member of the *Minindel* may be sent overseas, but so can persons from other ministries or institutions. The latter simply transfer to the *Minindel,* perhaps without a paper transfer. Certainly, KGB personnel are assigned to posts abroad with or without the Ministry's blessings: they receive their travel orders and, according to the nature of their assignment, go under *Minindel* cover or are attached to less conspicuous units. Similar flexibility governs appointments to higher-level positions; there is a constant interchange between Ambassadors and Division Chiefs. In other words, due to the highly integrated nature of the Soviet party and government apparatus, the *Minindel* is utilized as circumstances require, without regard for the bureaucratic standards which loom so large in the West.

• RED CHINA — In general, the principles directing Red Chinese foreign relations are akin to those of the USSR except that they

---

[13] It is interesting to recall that the *Minindel* for many years had another advisory body, the "Institute of Economics and World Politics." This institute was absorbed by the Soviet Academy of Sciences in 1947 and some of its activities were transferred to the Moscow University School of Politics.

embody an even more pronounced aggressiveness and revolutionary intent. The basic statement containing Peking's concept of foreign policy can be found in the "Common Program of the Chinese People's Political Consultative Conference" of September 29, 1949. Article 54 of this Program, while protesting peaceful intentions, vows opposition to "imperialist policy of aggression and war." The following articles emphasize enmity toward the Kuomintang, Chiang Kai-shek's ruling party, and make clear the wish to deal only with states which have "severed relations with the Kuomintang reactionary clique."

The "Constitution of the People's Republic of China" is more austere than the Soviet Constitution, but just as meaningless. It vests state power in a dummy parliament, the National People's Congress. This Congress is represented by a Standing Committee which conducts the Congress' business during the year between its sessions and is the most important policy-making body in Red China. The State Council, like the Soviet Council of Ministers, is the executive organ of the central government; one of its duties is to implement foreign policy through the Minister of Foreign Affairs, a Council member. The Standing Committee which supervises the work of the State Council also ratifies or abrogates treaties with foreign states, decides in issues of war and defense, and appoints or recalls envoys. Like its Soviet counterpart, the Constitution fails to indicate that the real power of decision in both domestic and foreign affairs lies in the hands of the Party Chairman and his six-member Secretariat.

The Secretariat and the somewhat larger Politbureau are not separate units outside the Central Committee but substitute for the Central Committee while the latter is not in session. Decisions concerning foreign policy are made by these bodies. As in the USSR, most members of the Secretariat and the Politbureau are also high government officials. The Chairman of the Party may also be the Chairman of the Republic; Mao Tse-tung occupied both positions until, in 1959, he resigned the state chairmanship, ostensibly to rid himself of less important functions, but in reality because the catastrophic failure of the Big Leap Forward forced him to take this step, urged upon him by leading party members. We know now that he bitterly resented their pressure and had many of them purged during the "great cultural revolution."

The position of the Foreign Minister is not important *per se*; it derives its influence from the standing of the incumbent. A man such as Chou En-lai, who has other administrative functions, adds luster to the Foreign Office simply because he sits in the high party councils and for that reason may actively help shape policy and suggest ways of implementation. A lesser man would play a lesser role.

The role of the leaders of the Chinese People's Liberation Army and their influence on China mainland's political development have greatly increased during the past few years and, particularly, during the "cultural revolution" when Mao had to rely on the Army to remain in power. It is possible that, after Mao's demise, the Army will play a decisive role in post-Maoist affairs, a role never equalled by the Soviet Army which has always been under firm party control.

Communist Chinese foreign policy is not the result of constitutional law but rather of the ideology determining this law. Specifically, it is what Peking terms "the thought of Mao Tse-tung" which directs Red China's methodological approach to the long-range goal it shares with Moscow. This "thought" is Marxism–Leninism, mixed with elements of Stalinism and "adjusted" to the conditions and requirements in Communist China. It is derivative rather than inventive: Mao has been overestimated as an original thinker.

The preceding highlights of constitutional and administrative procedures which characterize certain key countries' conduct of foreign relations were presented to clarify the fundamental theories and practices underlying the methods used. They demonstrate not only the actual difference between democratic and totalitarian principles governing the origin and administration of foreign policy, but also the conceptual reasons for the schism between the two camps. They throw light on the diversities among Western nations with which Japan is affiliated, but, while they testify to the pluralistic systems of constitutional laws, these differences are minor and philosophically unimportant. On the other hand, a comparison between Eastern and Western constitutional laws and applications of these laws should reveal the enormity of the chasm between them.

Who Formulates Security Policy?

There is a marked difference between totalitarian and democratic techniques of policy-formulation and decision-making. Soviet leaders face little if any internal opposition to their foreign policies. The Supreme Soviet, properly coached, votes for any proposal the Polit-bureau sets forth. The executive branches of the Soviet Government are charged with implementing the policy and told what methods to use: there is no recourse; the orders of the Party must be obeyed. Since the Party has earmarked funds necessary to carry out the policy, no further monetary discussion is required. The same is the case in Communist China.

Techniques are more complicated for the governments of democratic states where the parliaments control the nation's purse. Major policies announced by the chief of state or the government can be implemented only after the parliamentary body has agreed to furnish the necessary appropriations. Even if money is not immediately needed, parliamentary consent is highly advisable. Congress or Parliament may overrule the executive branch of the government. Theoretically this is more likely in the United States than in Great Britain: the Prime Minister controls the parliamentary majority whereas the legislative and executive branches of government in Washington have been known to work at cross purposes.

There is no hard and fast response to the question of how decisions are made except that techniques vary and imponderables can neither be measured nor systematized. Decision-makers are only human. Not only are they subject to pressures from within their own frontiers and from public opinion the world over, they also must be recognized as the products of their civilization, their upbringing, and their physical, glandular, and psychological constitution. Idiosyncrasies of the policy-maker play a vital role in the final determination of policy. His decision may depend at least partially upon his attitudes toward foreign statesmen with whom he is acquainted. It will be influenced greatly by his ideological concept of the world. It may be colored by little tricks of fate which, through human error, play havoc with decision-making: a breakdown of the messenger service; a missing or misrouted document; the failure of inter-office coordination; or the absence of an important adviser. It may be affected by an upset stomach or by marital arguments. There is no denying that a statesman worthy of the title will stay aware of the real problems with which he is confronted and that he will do his utmost to solve them.

But he would be superhuman if he remained unaffected by the hazards of prejudice nurtured by heredity and environment, emotional involvements, physiological conditions, and political schizophrenia.[14]

Thus decision-making is complicated by intangible hazards against which no foolproof system exists. The evolution of a foreign policy from original idea to final formulation can be systematized and its progress described in detail. But the decision of that final arbiter of foreign policy, the chief of state or government, on whether or not to use the formula, whether to modify it or ask for the creation of a new one, is suffused with imponderables. In the West, this is tacitly understood but rarely admitted. In the East, the communist party permits its foreign affairs "workers" less freedom of movement and shows little understanding for imponderables. Although its men may have a certain amount of leeway to determine their own tactics, they must do so at their own risk — which they are loath to take. In cases of important policy decisions, even the methods of implementation are strictly outlined.

Yet taking into account the sharp differences of political strategy and tactics between the opponents, one is confronted with the brutal fact that, however carefully prepared, final policy decisions are, so to speak, an act of God, communicated through carriers of power who are beset by all the tricks of fate and frailties to which humans are inevitably subjected. The communists may disagree with this somewhat fatalistic view, but they are not superhuman, however much they want to be.

Both sides make great efforts to minimize human error to the greatest possible extent. In the West this has led to a machinery in charge of what is called "security policy" and which comprises more than foreign policy; rather, it is a combination of political, economic, technological, and military considerations which, through coordinating processes, are supposed to deliver foolproof recommendations. This technique is highly developed in the United States and legally set forth in the National Security Act of 1947. In it, Congress expresses its intent to "provide a comprehensive program for the future security of the United States; to provide for the establishment of integrated

[14] Cf. Chapter 2, p. 19 ff.

policies and procedures for the departments, agencies, and functions of the Government relating to the national security; . . ." in other words, a concept of national security policy was developed which required collaboration and coordination between the Department of State, the military establishments, and several other departments of the Federal Government.

The result of this legislation was the National Security Council (NSC), composed of the President as Chairman, the Vice-President, the Secretaries of State and Defense, and the Director of the Office of Defense Mobilization. In addition to these permanent members, there are "standing requests" for participants who, though not statutory members, attend the NSC meetings more or less regularly.[15]

In addition to being responsible for policy coordination, the NSC "advises the President with respect to the integration of domestic, foreign, and military policies relating to the national security so as to enable the military services and the other departments and agencies of the Government to cooperate more effectively in matters involving national security."[16] This is a clear statement of the recognition that foreign policy is no longer a "thing in itself" but part of the entire body politic of the nation. It sweeps away barriers between foreign and domestic policies, just as it integrates them with defense strategy.

The NSC is supposed to be the focal point of such integration but its role and effectiveness have been the subject of protracted argument. Its tasks and importance have varied in accordance with the inclinations of different presidents. During the Eisenhower Administration, both legislators and political scientists criticized this decision-making machinery as inefficient. Summarizing all the components involved in the coordination process, Senator Henry M. Jackson of Washington stated that the "pretty picture" of the many security organizations allegedly cooperating closely has "little or nothing to do with reality. The NSC is not and cannot be an effective planning agency, except in the most Olympian sense. . . . The proper role of

---

[15] See T. V. Stanley with H. H. Ransom, *The National Security Council*, Harvard University Defense Policy Seminar, January 12, 1957.

[16] The National Security Act of 1947, as amended through August 1956, Title I, Sec. 1(a).

the NSC is to criticize and evaluate departmental planning and proposals in light of the knowledge, interests, and possibly conflicting policies of other departments. In this way what we would call a coordinated view may be developed, and such a view may be very helpful to the President in making a clear determination of the executive will."[17]

The Senator's main objection appeared to be that the coordination process within the NSC runs the risk of too much compromise and "departmental jockeying," resulting in a dangerous lack of consistency. Planning, in the Senator's view, should be undertaken by departmental experts who would present the NSC "with the most sharply defined political issues and choices, not with papers which have already lost their cutting edge by a process of compromise at lower levels."[18] The Senator believed the creative effort of the executive branch is stultified by the NSC because "the departments are relieved of responsibility for identifying upcoming problems and for generating new ideas. . . . The result is that a vast reservoir of talent goes largely untapped."[19]

President Kennedy may have shared Senator Jackson's views. During the first months of his administration, he made very little use of the NSC. But the Berlin crisis and the Cuban invasion failure prompted a change of mind. From then on, the NSC met more frequently. Under President Johnson, the fortunes of the NSC declined once again. One might surmise that when it now holds one of its infrequent meetings, the Council presents a sampling of views to its chairman, the President, without trying to force the chief executive's hand in decision-making. Such meetings probably are useful; there is nothing wrong with high-level bull sessions so long as the NSC remains an advisory body.

The NSC is a reflection of the committee system which has invaded the US Government and is here to stay. It certainly is a democratic

---

[17] H. M. Jackson, "To Forge a Strategy for Survival," *Public Administration Review*, Summer 1959, Vol. *XIX*, No. 3, p. 159.

[18] *Ibid.*, p. 160.

[19] *Ibid.* See also *Organizing for National Security* and *Interim Staff Memorandum*, Subcommittee on National Policy Machinery, Henry M. Jackson, Chairman, December 4, 1959.

way of coming to some agreement on policy or views on specific issues, but, again, there may be some question as to whether majority reports are necessarily best for the country. Majorities have been known to be wrong. For that reason and others, government officials and political scientists have often questioned whether a committee can make policy, and at least some of them have concluded that the committee system has failed. A specific complaint has been voiced that "the men who meet in the NSC and its subsidiary boards are not free agents but instructed ambassadors representing the particular interests and the particular points of view of their respective agencies."[20] Further charges stress that the "imposition of budgetary limitations on all levels of policy planning distorts and inhibits the planning process from the outset"; that "diplomatic politeness" has led the NSC to the tendency "to shy away from bold innovation in favor of a compromise" . . . or to evade a decision altogether.[21]

These serious criticisms constitute somewhat of an indictment against democratic processes which, if true, would not only jeopardize security planning but, at an earlier stage, compromise the coordination process of national intelligence estimates. While there seems to be a suitable framework for shaping national security policies, the democratic technique of compromise in coordinating substantive findings often prevents not only clear-cut decisions but also original and imaginative ones. Vested departmental interests are strong, and thinking is impeded either by lack of time or by "political" caution. On the other hand, experience has shown that committee work in government has achieved no mean feats, particularly when dealing with complex security problems. A properly chaired committee becomes a team pooling its intellectual resources. If disagreement ensues, instead of compromising, the majority view should be adopted with the proviso that the findings be reviewed by superior bodies. The final decision still depends on one man only.

Within the framework of this book it is not possible to examine

[20] H. J. Morgenthau, "Can We Entrust Defense to a Committee?" *New York Times Magazine,* June 7, 1959.
[21] *Ibid.*

in depth the problems raised here; the chief purpose is to point to their existence and nature. There is proof that the organizers of security and foreign policies are increasingly aware of their responsibility to develop ways to cope with new issues, some of which stagger the imagination. One cannot expect so recent a development as coordinated security policy to function perfectly. But one point needs strong emphasis, namely, that it is imperative "to stimulate deep, sustained, creative thinking about the whole range of problems facing our nation and society."[22] Ever since Franklin D. Roosevelt, US presidents have recognized that the growing complexity of problems, both domestic and foreign, require expert advice by the best talents available outside the government. Not all presidents felt as strongly about this need as did President Kennedy who gathered around himself a group of outstanding experts in various fields of politics and science. To some extent, President Johnson has emulated this example. However essential the cooperation of the nation's non-governmental experts, the NSC should remain the indispensable deliberating body it is supposed to be and should contribute to the clarification of issues and policies.

There is great danger that the "brain trusts," due to the pressure of current issues, cannot concentrate on long-range problems. These problems face the entire non-communist world; few governments provide their policy-planners and idea men with sufficient thinking time. The communists do not seem harassed by such problems; their planning is intrinsically long range while current events are dealt with as tactical matters.

In Great Britain, as in the United States, the formulation of security policy involves coordinating the views and interests of several government departments. The principal instrument of this coordination is a high-level Cabinet committee, the Committee on Defence and Overseas Policy. Under the chairmanship of the Prime Minister, it includes the Secretaries of State for Defence, Foreign Affairs, and Commonwealth Relations, and the Chancellor of the Exchequer. The Committee is advised by the Chief of the Defence Staff and the Chiefs

[22] Jackson, *ibid.*, p. 162.

of Staff of the three military services. The Committee's role is comparable to that of the American National Security Council. The British Committee, however, is a more powerful body since it is not merely advisory and its membership insures that its decisions will be determinative. It is a reinforced inner Cabinet considering and deciding problems over the whole range of national security, political, economic, and military.

In 1964, the Ministry of Defence, which had been established like the US Department of Defense after World War II, absorbed the Admiralty, War Office, and Air Ministry. The Ministry's political head, now called the Secretary of State for Defence, serves as Deputy Chairman of the Committee on Defence and Overseas Policy. Under him serves a Minister of Defence for each of the armed services; they have general responsibilities in the Ministry as well. The Secretary of State, the Ministers of Defence, the Chief of Defence Staff and the service chiefs, the Chief Scientific Adviser, and the Permanent Under-Secretary of State compose a Defence Council which directs the military establishment in accordance with the policies and decisions of the Cabinet Committee on Defence and Overseas Policy.

However, the Foreign Secretary's role in the Defence Committee is considerable and scarcely less important than that of the Secretary of State for Defence. One might speculate that the weightiest ballots cast in the Committee meetings are those of the Prime Minister, the Secretary of State for Defence, and Foreign Secretary. At the same time, the Foreign Secretary's influence depends to a considerable extent upon his personality, political judgment, and diplomatic skill.

The American concept of coordinated and integrated security policy has also been adopted, albeit in limited form, by the Fifth French Republic. It is referred to in the official announcement of the new Defense Organization[23] whose most important measures were the creation of two committees: The Defense Committee and the Restricted Defense Committee. It is the Defense Committee's task to formulate basic defense policy which is both military and political in nature. The President is chairman; members are the Premier, the Foreign Minister, the Ministers of the Armed Forces, the Interior,

[23] *Journal Official,* Paris, January 7, 1959.

and of Financial and Economic Affairs. The Restricted Defense Committee, also chaired by the President, is convoked by the Premier for the discussion of *specific* defense policies. Participants are selected by the Premier in accordance with the problems to be deliberated.

The value of these committees under the heavy hand of their chairman, President de Gaulle, is difficult to gauge. Their basic concept is sound and certainly is a novelty in the history of the French Republic. During the monarchy, the crown councils of the kings are somewhat comparable: their voice under the absolute monarch was weak. While it would be absurd to compare the powers of Louis XIV with those of Charles de Gaulle, there are some parallels. It is fascinating to observe the highest policy-makers steer between presidential influence and constitutional safeguards.

In both the Federal Republic of Germany and Japan, the concept of coordinated security policy has made slow progress. This is due to the fact that both countries were engaged, after the end of the war, in rebuilding their administrative apparatus, and that their security problems differed from those of the wartime Allies. As their political and military importance to the free world increases, the eventual creation of machinery for coordinated security policy seems inevitable.

Coordination of security policy poses a much lesser problem for Moscow, Peking, or other communist capitals. Their doctrine and organization have always been integral and "interdisciplinary." In this sense, the USSR had a coordinated security policy long before the US established its own. The communist leaders have at their disposal, and under their control, all branches of parties and governments; their Central Committees, represented by Politbureaus or State Councils, have the power to make decisions and coordinate the pertinent machinery to implement them. Metaphorically speaking, the Politbureau of the Soviet Communist Party *is* a Security Council. In fact, it is much more, since it does not differentiate between internal and external policy problems.

So much for the organizations of security policy. The American NSC is a high-level debating club whose discussions may or may not contribute to clarifying issues in the mind of the President who must make the vital decisions. The British Defence Council is a policy-making body which arrives at decisions democratically; the Prime

Minister can hardly afford to disregard its recommendations unless he is willing to risk mass resignations from his Cabinet. The French Defense Committee is chiefly a sounding board for a discussion of the President's views — which prevail anyway. The only committee-type body in the USSR and in Communist China which has real significance is neither the Presidium of the allegedly highest governing body, the Supreme Soviet, nor the Standing Group of the Red Chinese National People's Congress. They are the Politbureaus in Moscow and in Peking. There is little doubt that the members of these bodies can debate issues — provided they remain within the doctrinal framework in which they are expected to think and work. The chairmen of the Soviet and the Chinese Politbureaus have the final word.

Organizations are not at a premium but ideas are. Who produces them? The men in the high councils? The experts of the rank and file? Professors, writers, or other outsiders? Very rarely does one man generate policy recommendations. Generally a fusion of suggestions will eventually emerge in broad outlines as a product of the lower or middle level desk officers of the government with the help of research and analysis. They will then be refined by the higher echelon of the bureaucracy, often in cooperation with non-governmental experts. Regardless of where the ideas originate, they rarely stay as they were born. Suggestions, criticism, additional facts, and multifaceted analyses add or subtract substance, effect changes, and finally mold thoughts into articulate ventures.

The evolution of policy from recommendation to acceptance or rejection cannot be altogether systematized; it changes because the nature of policy issues changes constantly. Even in the routine business of international relations, hardly any two problems are alike, all the more so since policies recommended toward individual nations must conform to overall regional policy, and, in some cases, to a policy of global validity. Regional policy is often concerned with world politics and is certainly far more intricate than policies of country or area level. The issues of global significance with which security organs are primarily concerned go beyond routine policy formulation and no longer fall within the exclusive domain of the foreign offices. They are subject to deliberation in the organs of national security policy such as the NSC or the British Defence Council.

When decisions are reached at conferences held between cabinet ministers and chiefs of state or government, foreign affairs experts and administrators can only advise and recommend. The issues at stake outweigh those concerning any one country. In trying to attain the best possible "deal" for his nation, the decision-maker is bound to consider the consequences of his policy on the fate of his allies as well. He must keep in mind the strength and unity of his group; if he does not, its strength may diminish and thereby jeopardize the security of his side vis-à-vis the opposition. This requires large-scale coordination, and confronts the policy-makers with formidable difficulties: they have to forge into a common denominator both national interests and international obligations.

There is another problem with which statesmen have to grapple when pondering global issues: the interests of their nation and those of their allies must be related to the requirements of the United Nations, which was created to solve disputes peacefully. Totalitarian and democratic attitudes toward coping with these tasks differ strikingly. In view of its ideological objectives, a totalitarian government compromises with trends toward international cooperation only if it can avail itself of no other means to achieve specific ends. From its point of view, the company of nations it has to put up with is not very desirable. Although it collaborates when to do so promotes rather than prejudices its plans, a dictatorship can never be expected to recognize the right of majority opinion. It vetoes any distasteful compromise and boycotts decisions which cannot be vetoed. Its party leaders formulate policies based on its ideological principles regardless of the will of non-totalitarian nations.

Under democratic constitutions and governments, policy decisions of world-wide import require not only governmental but direct or indirect parliamentary approval. This is particularly true of Anglo-Saxon democracies where consultations between executive and legislative branches of government are the rule. However, the primary responsibility remains in the hands of the policy-makers whose recommendations are influenced by the views of their political and economic advisers, the attitudes of the chiefs of state and their parliamentary bodies, and the opinion of the mission chiefs abroad. Inevitably, this makes their tasks much harder than those of communist leaders.

In general it appears that the decision-making process in the two opposing camps varies organizationally, but the differences are almost as great within the Western and Eastern nation groups as between them. However, at the risk of repetition, it must be re-emphasized that the communist break with tradition has torn away the bases of habitual historical reasoning and compelled the communist leaders to seek new departures. Their doctrines provided them with the theoretical underpinnings. In the West, on the other hand, there has been no fundamental change in thinking habits. This contest of political ideologies requires as much research and study as does the new technology. The study of international relations is no longer pat and standardized but needs the same investigative and experimental approach as the natural sciences. Our facilities for political research are as yet insufficient. Governments and academic institutions would be well advised to support "clinical" laboratories in which foreign affairs experts could undertake inter-disciplinary studies and gradually eliminate antiquated approaches. Unless we understand the strange new world of the "socialist system," we cannot expect to obtain and put to work new ideas.

Fountainhead of Policy Planning: Intelligence

Theoretical Aspects

If foreign policy determines the character of relations between states, information on which to base it determines policy planning. Without information, the policy-making machinery would slow down or idle. Worse still, statesmen who lack adequate information, neglect to study it, or misinterpret it, arrive at wrong conclusions which endanger national security. Those responsible for recommending or making decisions often enough are forced to shoot into the dark, but their chances for a hit further diminish if information gaps prevent their taking well-calculated risks.

Such information, which we call intelligence, is vital to a country's security and is the foundation of policy decisions. Indeed, no foreign policy can ever be stronger than the information upon which it is based.[1] To obtain reliable information of genuine importance is no easy task. A nation's intelligence organization, in order to be the guardian of national security, requires a generous budget, an efficient administrative structure, highest caliber personnel from all disciplines of the social and natural sciences, and recognition by those government bureaus responsible for formulating policies. It is not too much to say that if foreign policy is the shield of the republic, intelligence is the material of which the shield is forged and the form into which it is shaped. If the shield is brittle or ill-fashioned, the defending knight stands no chance against the sharp sword of his antagonist.

---

[1] K. London, *The Making of Foreign Policy — East and West* (Philadelphia: Lippincott, 1965), p. 114.

The enormous complexity of intelligence production requires a delineation between its different types. In general, its organization logically follows its substance and the specific needs for which it is created. An intelligence organization may be visualized as a pyramid. Its sub-base consists of those facts of national and international life which produce a country's assets and liabilities. Information on the polity comprising all possible aspects of life is an absolute necessity. Some of these elements (geography, natural resources, demography) have been discussed above.[2]

The base of the pyramid encompasses primarily historical investigation, to be used as background for evaluation purposes and for the instruction of foreign-affairs personnel. Contemporary problems can be fully understood only as the outcome of historical antecedents, and one cannot expect all diplomats to be thoroughly familiar with historical detail. Invariably, not only political but also social and cultural developments have their historical reasons, as have attitudes. There is no new departure in policy which cannot be related to historical causes, not even twentieth-century ideologies. Only two factors are utterly new and demand correspondingly new approaches: nuclear power and missile developments. Research in and interpretation of the history of nations, with respect to their political, economic, and social progress, will thus be the first and foremost task of the research offices. In particular, the history of relations between two countries must be thoroughly investigated. In tracing it, the researcher may well find significant aspects which shed new light upon contemporary problems, and thereby enable policy-makers to gain clarity concerning the issue at stake.

The middle layer of the pyramid consists of fact-finding, involving the study of the daily incoming material and covering all pertinent aspects of the analyst's specialization. This material comprises not only confidential sources and government reporting; the larger part is derived from such overt sources as newspapers, journals, books, and radio broadcasts from all over the world. These are the chips from which the mosaic eventually can be pieced together. Moreover, an accumulation of facts in the minds of intelligence analysts not only

[2] Cf. Chapter 3.

contributes to current understanding, but also builds up a knowledge and appreciation of areas or functions for which the analysts are responsible, thereby enhancing their stature and value. Frequent turnover of personnel is the worst that can happen to an intelligence office: it diminishes the overall efficiency and wastes time and money.

There is also the task of investigating the "facts behind the facts." Special research projects of this type, requested by interested bureaus, may concern such matters as ideology, politics, sociology, economics, and cultural life. For example, there may be a request to investigate, on the basis of actual evidence or deduction, whether or not or to what extent orthodox Marxism–Leninism still forms the core of Soviet doctrine, what the post-Stalinist modifications of Leninism amount to, and whether these changes may indicate a significant departure from basic ideology. Such complex projects involve both the study of a wealth of material and a careful analysis of political statements, economic plans, constitutional revisions, social conditions, and so on. Analysis of the press and of radio broadcasts, plus information from the embassies throughout the bloc, would also have to be culled. The project would be difficult and costly, but might well result in a clarification of issues from which policy consideration would greatly benefit.

Another important task in this general area of intelligence is the evaluation of information and propaganda from abroad. It may be possible, through study of propaganda output, to deduce an opponent's policy line or, at least, his methods of policy implementation. In fact, propaganda analysis has become one of the most enlightening of information sources with regard to a foreign government's probable intentions and now is indispensable to policy-makers as well as intelligence analysts. Moreover, research and analysis, dealing not only with facts but also with attitudes, must be permeated with the methods of psychological diagnosis. The evaluation of a people's "national character" and behavioral tendencies demands close scrutiny. For events happen which cannot be explained in terms of known facts alone. Neither can the success or failure of socio-political movements. Certainly the political religions of the twentieth century require extensive psychological, in addition to philosophical, analysis.

To achieve these difficult tasks, governments must seek outside help from scientific institutions, universities, and individual experts. The issues of international relations are indeed so manifold and complex that, if its government research proves inadequate, a nation's intellectual resources should be tapped and pooled. Communist governments can commandeer the total manpower resources for any project they wish to undertake. The free world has no such control, but indications are that more and more academic experts are requested by their governments to contribute or collaborate. At the same time, numbers of learned societies and institutes lend their resources to government research. Many lively exchanges have been instituted between governmental and academic personnel with considerable advantages to both. It is of particular importance for non-governmental specialists to recognize that intelligence has two aspects: the analytical and the operational. Here we are concerned with analysis, and since operational activities are unpopular in the United States (much more so than in other Western countries), it is essential that the mixture of fascination and revulsion towards espionage and other types of operations not be transferred to the very academic work of research, analysis, and estimation. The sooner intelligence is recognized as a science, the easier it will be for scholars to collaborate, shedding former prejudices and contributing knowledge in exchange for new intellectual horizons.

We now come to the summit of the pyramid: strategic intelligence. This intelligence end product most concerns the policy-maker and has become the subject of a growing literature.[3]

Policy-making officials presumably are familiar with the historical and statistical facts concerning the area of their responsibility. But they need factual information of primarily current significance. These facts must be put in their proper context because, in themselves, they

[3] Aside from numerous articles, the following books on analytical intelligence may be noted: A. W. Dulles, *The Craft of Intelligence* (New York: Harper and Row, 1963); R. Hilsman, *Strategic Intelligence and National Decisions* (Glencoe, Ill.: The Free Press, 1956); S. Kent, *Strategic Intelligence* (Princeton, N.J.: Princeton University Press, 1966); K. E. Knorr, *Foreign Intelligence and the Social Sciences* (Princeton, N.J.: Princeton University Press, 1964); W. Platt, *Strategic Intelligence Production* (New York: F. A. Praeger, 1957); and H. H. Ransom, *Central Intelligence and National Security* (Cambridge, Mass.: Harvard University Press, 1959).

may appear meaningless. They become articulate through expert analysis and evaluation, through their relationship with other world political developments, and through an estimate of possible future developments. Strategic intelligence must be coordinated, integrated, and comprehensive. It is both horizontal and vertical. Whether it deals with one country, one area, or the globe, it is ever mindful of the totality of a problem. It is the highest derivative of the entire intelligence process and has become a product without which security policy and strategy cannot be formulated successfully.

Strategic intelligence is concerned primarily with estimating the capabilities, vulnerabilities, and intentions of intelligence "targets." It is distilled from information comprising all other layers of the pyramid, an encyclopedic arsenal of facts, figures, and analyses. It requires extraordinary substantive comprehension combined with a supercharged intuition, tempered by knowledge, experience, and complete objectivity. A strategic intelligence estimate should be written in clear and meaningful prose by men who are both scholars and soothsayers.

The great importance of this product requires that provisions be made to minimize human error and fallibility. Two approaches might achieve, to some extent at least, a diminution of errors. First, it must be recognized that the end product of intelligence can rarely be the result of the labor of a single man or office. Intelligence is teamwork in all its stages, particularly the final one. In practical terms this means consultation and coordination not only within one office but among the pertinent or interested government departments. At the least, strategic intelligence estimates must be coordinated with the foreign office and the intelligence bureaus of the military services; frequently, other specialized agencies must participate. For example, in the United States, the Office of National Estimates in the Central Intelligence Agency prepares estimates based on contributions from various departments and finally coordinates them through the United States Intelligence Board, chaired by the Director of Central Intelligence. With variations, the production of strategic intelligence follows similar lines in Great Britain and other Western countries.

The second technique for minimizing human error is the insertion of alternative premises. In other words, an estimate's conclusion may be based on a definite supposition, but, should this supposition change, it must provide the policy-maker with political recoil. This technique is less applicable to short-range than to long-range estimates, but in the case of the latter alternate assumptions should allow for alternate policies *before* rather than after events.

If strategic intelligence is the sum of all intelligence efforts, what are the organizational and substantive details that lead to the final estimate? Where does the information originate? How is it processed and disseminated? To whom is it directed?

Let us begin with the sources of information. It should be made quite clear that intelligence obtained from clandestine operations constitutes only a fraction of the entire output. It has been estimated at 10 per cent, but is probably even less than that. Of this information, only a small part is of real value; the bulk may consist of already known facts, items of marginal interest, or outright fabrication. Of course, there may be reports whose value renders worthwhile such long-term operations as Klaus Fuchs' theft of atomic secrets for Soviet intelligence. But such instances are rare and, frequently, information of great value may be unappreciated or simply disregarded by the recipient.[4]

A great volume of information is produced by diplomatic missions and military attachés, as well as other specialized attachés in such fields as agriculture, commerce, science, or culture. Reporting by these groups has long been recognized as a perfectly honorable and accepted occupation. Every nation's foreign representation is charged with gathering data which it often openly requests from the host government. An invitation by the host country to service attachés to attend a military parade is no mere courtesy but an overt exhibition of military power. All the more hypocritical are periodic communist accusations of spying by non-communist accredited personnel.

The diplomatic staff of a mission collects information on current problems of the host country. It tries to assess the general attitude of the "receiving" government to the "sending" one, analyzes and interprets official statements as well as mass communications. It seeks to

[4] See also H. H. Ransom, *Central Intelligence and National Security* (Cambridge, Mass.: Harvard University Press, 1959), p. 44.

clarify the policies of the host state, the behavior and influence of the men in power and those regarded as potential leaders. It probes public opinion regarding domestic and international problems, significant cultural developments, and the overall socio-political trends. The prevailing type of government, the constitutional law and ideological posture, the effectiveness of either parliamentary or dictatorial control, the forces jockeying for power within the country's political parties or party factions, all must be constant objects of the observer's attention. Information concerning the leaders is particularly essential, for those in power direct the country's trends and alliances, color its ideological outlook, and shape its social conditions. The complete picture of the political, economic, social, and cultural status of the target area will gain additional meaning through military and scientific reporting. No detail is too small or too insignificant to be included: it may provide the missing piece of the mosaic.

So great is the volume of incoming material and so much information does it contain that the process of stripping it down to essentials requires a great many analysts of skill and experience. After such processing it can be presented to policy officials. If they even began to peruse the bulk of incoming reports they would never have time to formulate foreign policy. Only in extraordinary cases will they read cables *in extenso,* for example, those which contain vital security intelligence or describe the political position and character of the men with whom they may have to deal. It would be difficult to list all the subjects on which the policy-makers require information. Apart from special issues and the ever present problems arising from the protracted world crisis, there are always areas of controversy between nations, even those basically on friendly terms.

Most of these efforts are self-generated and fall within the responsibilities of the mission staff. Special requests for information may originate in the home office. The more urgent messages are cabled, those less urgent — but not always less important — are dispatched via diplomatic pouch, one of the safest though not necessarily the fastest means of communication between the foreign office and its missions. Although classified cables are coded, their safety is relative since the possibility is ever present that a foreign agent may succeed in obtaining the code key; in wartime this has happened often. Every foreign office employs experts whose task it is to break the codes if they cannot be obtained clandestinely. Since governments reckon with these attempts, they frequently change their codes.

With few exceptions, material derived from this type of official reporting is classified. There is, however, another vast source of intelligence that is available to everyone: books, newspapers, journals, radio broadcasts, and film reporting. Television, too, may contribute information.

To this category belong first of all those writings published by political leaders chiefly before they actually came to power. Examples abound: Lenin and Stalin; Mao and Lin; Hitler and Rosenberg; Mussolini and Gentile; Peron and Nasser prove the point. It is incredible that leading free world statesmen have paid so little attention to these works and that their advisers did not study them more intensively. Even the actual implementation of the evils contained in these books persuaded neither the leaders nor the peoples of the West to take such writings seriously. Yet these blueprints for conquest exhibited not only the stated objectives of the revolutions but also the means with which to attain victory. It stands to reason that, in the years between the wars, intelligence officers either did not read these books or shrugged them off as manifestations of sick-minded megalomaniacs. In the case of communist literature, this attitude was even less condonable because, ever since the time of Marx and Engels, a large number of books on the subject has been published. But even after World War II, when serious students of communism suggested that the books containing the Marxist–Leninist–Stalinist gospel be studied and analyzed in depth, most political and many intelligence experts felt that the doctrines expounded were no more than disguised power-politics, that the traditional efforts to achieve a balance of power determined political issues, and that the communist political philosophy was too intangible.

Obviously, the type of information derived from such books is less of current than of long-range value. It is indispensable for strategic intelligence estimators concerned with possible future developments. These specialists should know how past and current conditions have developed under the influence of doctrine and what methods were used to implement them. This does not imply that they should take at face value every work written by the ideologists, but it does mean that without considering the essentials of these writings they cannot hope to arrive at correct appraisals of the current situation or of likely coming events.

The study of mass communications media has become one of major significance for intelligence. This information can be distilled from pamphlets, newspaper and magazine articles (including items that appear innocuous), radio broadcasts, and, to a lesser degree, visual media. Two major types of intelligence can be garnered from mass media. One consists of personalia, inspired editorials, statistics, news-slanting (in emphasis and omission), and expositions of important problems. This kind of material is comparatively easy to select for dissemination and analysis. The other is far less simple in that it requires painstaking search for seemingly marginal facts of no apparent importance (promotions, relocations, deaths, marriages, festivities) which, when correlated with existing political, economic, and military information, may become highly significant. This type of research is not *de rigeur* in most intelligence bureaus but is left to the discretion of individual analysts who may not have the time to engage in such activity. A classical example of the worth of information gathered in this fashion is the case of the journalist Berthold Jacob who, prior to World War II, was kidnapped in Switzerland by Nazi agents after publication of a book in which he had been able, merely by studying the "fine print" in German newspapers, to sketch correctly the organization of the new Nazi army.

Mass communications media such as radio and newspapers are a never-ceasing source of intelligence information, not only for hidden meanings as exemplified in the Jacob case, but in overt articles and expositions of policy. The enormous variety of Western editorial opinion probably makes it more difficult for the East to discern a political line than it is for the West to survey the communist press, which is notable for its dull uniformity. However, against the glaring publicity attending statements and opinions in the Western papers stand the censorship and distortion of facts in the communist press which necessitate reading their publications "between the lines." Thus, what appears to be dullness may offer fascinating problems of interpretation and esoteric intelligence.

Following a nation's intellectual production, whether censored or not, reveals many things to the skilled eyes and ears of analysts and monitors. They uncover the social atmosphere and the political climate of the people in question just by perusing their literature, stage plays, radio and television broadcasts, and motion pictures, especially the news reels. Such intelligence sources are particularly important in countries which restrict or prohibit the free flow of information.

In addition to these major sources of overt intelligence are the windfalls of unexpected information from tourists, defectors, and the slackening of the target area's alertness. In countries where the mass media of communication are free and unfettered, many such windfalls provide easy intelligence for foreign observers. In the United States particularly, where the "right of the public to know" often supersedes the "need to know" concept of intelligence, discussions of issues pertaining to national security in newspapers and magazines are frequent. It is significant that overt literature concerning problems of intelligence organization exists almost nowhere except in the United States. Elsewhere, books covering the topic of intelligence are limited to past clandestine operations of the "now it can be told" variety. In the communist countries, not even such books have been published, and whatever has been written in this field concentrates on alleged activities of "imperialist spies." Although the student of international relations has a justifiable need to comprehend the problems of intelligence, the governmental bureaus charged with this responsibility must, by the very nature of their work, shun the light of publicity — a fact which Americans, for whom this field is new, fascinating, and repulsive, have yet to absorb.

Perhaps a word on clandestine intelligence which is as old as human society, is now in order. The literature on espionage, counter-espionage and sabotage is super-abundant. Most of it must be taken with more than a grain of salt. There is something fascinating about undercover activities, but in reality, the work is sheer drudgery, requires utmost anonymity, earns seldom more than mediocre pay, and altogether makes for a dangerous yet unromantic life.[5]

Besides, rarely does an agent's effort result in the spectacular suc-

---

[5] An excellent and authentic example of the life and work of a secret agent is A. Foote's *Handbook for Spies* (Garden City, N.Y.: Doubleday and Company, 1949).

cess of a genuine intelligence coup. From surveying published accounts of clandestine operations one gains the impression that the bulk of information differs little from that gleaned by foreign service personnel or mass media analysts, except perhaps in its concentration on detail. It may contain conjecture if not actual invention written by men with political axes to grind. Only a fraction of the output is valuable enough to justify the cost of an entire intelligence organization; however, the knowledge gained this way may indeed be crucial for a nation's security. Such successes have occurred from time to time and will be repeated in the future. From the national security point of view, they justify all the money and effort expended over long periods of time when nothing spectacular was achieved.

Having discussed the sources of information, we can now turn to its processing, which is as essential as its collection. This activity is carried on both abroad and at home. It is true that this results in overlapping or duplication by intelligence bureaus of the various government departments. But intelligence is a costly affair, and the government which economizes at the expense of securing information is ill-advised. Duplication is sometimes beneficial because it corroborates findings in both fact and interpretation. Furthermore, policymakers need to know not only facts but also trends; not nearly enough attention has been paid to the intelligence of intangibles.

In the main, processing raw intelligence takes the form of condensation, analysis, evaluation, interpretation, and attempts to put the findings in their proper context, i.e., relating them to pertinent events past and present within the framework of existing conditions. Condensation serves for quick preliminary messages, often followed by more extensive reports. Analysis dissects the facts and aspects contained in the information and investigates their relative significance. Interpretation explains and clarifies them in terms of prevailing policy. Evaluation deduces rather than explains; it searches for the reason behind facts and events and judges them in the context of overall conditions, including an appraisal of the source from which the raw intelligence has been secured.

Intelligence of this type is an "intellectual process"[6] of a very high

[6] W. Platt, *Strategic Intelligence Production* (New York: F. A. Praeger, 1957). Chapters III and IV.

order; it proceeds along various organizational levels; and it requires correlation of facts and coordination of efforts — in other words, skill in solving jigsaw puzzles, and teamwork. Beyond these rock-bottom requirements (among which should be a capability of keeping secrets well) are ingenuity and intuition; a fine sense of perception, a solid political judgment; and, last but not least, a talent for the inductive and deductive reasoning indispensable to crystal-ball gazers. Indeed, intelligence service requires a combination of acumen, scholarship, and self-denial which no other profession, governmental or otherwise, demands. Good intelligence is both an art and a science — a very complex process which needs generous funds, effective organization, and the best possible personnel.

Organizational Aspects

The description of intelligence organization is handicapped by its confidential nature. This is to be expected; no government can afford to reveal the secrets of its security operations. Nevertheless, there does exist a body of information, published in numerous books and articles, which affords a reasonably clear idea of how, in general, intelligence works. The principles of organization and activities probably are similar, at least in non-communist countries; thus, existing literature on American intelligence permits us to draw at least limited conclusions. As may be expected, considerable differences can be found between Eastern and Western intelligence concepts.

Since World War II, United States intelligence has developed from a very minor to a major source of security information. The experience of the war, the surprise attack on Pearl Harbor, and the exploits of the Office of Strategic Services (OSS) led American political and military leaders to the inevitable conclusion that the realities of a world rent by basic, irreconcilable conflicts required a reorganization of the national security concept and the components charged with its implementation. Congress passed the National Security Act of 1947, with subsequent amendments in 1949 and 1956.[7] This Public Law 253 decreed the unification of the armed

---

[7] National Security Act of 1947, as amended in 1949 and 1956 (Washington, D.C.: U.S. Government Printing Office, 1957).

forces by creating the Department of Defense, the Department of the Air Force, and the Joint Chiefs of Staff; it created the National Security Resources Board, which under Reorganization Plan No. 3, of 1953, became the Office of Defense Mobilization; and it established the National Security Council (NSC) and the Central Intelligence Agency (CIA).

The role of CIA as coordinator or, as some have called it, "holding company" of US intelligence, is reasonably well defined in its statute. So are the provisions regarding the appointment of the Director and his Deputy. But beyond these specifics, the law is somewhat vague and leaves ample room for interpretation by the National Security Council. Since its directives must perforce remain secret, the political scientist can only indulge in somewhat of an interpretation himself. He may feel that the concept of CIA as a coordinating agency is insufficient and possibly not even intended by the law. According to paragraph (4), CIA should perform "such additional services of common concern as the National Security Council determines can be more efficiently accomplished centrally."

Fear has been expressed by intelligence specialists that departmental intelligence might be squeezed out of business if CIA assumed more substantive functions. But the law is quite specific in pointing out that departmental bureaus will continue their work nor does there seem to be any published indication that either the military service intelligence offices (since 1961 integrated into one Defense Intelligence Agency, DIA) or the State Department's Bureau of Intelligence and Research (INR) have been impaired. Their primary function is to serve the immediate needs of their agencies, and similar cases can be made for the more technical departments such as the Atomic Energy Commission. However, they contribute to the strategic intelligence estimates of CIA.

The question arises as to whether the CIA should be "central" only in coordinating intelligence or assume central responsibility for substantively and organizationally efficient intelligence work. It would seem that, in this day and age, atomization of duties is no longer permissible. If a central intelligence agency is to produce integrated strategic intelligence for the National Security Council whose Chairman is the President of the United States, then it should be in a position to take over all those functions which are non-departmental in order to streamline the production process and control the substantive standard of the production.

In his pioneering work *Strategic Intelligence,* Sherman Kent suggests "six lines of administrative activity": the establishment of "clear jurisdictions for the various departmental intelligence organizations"; the policing of departmental jurisdictions in order to avoid duplication, to stimulate proper exploitation of jurisdictional fields and to increase "established jurisdictions by the addition of new subject matter" if necessary for national security; continuous surveying of departmental intelligence for quality; discovery and correction of trouble; management of interdepartmental intelligence projects; and recognition of problems regarding personnel policy.[8]

One can agree fully with these suggestions, but it is difficult to accept the proposition that a central intelligence agency should stay out of substantive work. The coordination of strategic intelligence is not mechanical; it is a creative and substantive process. To absorb departmental intelligence and mold it into a new creation requires more than the twelve wise old men who, according to Kent, would counsel the production of intelligence estimates. It requires more than a small group of skilled draftsmen possessing the talent to shape into lucid sentences such strategic analyses as may be required. These groups must depend upon departmental intelligence but may find it inadequate for their task. They may disagree with departmental points of view; they may need further research and analysis which they cannot order and quickly obtain from departmental offices and for which they themselves have no time.

Coordination of strategic intelligence is the second step only — the first one being the specialized and departmental intelligence contribution toward the coordinated estimate. The third and most important step is the crystallization of a broad and deep world view.

Strategic intelligence needs a very broad base of substantive support at the immediate disposition of the estimators. Such support should come both from its own bureaus and from the departmental offices, regardless of whether or not occasional duplication occurs. Since strategic intelligence is most essential for national security — as

[8] S. Kent, *Strategic Intelligence* (Princeton, N.J.: Princeton University Press, 1966), pp. 91–94.

the National Security Act clearly implies — it cannot be measured in dollars and cents; a nation's security is priceless. The law sought centralization of national defense; it could not have advocated decentralization in national security information. Therefore, one may conclude that since CIA is charged with furnishing such information, it must be the guardian of national intelligence production and provide facilities which do not elsewhere exist.

Whether or not an intelligence agency should also be involved in psychological warfare of operations of a military or political nature (the Bay of Pigs, Iran, Guatemala) is debatable. It depends on whether other government departments are in a position to do such a job — which is unlikely. If the political and military leaders of a country decide on a plan of action which may achieve their aims short of war, *someone* must implement it. In view of the secrecy which necessarily shrouds intelligence activities, it seems logical for an intelligence organization to be put in charge. There is nothing sinister about this; every state, democratic or totalitarian, engages in such activities. Americans are squeamish about these matters; if other peoples are less so, this is because they are told less about it. Secrecy is not violated everywhere in so grand a style as in the United States.

There has been considerable uproar over CIA financial help to civilian organizations even though such help is in the interest of US security and was approved by at least three administrations. Since a shift of funds from the CIA to the State Department or other government agencies was ruled out by certain members of Congress, the CIA was the natural fountainhead of funding. The cutoff of these monies may have satisfied the delicate feelings (genuine or alleged) of many Americans but it has not helped American foreign policy. It is time that a more sophisticated understanding of political operations in this complex era replace the country bumpkin approach toward both intelligence and propaganda which is still prevalent in the United States.

It was noted above that American publications on intelligence provide a rather clear picture of its concept and organization. The CIA obviously has not published its organization chart but has permitted much of its coordinating work to be made known. The State Department has published an unclassified chart of its INR.

In other countries, public information on intelligence is rare. It is known, however, that the British Foreign Office, having had far fewer budgetary troubles than the US State Department, has been able to continue to develop its coordinated and efficient intelligence service. Formerly, political intelligence was processed in the "Library," a comprehensive department with many duties. In 1943, two of the most important British intelligence units, the Political Intelligence Department of the Foreign Office and the Press Section of the Royal Institute of International Affairs, were amalgamated and became the Research Department of the Foreign Office. Once organized, this Department coordinated its work with the Library, functionally and physically. Set up along geographical lines, its foremost task is the study of historical backgrounds of current foreign policy problems for the use of the political departments.

In addition to this organization, roughly the counterpart of INR, and the various specialized intelligence bureaus including the military one, Britain also has a small intelligence coordination organization, the Joint Intelligence Committee (JIC) of the Ministry of Defense. Its functions may be compared with those of the United States Intelligence Board (USIB), but it has only a small supporting staff and must rely on the dozen or more intelligence outfits throughout the British government. It is primarily the JIC which furnishes coordinated strategic intelligence to the British policy-making body, the Cabinet.

Such coordination probably does not exist in France, perhaps because the inherent French spirit of individualism does not lend itself to centralization. As far as is known, research and analysis services are scattered throughout the Ministry of Foreign Affairs and to a considerable degree depend upon the assistance of such organizations as the *Institut des Hautes Etudes des Sciences Politiques* and the University of Paris (Sorbonne).

One might add that the popular fame of both British and French intelligence has little to do with its political aspects but rather with its espionage and counter-espionage activities. In Britain, Military Intelligence (MI) is responsible for this work, but its many branches are frequently handled by civilian experts. In France, the famed *Deuxième Bureau* was the protagonist of many a spy thriller which made it almost as famous as Scotland Yard.

Different from this decentralized concept of intelligence is that of postwar West Germany. A German publication has given a rather open, if slanted, account of what is purported to be the present-day German intelligence service.[9] While the greater part of the article indulges in descriptions of secret agent operations, it admits that the "broad picture of the economic, military and political situation of the USSR and its changes are of the greatest importance. Detailed news is of interest only when it contributes to the clarification of larger issues." This broad picture "generally is easier to see through intensive comparison of publications, statistics, geographic, and archivistic material, diplomatic reports and official sourcebooks than through individual agent communications." A hard core of officers and functionaries has been joined by experts on economics, technology, and the natural and political sciences. No reference is made to coordination methods of intelligence thus gained, but the article was published in 1954, and one can assume that since then the development of various West German government branches, the growing importance of the Federal Republic as a NATO partner, and the example of US strategic intelligence production have enabled Bonn to develop an adequate information and evaluation machinery.

There are, in addition, some private or semi-private organizations gathering information, primarily concerning conditions in East Germany and the East European states. The Social-Democratic Party (SPD) has for years conducted such investigations and analyses in its *Ostbureau* (Eastern Bureau); its output is relatively objective and of good quality. In fact, qualitatively and quantitatively, it provides one of the best sources of information in its specialized areas. The *Friedrich Ebert Foundation* also has produced much useful material, particularly on the Third World. While it, too, is a creation of the SPD, its value has been recognized by the Federal Government which supports the Foundation's activities to some extent with public funds.

Little is known about NATO's intelligence functions. One may assume that they involve coordinating intra-national strategic intelligence to which the member governments contribute their analyses

9 "Des Kanzler's Lieber General" (The Chancellor's Dear General), *Der Spiegel*, Hamburg, September 22, 1954.

and estimates for NATO's leading political and military officers. Obviously, the material made available to such a central intelligence bureau would be highly selective; it would exclude information which the partners prefer to keep to themselves. France, in particular, has been reticent in providing intelligence to NATO, and with the removal of the organization's headquarters to Belgium, few significant contributions can be expected. In sum, NATO intelligence is at best patchwork which is understandable but nonetheless regrettable. It bespeaks distrust and jealousies which separate allies who have banded together for the sake of their common security.

The secretiveness of Soviet intelligence services is absolute. Were it not for depositions of defectors formerly employed by the Soviet secret service, it could scarcely be appraised at all. We know, of course, that Soviet intelligence has many aspects and that it is "a powerful weapon of the cold and hot war against the non-Soviet world. It is aggressive, ever-watchful and untrammelled by any moral or economic limitations. The inherent aggressiveness of the totalitarian system forces the Soviet police to go much further than the mere collection of information. The Soviet intelligence agencies are not satisfied with merely knowing facts. They aspire to influence the policies of the free countries in a way favorable to the Kremlin by using all their freedoms and institutions."[10] In spite of their own preoccupation with clandestine and subversive activities, they constantly denounce alleged Western espionage. Among the many cases of framing and jailing Western visitors to the USSR, that of Professor Frederick C. Barghoorn has become well known because of the late President Kennedy's personal — and successful — intervention. There are other instances in which legitimate American scholars engaged in scientific research have been accused of espionage or "counterrevolutionary propaganda." Moreover, Soviet newspapers and journals have attacked scholarly accounts dealing with intelligence aspects of international relations.[11] Such hypocritical tactics are particularly aggra-

---

[10] S. Wolin and R. M. Slusser, *The Soviet Secret Police* (New York: F. A. Praeger, 1957), p. 138.

[11] E. P. Dimitriev, "The Total Espionage Machine — Weapon of American Warmongers," in *Sovietskoe Gosudarstvo i Prava*, No. 4, Moscow, 1951. In this

vating when one considers the character of intelligence in communist-ruled countries.

Information received on these activities, which are concentrated mainly on espionage and subversive activities, discloses a bewildering array of multiple, intertwined organizations, manned by professional secret service, police, and military agents. There is no separation between external and internal investigative responsibilities. Formerly, the Ministry of Internal Affairs (MVD) was heavily involved in foreign intelligence. However, the MVD, an all-Union organization, was abolished in January 1960, and its tasks, apparently narrowed down to domestic affairs, were transferred to the Union Republics. The State Security Committee (KGB) now seems to reign over foreign intelligence. Its extraordinary status was vividly described by Peter Deriabin, a former officer of the KGB who defected to the West and reported his experiences in a fascinating book.[12] The table of organization of the KGB published in this book clarifies its duties for the first time.

The KGB works in the closest possible contact with the Party Politbureau, and its most important reports are transmitted directly to the Party's Secretary General. Many of its officers are highly trained and all of them occupy a special position in Soviet society. The Western concept of securing information would be unsatisfactory to Soviet intelligence. Instead, it is "an active, aggressive political arm of the regime. Its purpose is not only to acquire information, but to manufacture information, terrorize, assassinate, and proselytize, as occasion demands. In short, Soviet intelligence sets out to subvert the political and social life of a foreign country, while at the same time taking utmost pains to see that no foreigners succeed in pene-

article, the writer attacks S. Kent's *Strategic Intelligence,* E. Plischke's *Conduct of American Diplomacy* and K. London's *How Foreign Policy Is Made* as works of "imperialist spies."

More recently, the 1967 disclosures regarding CIA aid to US student organizations let loose an unequalled outcry in the Soviet press which promptly accused a number of American scholars in Russia of alleged intelligence activities.

12 P. Deriabin and F. Gibnay, *The Secret World* (New York: Doubleday and Co., 1959).

trating the international curtain which the KGB throws around Soviet citizens inside and outside their country."[13]

The organization of the KGB, according to Deriabin, comprises geographical, functional, and "special" sections. For example, the Advisory Section is charged with the surveillance of conditions in satellite countries; the Illegal Section is concerned with espionage and counterintelligence, and the support of illegal "residencies" in foreign countries. The most sinister of these sections is the Special Operations Section (Spetsbureau), which engineers terrorist actions such as assassination, murder, and large-scale sabotage. (The murders of Trotsky and Krivitsky were carried out by the Spetsbureau.) KGB is also responsible for training terrorists, saboteurs, wreckers, and diversionists. It directs organizations that penetrate the penetrators, i.e., supervise the activities and loyalty of Soviet citizens abroad, from ambassadors to chauffeurs.

The quantity of information gained by Soviet services is unquestionably much greater than that of the West. The USSR and other communist countries have the advantage of many collaborating communist parties, legal or illegal, communist sympathizers, and the so-called front organizations. The latter ostensibly have no party affiliation but are under the control of and dependent upon the organizational and financial resources of the CPSU or the Chinese Communist Party (CCP). Among these organizations are the World Federation of Trade Unions, the World Peace Council, and the International Student Union. They provide Moscow or Peking with Trojan Horse crews throughout the non-communist world. It is well known that Soviet intelligence is an arm of the Kremlin's military and foreign policy at home and abroad. Strengthened by the assistance of communist parties abroad and by fellow-travelling front organizations, this intelligence network is uniquely Leninist–Stalinist. While the Comintern and Cominform still functioned, their international branch offices directed much of this work; their task was not limited to securing intelligence, it included implementation of propaganda and agitation campaigns. Since these organizations no longer exist, their work is done more subtly by Soviet diplomatic missions,

13 *Ibid.,* p. 183.

communist party members, and all ardent believers in the communist "wave of the future." Moreover, the stronger the "socialist camp" becomes and the more territories it controls, the vaster will be its intelligence resources.

Communist China's intelligence activities are somewhat handicapped by the ethnic characteristics of Chinese agents. In many parts of the world, Peking must rely on sympathizers and agents other than Chinese. Moreover, while Soviet intelligence undoubtedly has attained a high level of sophistication in the interpretation of information, this probably is not the case in China where cultural and ideological differences could create serious miscalculations in analyzing Western developments.

Being concerned here mainly with strategic intelligence, we should examine the manner in which we presume it is collected, coordinated, and processed. Again, in view of the different organization of the Soviet state and the doctrine that basically determines its actions, the answer cannot be clear-cut. To begin with, there is little doubt that strategic information reaches Moscow in quantity. Until Stalin's death, the quality of these reports must be presumed to have been low. The desire to please superiors with tailor-made ideological interpretations or the fear of saying the wrong thing even if it was substantively right could only have produced heavily slanted and unrealistic information. With the succession of Khrushchev, a firm believer in his "religion" but rational enough to keep an open mind, a more realistic reporting was encouraged, if not ordered, a policy continued by Khrushchev's successors. This down-to-earth approach undoubtedly has contributed to more realistic, less doctrinaire analyses, with the probable result of better information and, one hopes, better understanding. Presumably, Western publications are now being studied in the USSR with greater objectivity. How is this information coordinated and processed?

We can only deduce from the limited information available. It seems logical that at least some processing and interpreting is done in the Ministry of Foreign Affairs (Minindel). It is doubtful that the Foreign Bureau of KGB would do much if any interpretive work in matters concerning relations with other countries. However, the Minindel, as all Soviet government departments, is essentially a technical ministry; it suggests policies but never makes them. That is the sole prerogative of the Party and, more specifically, the Party Politbureau. Nevertheless, the "Collegium" of the Minindel, referred to above, which consists of the ranking area division chiefs, probably submits to the Politbureau its analyses and estimates of relations with other countries. Furthermore, the Minindel, and, for that matter, the Politbureau, may avail themselves of all outstanding bodies of experts. They may order the Academy of Sciences to participate and unquestionably often do so. They may commandeer the services of a variety of institutes working on political, social, cultural, and economic aspects of foreign areas. Naturally, the universities will have to play their part.

If a coordination process exists in the USSR, most likely it is located in the Party Secretariat and Politbureau with the assistance of the Collegium. To some extent, the material may have been pre-selected or pre-coordinated by the State Security Commission organs. Nevertheless, voluminous overt sources of information must be absorbed and analyzed by professionals both in the field and at home. Such specialists unquestionably are to be found in the Minindel where the geographic bureaus, just as elsewhere in the world, will do the job. The Deputy Foreign Ministers in charge of areas may then be expected to submit their estimates and recommendations. They will be careful to combine realistic appraisal with doctrinal yardsticks; they know that their submissions will be scrutinized by the Party, which has its own experts in foreign affairs.

The question of which office prepares final strategic intelligence estimates cannot be answered with certainty. Knowledge of the communist apparatus and the doctrines concerning communist relations with the non-communist world lead to the deduction that quite possibly coordinated strategic estimates are not produced.

The West regards the development of history with some degree of fatalism: the course of events is unpredictable, the old cliché "history repeats itself" notwithstanding. The communist's world view is utterly different. He makes a tool of history because he believes that the "forces of life" compel it along the road of his choice. Thus his picture of the world is not one-dimensional but stereoscopic; he professes to see with greater depth because, for him, the future is an open book. Philosophically, his world conception is fully systematized, at least in broad strokes; details may change as do tactics, but these do not alter the fundamentals. Since the system is materialistic, unexpected oscillations such as occur under the influence of emotional idealism or transcendental spirituality would not ruffle its construct.

This communist *Weltanschauung* entails a vastly different interpretation of prevailing circumstances, thereby preconditioning opinions concerning future developments. The visible world is measured against the system and adjudged accordingly. Having deliberately cut itself off from Western tradition, the East uses its ideology as a "guide to action" and an intellectual framework for a future world peopled with men and women whose thinking and reasoning are totally different from either occidental or oriental civilizations. It follows that a Soviet strategic intelligence estimate would speculate primarily on timing for, if the course of history is predetermined, what matters is when certain events may be expected to occur.

Furthermore, while Western strategic intelligence must be the product of coordination, i.e., of democratic "negotiation" between departments and experts, it is hard to conceive that in Moscow matters of high security policy would be permitted to become subject to negotiation at all. Rather, one may assume that top-level Party leaders, briefed by specialists from the Party or the pertinent government departments, determine policy without the benefit of coordinated strategic intelligence. It is doubtful whether members of the Party Politbureau, the most powerful Soviet policy-making body, permit experts to attend their meetings. So far as the Politbureau is concerned, the experts are technicians; they present the facts and submit their views, but the Politbureau determines the course of action. There is no recourse; the assent of the Supreme Soviet, nominally the highest authority of the land, is an *ex post facto* formality, providing the rulers with a platform from which to proclaim their decisions.

This approach probably is exaggeratedly prevalent in Red China. The Politbureau's Standing Committee, that small group which determines the fate of China mainland, undoubtedly calls for advice but woe to the expert who does not slant his analysis toward the "thought of Mao Tse-tung." There must be highly intelligent and knowledgeable specialists in both government and party whose insight and understanding would benefit the regime but, while the "Red Sun" lives, their reports almost certainly will conform to the party line — a dangerous technique which precludes accuracy of intelligence.

Thus, the conceptual difference between communist and non-communist world views cannot but lead us to conclude that the respective approaches to intelligence reflect this difference. Although there is no hard-and-fast evidence for the above assumption, in the light of other experience it does not seem too risky. It may strengthen the argument to add that the term "strategic" has a somewhat different connotation in communist usage. Strategy is subordinated to the ultimate grand goal, communist world conquest. To achieve this overall objective, various strategies — or stratagems — are devised. They are flexible so far as timing, function, and area are concerned. In turn, strategies are implemented by even more flexible tactics. It is frequently difficult to establish the border line between strategy and tactics; all too often, Western statesmen confuse the terms. In any event, doctrinally, strategic intelligence has a basically different connotation in each camp, thereby creating another important divergence between Eastern and Western approaches to intelligence.

The importance of intelligence for national security and the fate of the world is enormous and it is time that romantic or sensationalist ideas be discarded and more realistic aspects considered. The task of an intelligence organization is to procure, analyze, and interpret information. The emphasis is on interpretation, and here, once more, we are confronted with the problem of understanding the opponent's motivation and actions and the effect of his attitudes toward the world at large. The best information is useless without correct interpretation.

..9....

Bipolar Conduct of Foreign Affairs

Vanishing Diplomacy

The most ingenious policy is no better than its application. Political thought of the highest intellectual caliber remains idle theory unless it becomes a living principle of one nation's relations with other nations. The value of a policy formula is determined not only by its perceptive depth and accurate foresight, it must also be founded upon practicability of implementation. On the other hand, the failure of a policy to meet with response need not imply that the policy-makers have come to the end of their rope. It is a rare occurrence indeed if a policy, once introduced, finds immediate success in its envisaged form. As a rule, modifications in substance and method occur gradually; sometimes an entirely different approach has to be explored. In general, policy substance is treated flexibly in the West and rigidly in the East, while methods of implementation change slowly in the traditional West and rapidly in the revolutionary East.

Time was when the execution of foreign policy was the domain of diplomats. This period of classic diplomacy developed after Richelieu with the adoption of the French diplomatic fashion and language throughout Europe. It experienced its climax during the Congress of Vienna, then gradually deteriorated. Still, diplomats knew what and whom they had to face; above all, they shared a common platform of culture and civilization which made eventual understanding possible. Their work (if not their play) was protected from the glare of publicity; the problematic Wilsonian concept of "open covenants, openly arrived at" had not yet been introduced.[1]

---

[1] Cf. J. Poorterman, "Des Diplomats et de Leur Statut," in *International Review of Administrative Sciences*, Vol. *XXIV*, No. 4, Brussels, 1958. See especially pp. 431–432.

It is quite possible that the lack of secrecy in negotiating, resulting from the ever-widening demand for public information, accelerated the demise of old-fashioned diplomacy which functioned best under conditions of confidential negotiations. According to Harold Nicolson, "covenants should be open, but not openly arrived at." Yet, of the factors contributing to the decline of diplomacy during the first half of the twentieth century, this was only one. Other important factors were the ideological divisions of the world and the resultant rigid if not crusading attitudes of the opponents; the arrival of the nuclear age; and a communications system that enabled chiefs of states and governments to be mobile and less dependent upon envoys. In special cases, seemingly beyond the range of diplomatic competence, "trouble-shooters" are called to the scene. Combining the prestige of an official representative of the Chief of State with that of a high official from the dispatching government, they have frequently proved to be of great consequence in settling thorny problems.

Nevertheless, for handling routine day-to-day international affairs, traditional diplomacy remains irreplaceable. Both East and West use its facilities, with this difference: in the East, the trappings of diplomacy are mere tools for accomplishing objectives; in the West, form and content are inseparable. This is explained by the fact that *totalitarians consider diplomacy and propaganda to be one and the same* while the free world differentiates quite emphatically between the two.[2]

Originally, envoys were personal representatives of their monarchs and accredited to foreign sovereigns. Modern diplomats in effect represent their government and, thereby, their peoples (or their political parties). Before departing for his post, the envoy of the past received detailed written and oral instructions, but once he had left, his independence was almost complete and his power of decision uncontested. There was no other way to handle the affairs of even the most autocratic ruler because communications were either slow or non-existent and, more than time-consuming, the exchange of messages by courier was unsafe. The modern diplomat also receives

[2] S. D. Kertesz and M. A. Fitzsimmons, *Diplomacy in the Changing World* (South Bend, Ind.: University of Notre Dame Press, 1961), Chapter 10.

rather detailed instructions before departing, but his day-to-day business is guided through close contact with his foreign office by radio, telephone, cable, teletype, or rapid air travel. He makes few decisions on his own. Since policies require daily adjustments to a rapidly changing world situation, the envoy is guided not only by the incoming flow of information, but also by a stream of directives from his home office, headquarters comments to his dispatches, and suggestions as to procedures. He receives guidance for implementing policies he may have had no part in formulating. In other words, he is not a free agent but rather the mouthpiece of his government. He negotiates to attain limited objectives assigned to him, yet if his chief of state decides to undertake personally negotiations on very important issues, he can only prepare and assist.

In earlier times, the envoys were "plenipotentiary" in fact as well as name. They alone negotiated; the sovereigns rarely met, and if they did, they left it to their ambassadors to prepare the way to a general agreement on policy, the details to be worked out by the experts. Generally, a monarch's crown council contained one member who specialized in foreign affairs and assigned to the envoy definite responsibilities and tasks. The expert was not only a political and economic negotiator whose responsibilities included territorial and population adjustments; he also was marriage broker, chief intelligence agent, and propagandist. Contrariwise, the contemporary diplomat receives meticulous guidance from his foreign office comprising practically all the steps he may or may not undertake to achieve his country's policy objectives. His decisions are not independent; he cannot determine, only suggest how crucial problems are to be solved; he can only explore a problem to the point where the Foreign Minister and the head of his state or government meet with their opposites in international conferences, which he attends in an advisory capacity. This new concept of diplomacy by conference, unilateral visits of the heads of state, and "summit" meetings have contributed to a deflation of the envoy's former influence.

Diplomacy has lost most of its glamour. Its tasks have become harder and more grueling, and more mundane than ever before. A diplomat is not limited to conducting negotiations and maintaining relations between his country and that to which he is accredited.

He must also be the "eyes and ears" of his government, reporting on the political, social, economic, and cultural conditions in his station and evaluating his findings for the consideration of the policy-makers at home.

The deterioration of international relations, which began its inexorable course shortly before World War I, the split between the traditional and revolutionary power groupings, and the fast shrinking of the globe due to technological developments, all have rendered diplomacy a hard and burdensome profession. The motion-picture illusion of the diplomat as a carefree clothes horse living brilliantly is hopelessly out of date. To be sure, a few glittering affairs still conjure up olden times; even the communists indulge in them now and again. But they no longer characterize diplomatic life in the twentieth century and occur far less often and with far less lavishness than in previous centuries. The often derided cocktail and dinner parties which are part of diplomatic life nowadays serve as informal meeting places where office work continues in a different — and hopefully more relaxed — atmosphere. They are the bane of the profession for the diplomat and, often enough, his wife. They reduce his free time to almost nothing. They are a labor, not a pleasure.

Social graces, though helpful, are no longer decisive for diplomatic success. High birth and personal fortune have lost much of their former magic. To be sure, the man whose personal magnetism impresses foreign officials and his diplomatic *confrères* is preferable to one with an unfortunate personality. But much more important for success in implementing policies are sound political judgment, talent for quick acquisition of area knowledge, ability to adapt to a country's social and psychological climate, and understanding of the problems concerning the general area in which that country is situated. Few things are more dangerous than an amateur diplomat who relies on half-truths.

The free world envoy's only area of independence is the freedom to choose his techniques of persuasion, pressure, or negotiation. Conditions abroad always vary somewhat from their appearance at home and changes in these conditions occur so frequently that theoretical reasoning may not correspond to reality. In this respect, the foreign office must rely on the envoy's initiative to modify methods, recommend changes in timing, or request instructions. More often than not he is forced to implement policies with which he does not fully agree, and the only way to resist them — should his protests go unheeded — is to resign. Frequently he is blamed for failures which are not necessarily of his own making, nor can he be sure of credit where credit is due.

Formerly, the Western diplomat possessed more freedom of action to carry out his government's policy than did the representative of an authoritarian government who came to the conference table laden with rigid orders which only his headquarters could modify. This difference has gradually lessened. In the first place, the diplomat's chief, the foreign minister, is apt to attend conferences of major significance with advisers of whom the envoy is only one. The really great decisive issues are negotiated by the chiefs of state or government themselves. In the second place, modern communications keep him in daily contact with his home office so that there is no need to proceed independently to implement an already coordinated policy. Thus the diplomat's role has become increasingly technical. Few contemporary envoys have had a genuine impact on the relations between their countries and those to which they were accredited. There are exceptions, of course: it cannot be denied that compellingly cogent observations and policy recommendations, made by an exceptionally capable diplomat, may create among policy-makers a residue of thinking which affects their decisions. Also, if a diplomat succeeds in establishing close personal relations with the head of the state in which he serves, he may be in a position to advance his country's policies and influence those of his host. But in the great majority of cases, envoys are administrators rather than diplomats, and figureheads of their embassies rather than creative negotiators.

If free world envoys compare poorly with their predecessors of another age, envoys from totalitarian states are even worse. They carry imposing titles but are merely messengers of their government. Their every statement or action must be specifically directed by the ruling party. Even their public mood is prescribed: they must smile or scowl in accordance with prevailing tactics. They are sometimes not even in personal control of their embassies. In fact, calling them diplomats is a misnomer.

In the free world, the diplomatic and consular personnel assigned to diplomatic missions abroad are usually drawn from the foreign offices. After being chosen with utmost care from numerous applicants, they receive a specialized though not all-too-thorough training in the techniques of foreign affairs. In contrast to previous centuries, they are selected predominantly on the basis of their education and personality; birth and money no longer play an essential part although in some Western European countries aristocratic family connections would certainly not harm an applicant's chances.

In communist countries, the situation is entirely different. There is complete interchangeability between the personnel of the foreign office and that of other agencies. An individual who appears promising for foreign service is drafted, regardless of age, position, or experience. He is sent to an institution for area and language training. He may be given brief special missions to test his abilities. Should he prove successful, he may be given a long-term assignment abroad. However, though he appears to be one of the Embassy Secretaries reporting on political or economic events, he actually may engage in political activities inside the Embassy (where even the ambassador is subject to surveillance) or try to organize espionage networks. He may become the leader of the mission staff's "Activ" whose members are stimulated to excel in work useful to the Party and the government. He is nearly always a member of the Communist Party.

The Soviet government and, for that matter, any communist-ruled government, can select with confidence among young unproven candidates. The life of citizens in such countries is an open book to the authorities; since people's reactions and tendencies are recorded from the time they enter the day nursery or kindergarten, it is a simple task to judge a candidate's character and loyalty. Scholarship in some fields is also required. Candidates most likely have completed the equivalent of a college education and, above all, thorough language training. If appointed, they attend party schools and area study courses so as to be knowledgeable of the country to which they are assigned. Only the most promising students are given this opportunity. But no student is admitted to the ranks of foreign service unless he has successfully completed an intensive course on Marxist–Leninist ideology.

It is of particular interest to note that Soviet and East European foreign service officers have adapted themselves to the Western style of diplomacy. They vary their degree of sociability in accordance with existing tension or relaxation, but at least they try to be "cultured" and maintain a façade of civility if they come in contact with their non-communist colleagues. The same cannot be said of the Red Chinese who seem to hold diplomacy and all it stands for in contempt. They appear to be extremely hard-working transmission belts for their government's propaganda machine, inflexible negotiators, and somewhat clumsy collectors of intelligence. They work in teams rather than as individuals. They disdain haberdashers and adhere to their drab civilian uniforms. Their faces are unsmiling and they always seem to feel uncomfortable. They show contempt for their foreign colleagues. By comparison, Soviet foreign service personnel appear quite polished.

East–West Negotiations

The schism between East and West has widened the gulf between traditionalists and revolutionaries. Misunderstandings, due to differences in ethical concepts and customs and to conviction of the adversary's wrongness, have created contradictions which render it extremely difficult for traditional diplomatists to negotiate with communist representatives. The repercussions of the Marxist–Leninist creed, substantiated by growing communist power, have wrought changes even in negotiations among the traditional powers: although the totalitarian menace is recognized, opinions differ as to its extent, depth, and nature.

Nevertheless, the traditionalists still speak the same diplomatic language. The accent may differ, but the idiom is little changed. Western diplomats and representatives of highly developed Asian countries such as Japan share similar convictions. Different as their cultures and racial antecedents may be, they continue to think and act along the lines of traditional diplomacy. The same is not true of the communists. Their ideological indoctrination and foreign-service training produce personalities who bear resemblance to conventional diplomats (China excluded), but in reality are the party cadres for eventual world revolution. The Western world has always believed that a diplomat must be "diplomatic," a term which connotes not only skill in negotiations but also a willingness to "give and take." Communist diplomacy wants to take without giving. It either indulges in euphemisms or covers its intentions with invective. In two words — it is horse trading. The apparent frankness of top-level negotiators is unstable and changes direction without warning. It is possible to reach broad, hazy agreements, which may become worthless in the hands of the lower-level negotiators, such as foreign ministers, ambassadors, and delegation leaders, because of their negative approach to details required to implement the overall agreements. Since they depend absolutely upon the final authority of communist headquarters, to parley with them is a "frustrating experience."[3]

Most "Soviet diplomats outwardly follow the procedures and concepts of traditional diplomacy . . ."; "the Soviet representatives have only a formal diplomatic status; they can hardly be considered diplomats in the customary sense."[4] Communism and traditional diplomatic practices do not mix. So long as diplomatic immunities and privileges are granted to representatives of totalitarian countries, they will be exploited for the subversive activities of foreign service agents. The very essence of diplomacy, in the Western sense, is compromise. Totalitarianism relinquishes only what is of little value or breaks the agreement whenever it is convenient. Communist efforts to obtain relaxation of international tension accompanied by smiling professions of goodwill, are deceptive. A change in behavior is all too often mistaken for a change in principles.

Although the post-Stalin period has produced numerous refinements in Soviet negotiating techniques, these are limited almost exclusively to party and government leaders. The existence of a nuclear stalemate and desire for "peaceful coexistence" have stimulated per-

---

[3] S. D. Kertesz and M. A. Fitzsimmons, *Diplomacy in the Changing World* (South Bend, Ind.: University of Notre Dame Press, 1961). Cf. especially Chapter 10. For further reference see J. R. Deane, *The Strange Alliance* (New York: The Viking Press, 1947); Adm. C. T. Joy, *How Communists Negotiate* (New York: Macmillan, 1955); and the memoirs of Churchill, Hull, Byrnes, and Stettinius.

[4] Kertesz and Fitzsimmons, *ibid.*, p. 149.

sonal and summit diplomacy. Since chiefs of state leave the discussion of details to their ministers, and communist leaders regard examination of their revolutionary objectives as "interference in their internal affairs," talks are limited to well-sounding, pious generalities. So long as the West realizes this, nothing is lost. If it takes communist peace protestations literally, it runs the risk of weakening its defenses. One reaches the gloomy conclusion that "diplomacy as practiced by communist negotiators destroys confidence instead of creating it. If the big lie is accepted as a routine means in diplomacy, as it frequently is by Soviet Russian representatives, then international negotiations necessarily have a limited value."[5]

Against the deterministic historical materialism of communist negotiators, free world diplomats need substantive and administrative protection. They should be familiar with the principles of Marxism–Leninism and their governments should provide them with clearly defined and well-formulated policies, combined with an efficient machinery for administering foreign affairs.

Both sides frequently receive support of a different type from official declarations of policies whose significance is indicated by their form, content, and tone, as well as by the very fact of their announcement. Official statements of policy serve several purposes. While clarifying, for the international record, the reasons for the policy, they commit a nation to a course of action. By trying to convince the citizens of the necessity for the measures, they propagandize and explain policies at home. They give diplomats abroad a suitable platform from which to conduct their negotiations. The form and timing of such statements are limited only by the ingenuity of presentation and the choice of the man to make the statement, but some universally recognized usages have developed. For example, speeches may be directed ostensibly to the domestic audience but intended for foreign governments' attention; interviews may be arranged with briefed interrogators; questions may be asked in press conferences or in parliaments whose answers serve as policy statements or interpretations. Moreover, policy may be promulgated by foreign offices to clarify the official position of their governments. The policies thus

5 *Ibid.*, p. 155.

stated will be defended by the envoy to the government to which the statement is directed. It is also conceivable that an announcement merely serves to cover up very delicate issues approachable only by indirection.

The envoy may have to negotiate problems with the foreign minister of the host country after receiving a thorough briefing from his headquarters. Should instructions fail to reach him before he is called into conference by the foreign minister, he may stall for time. If basic policy issues are at stake, the envoy's minister or his chief of state may take it upon himself to negotiate with the envoy in attendance. This trend is disturbing to at least some chiefs of state. President Eisenhower, although actively participating in personal and conference diplomacy, remarked at a news conference that he disliked the idea of foreign ministers becoming useless, and "only heads of government getting anything done." He called it "a step backward in diplomacy" and "a false doctrine that we should revamp our entire diplomatic procedures in order to get to a summit meeting every thirty days or so. . . ."[6] Similarly, Secretary of State Rusk made it clear that the Kennedy Administration would try to re-emphasize the use of traditional diplomatic channels to negotiate issues until their solution in a summit meeting is assured. President Johnson appears to continue this policy, as the Glassboro summit shows.

Unfortunately, communist tacticians have developed and stimulated certain techniques for dealing with international problems which democratic governments have been compelled to emulate. Depending on the form and circumstances, they are called personal diplomacy, diplomacy by conference, or summit diplomacy. Scholars in the field of diplomatic history will find little in these techniques that is diplomatic.

Top-level conferences are as old as history. In modern times the Congresses of Vienna, Paris, Verona, and Troppau are best known; they occurred in the nineteenth century and were dominated by the spirit of the diplomatic code which found its most significant expression in the regulations of the Vienna Congress in 1815. However, these gatherings of sovereigns were carefully prepared by their gov-

[6] *The Washington Post and Times Herald,* Washington, D.C., June 18, 1959.

ernments and ambassadors; the final meeting crowned the diplomatic efforts which preceded the "summit."

In the present divided world, such meetings differ from their historic counterparts in important respects. They reflect the inability of the "lower" levels to reach agreements; they fulfill, from the communist point of view, an effective propaganda function; in case of failure they serve the communists as a pretense to blame the "imperialists" for being "against peace." The democratic governments nevertheless felt constrained to accept the principle of "summit" meetings and even after the near disastrous Geneva Conference of 1955, agreed to another summit in Paris in 1960, which was torpedoed by Khrushchev. The need to cope with world opinion and combat the notion that the West is "war mongering," and perhaps the never-ceasing hope that somehow an agreement can be reached, may well cause the West to continue attending such conferences.

There are other, eminently practical reasons for participation. The West can neither refuse to negotiate with the leaders of the foremost communist power nor delegate second-string men to negotiate. First, this would be unacceptable to a protocol-conscious dictator. Second, the traditionalist attitude of free world diplomacy would not condone deliberate snubs. Third, even in democratic countries, decision-making is confined to relatively few individuals. As a result, personal contacts between the chiefs of state and governments have become a characteristic feature of postwar bipolar relations.

There have been quite a few communist "summits" and a number of similar Western conferences; there have been personal contacts between leaders of both sides such as the exchanges between President Eisenhower and N. S. Khrushchev in Geneva (1955) and in the United States (1959), between President Kennedy and Khrushchev in Vienna (1961), or between the British and French leaders with Soviet chiefs of Party and State (prior to and during 1959–1966). The next logical step was, of course, multilateral, bipolar "summits." Since most of these plenary sessions are open meetings, detailed negotiation of delicate issues is ruled out and they consist predominantly of recitals of the leaders' well-known official positions. Since there usually is little give-and-take in the more confidential preparatory meetings between ambassadors and foreign ministers, the plenary summits basically reiterate long-established policies without reconciling them.

The major shortcomings of summit conferences lie in the broadness, if not vagueness, of the discussions. Detailed implementation of agreed policy or reconciliation between controversial issues is left to the experts. During the conferences held by these "support" staffs, the vicious circle, alas, begins anew: the interpretation of broad policies inevitably leads each side to a different conclusion; the spokesmen can make decisions only when the solutions are consonant with their governments' policy, otherwise they must request instructions from their leaders; agreements may be difficult or impossible to reach; only minor issues are resolved while the significant ones remain in abeyance; the conference adjourns with a face-saving statement, and the unresolved questions are referred back to the leaders themselves. Personal diplomacy must take up where it left off and arrange a new summit meeting. And so on, *ad infinitum.*

This is one of the deplorable results of the schism which has rent the world into opposing camps. The communists have no basic interest in settlement except on their own terms or as a matter of temporary accommodation. They regard traditional diplomacy as an obsolete method which will be unnecessary in a communist world. In the meantime, they play the game, abiding by the rules or breaking them if expedient. No wonder traditional diplomacy finds itself stymied in the face of such formidable tactics. Regrettably, the revolutions of the twentieth century have left their mark on Western traditions: this is the dilemma of its diplomacy.

Under such circumstances, one can only conclude that diplomacy alone no longer is able to cope with the overpowering problems created by the doctrine of cold war strategy and tactics; it must seek new means to execute foreign policy. It needs a "new arm." This new arm exists. It has become enormously powerful and influential. It has caused a mutation of diplomacy and even foreign policy. It has left its imprint on world politics in indelible ink.

The new arm is propaganda.

..10....

Propaganda Versus Diplomacy

Concepts and Types

Propaganda is as old as the human race. From time immemorial, men have striven to convince others of the rightness of their views and actions. Political and military leaders have attempted to "soften up" their opponents' morale in order to undermine their resistance to political and military attack. In this age of ideological contests, when belief in a cause is almost as great a determinant of relations among nations as is power, governments must endeavor either to support or oppose such belief by propagating their policies with all possible means. The enormous growth of propaganda organizations in the twentieth century is the result of the development of communications media. Ironically, the same technology which engendered this development has reduced the influence of traditional diplomacy, which looks upon propaganda as an unfortunate necessity.

Modern political life is steeped in propaganda. Hardly a domain has remained untouched by it. In the realm of foreign affairs, international propaganda has emerged as an essential instrument in world politics, whether it be called open diplomacy, information, economic competition, cultural exchange, or education. Propaganda remains the generic term, and no euphemism can replace it.

The implications of propaganda's role in a divided world are immeasurable and crushing for traditional diplomacy. Governments appeal to foreign peoples over the heads of their governments. Chiefs of state and high officials lash out at each other publicly. Generals rattle their sabres frequently and audibly. International law is flouted by propaganda campaigns. Indeed, the era of international propaganda may be likened to the era of international lawlessness.

Who is to blame? The Western powers desired to confine propa-

199

ganda to war where it played a legitimate role. Following each of the World Wars, the information agencies of the victorious Allies were all but abolished. When the Soviet Union and its satellites, in cahoots with communist parties and front organizations everywhere, unchained a violent political warfare in 1945, the West was forced to reactivate its propaganda organizations. The guilt for immersing the world in an ocean of propaganda falls directly upon the Kremlin which initiated a world-wide propaganda system almost immediately after the successful October Revolution. The Nazis and Fascists learned the Kremlin's lesson all too well. Thus, much against the wishes of the West, the "new arm" of diplomacy became a fact. More than that, it changed the concept of diplomacy to the extent that policies now are formulated with an eye to the propagandistic effect of their substance, presentation, and implementation.

For these purposes, great ingenuity is required. The diversity of propaganda media permits a variety of approaches and the skilled propagandist knows how to play the registers of mass media, cultural presentations, and diplomatic moves — integrating socio-political, military, and economic aspects. The presentation is tailored to fit social strata or the entire population of the country to which it is directed. Media are chosen according to their practicability and availability.

The ideal of reaching all elements of a nation or group of nations can seldom if ever be achieved. Propaganda is destined to be directed to social and political groups. For example, political propaganda may be shaped to influence party or governmental leaders or intellectuals; in different forms it may try to penetrate the rural or urban working people. While propaganda output is not "addressed" to a given group, the form, content, and techniques of its transmission are disguised to appeal to the chosen target.

According to its needs, objectives, and targets, propaganda appears as information and education, cultural relations, or psychological and political warfare. The distinctions between these different aspects of propaganda require explanation.

In general, *information* is a polite term for propaganda. In particular, it is dissemination of news, news interpretation, and editorial comment. It also comprises such educational items as the history, politics, and civilization of the sending nation. There is still a school of thought in the West which distinguishes between information and propaganda. But information may be propaganda, just as propaganda can be informative. Even the truest, most genuine account of a country's point of view is designed to further understanding and therefore to persuade; *ergo* it may have propagandistic effect. It is questionable whether there is such a thing as absolute objectivity. However, truth can be slanted without malicious intent. For example, news items disseminated by a British Tory government are bound to differ from those of a Labour administration if only in selectivity. The political divergencies which exist between a Republican and a Democratic administration in the United States are necessarily, if indirectly, expressed in the American news output for foreign countries. Despite basic bipartisan policies in matters of international relations, political parties differ over details. Even the most objective *reportage* reveals such disagreements.

In its desire for clear and authentic news dissemination, Western information strives to present a balanced picture of events occurring in the informing nation and in the world at large. Further, it undertakes to interpret that picture. One cannot expect such commentary to be completely "neutral." The very word interpretation implies that the presented views are the result of an ideological disposition. Even if an interpretation is not written specifically for the program but comprises a composite quotation from press reports and editorials which reflect the political and cultural temper of the disseminating nation, the choice of items is determined by political guide lines. After decades of being exposed to propaganda most peoples have developed a sixth sense for hidden meanings. For example, they may feel that the selection of colorless editorials connotes a reluctance for commitments; the omission of negative comments may be interpreted as having been inspired; the televised speech of a high government official, in itself an act of objective reporting, gains a definite significance simply by being broadcast. News and information media often appear to be mere transmission belts, yet the political motivation behind the act of dissemination is meaningful.

Although one need have no illusions that absolute objectivity is possible, or even desirable, Western information services, when compared with those of the communist countries, are models of virtue. This is particularly well illustrated by the educational portions of information programs. The West seriously attempts to convey to the target areas factual descriptions of its civilization and cultural aspirations, of its political philosophy, economic beliefs, scientific achievements, artistic life, and social climate.

All information and propaganda output is affected by omissions which conceal the truth, emphasis where none is needed, and boastfulness where modesty is required. Communist propaganda is a past master in all these vices. One can hardly expect a country to undertake public self-analysis before uncomprehending listeners, but it should be possible to offer a reasonable array of both positive and negative factors which explain its national character, goals, and *Weltanschauung* to peoples with similar socio-political concepts. Objectivity vis-à-vis the totalitarians is a waste since they are strictly subjective and regard objectivity or understatement as indications of weakness and "bourgeois decadence."

Propaganda critical of the target area is not necessarily the most effective means of obtaining favorable results. It might create resentment rather than a favorable image of the propagandist. Clearly the most effective information technique is the reporting of true facts which in themselves constitute a powerful weapon of persuasion. The American stories of the Marshall Plan, the Berlin airlift, the development of nuclear power, and the accomplishments of US astronauts needed only to be told to be effective; the reports on the Soviet earth satellites, lunar rockets, and the excursion into space by USSR cosmonauts needed no adornment to be most impressive. The veracity of the facts was indisputable, only their significance was speculated upon.

This brings us to the question of whether or not the target people believe what they learn through information media. The answer varies with the area and the reputation of the source of information. Most of the world's population has been exposed to heavy propaganda for the past half-century and has acquired a self-protective cynicism toward it, a fact which should never be forgotten by those responsible for programming. There are only two ways to surmount this hurdle: one must either present incontestable, cogent logic to the educated segment of the populace or appeal to the emotional and material desires of the masses. The first is exceedingly difficult and requires propagandists of such high intellectual and substantive capabilities as to remain rare; the second is used by East and West with the difference that the latter tries to maintain a relatively decent ethical *niveau.*

In the introduction to a book on *cultural relations* among nations, Archibald MacLeish counseled that "the entire problem of the conduct of foreign affairs requires — urgently requires — re-examination . . ." and that "Foreign Offices are offices of international understanding of peoples whole and intelligible and complete."[1] This high-minded statement certainly should be implemented in the free world. Cultural relations with the communist bloc are quite another matter. They have become fashionable; in fact, Soviet cultural diplomacy is the *pièce de résistance* of "peaceful coexistence."[2] A host of cultural agreements has been concluded between communist and non-communist powers, notably between the USSR and the East European states on the one hand, and the United States and many countries in Europe, the Middle East, Africa, and Asia on the other. The resultant initiation of a considerable interchange of artists, scientists, and educators unquestionably has produced salutary effects among limited groups on either side.

Cultural relations programs are nothing new. Prior to World War I, Germany and France maintained such programs and expanded them between the wars. In 1934, Great Britain followed suit. The United States initiated a limited cultural program for Latin America in 1938. The Soviet Union sought cultural contacts only after establishing itself as a great power, when it undertook very limited participation until Stalin's death. Of the Asian states, Japan has sought cultural relations ever since the nineteenth-century Meiji reforms. Many smaller states tried to enhance their prestige through

[1] R. McMurray and M. Lee, *The Cultural Approach: Another Way in International Relations* (Chapel Hill, N.C.: University of North Carolina Press, 1947), p. 10.

[2] See F. L. Barghoorn, *The Soviet Cultural Offensive* (Princton, N.J.: Princeton University Press, 1960), *passim.*

artistic and scholarly efforts. Gradually all civilized nations came to recognize that their national culture, in whatetver form presented, would increase their prestige and contribute to a better understanding of their civilization by foreign peoples. The ingredients of power create respect but scarcely promote understanding: history proves that in the long run it was a nation's cultural achievement rather than its power which won the admiration of subsequent generations. Beyond their value as aesthetic expressions, such cultural emanations as music, literature, the fine arts, dramatic creations, and scientific achievements can establish an atmosphere of appreciation which may assist the exchanging governments in their search for a political *modus vivendi.*

The great question remains whether an East–West cultural exchange can be more than a temporary and specialized expedient for the communists who desire to convince the world that only under a "socialist system" can genuine "popular" culture flower. The free world is well aware of the East's political regimentation of the arts and the imposition of "socialist realism" as the only admissible style.[3] In the "thaw" following Stalin's death Khrushchev and his successors have permitted a less stringent interpretation of "socialist realism" despite temporary fluctuations of that policy. Some notable achievements, particularly in music and the ballet, have duly impressed the West. But the Soviet's primary motive for exporting and advertising its cultural products is to exert a psychological impact by presenting an overwhelmingly impressive picture of communist civilization.

The Western world and its like-minded Asian friends project their cultures abroad to enhance their stature and prevent misconception. By offering artistic feats and scientific–technical information, they boost their assets and gain national prestige. Plugging the gaps in understanding is propaganda, too, but it is conceived chiefly to win and keep friends rather than to foist their civilization upon other countries. The West's cultural relations programs are not aggressive; they do not penetrate the communist orbit sufficiently to present an

---

[3] K. London, *The Seven Soviet Arts* (New Haven, Conn.: Yale University Press, 1938), especially "The Struggle for the New Soviet Style," p. 61 ff.

effective picture of non-communist civilization. Furthermore, performances by visiting artists are accessible only to the privileged few. (Trade fairs are in a different category and probably more effective than cultural exchanges.)

In any event, most cultural relations programs seem politically innocuous; their influence on political philosophies is slight and they convince neither side that the other is right. While it is not suggested that cultural exchanges are altogether ephemeral, neither can they prevent continuation of the cold war. It is dangerous to overestimate their effects despite the spectacular publicity they enjoy. Furthermore, one must also consider the possibility that a more thorough understanding of the opponent through cultural relations could result in an increased dislike rather than sympathy.

Psychological warfare is propaganda with teeth in it. It seeks to disseminate among target peoples ideas and beliefs designed to weaken their moral fiber, turn them against their government, and arouse sympathy for their opponents. It tries to render *ad absurdum* the point of view of their own leaders. It is usually coordinated with carefully prepared propaganda campaigns whose strategic objectives and tactical means are minutely predetermined. Major campaigns using all available media must be coordinated with political, economic, and military planning. Their chances of success are unpredictable but certainly greater if the policy behind them is articulate, realistic, and purposeful.

The boundary between psychological and *political warfare* is blurred. The former primarily "uses the means of mass communications in order to destroy the enemy's will to fight."[4] The latter "adds the important idea that all instruments of policy need to be properly correlated . . ." with the other "chief instruments of policy in war and peace: diplomacy . . . economics, arms . . . Political warfare thus includes operations in relation to allies, neutrals, and the home audience. Psychological warfare includes propaganda directed against the enemy together with the use of arms to create the greatest impact

[4] H. D. Lasswell, "Political and Psychological Warfare," in D. Lerner (ed.), *Propaganda in War and Peace* (New York: G. W. Stewart, 1951), p. 262.

upon the enemy's will to fight at the least cost of capability."[5] One might comment that the "use of arms" is not necessarily part of psychological warfare but the threat of arms or, as it is now called, "atomic sabre-rattling," may well be. In any event, political warfare must be conducted with psychological skill.

In a time when there is neither war nor peace, propaganda automatically becomes psychological warfare. It comprises a variety of actions: political, economic, ideological, or cultural. Were such actions conducted only through communications media, they would achieve little effect. To translate them into practice, they must be "married" to policies whose implementation they permeate with the help of envoys and their staffs. In the tug-of-war between East and West, even the negotiations between diplomats or representatives of the opposing camps become instruments of propaganda. The waging of political warfare by envoys abroad has become an indispensable tool in international contacts, contributing greatly to the changed nature of contemporary diplomacy. It is not surprising that Western statesmen are intuitively leery of high-level conferences which are not minutely prepared. They realize that the communists use such meetings, "personal diplomacy," and summitry as tools for psychological and political warfare.

However much the democratic leaders desire a return to traditional diplomacy, their totalitarian opponents are unlikely to permit it to happen. Even if they did, it would do no good. First of all, the negotiators would proceed from utterly different concepts. Ideological contradictions can be camouflaged with pious clichés, but the moment details are discussed, revolutionary dynamics and traditionalist *status quo* meet head on. Secondly, as has already been noted, envoys and foreign ministers no longer make important decisions; only the chiefs of states or governments are empowered to sign on the dotted line. Often enough, when lower-level policy-makers and diplomats reach an impasse, they call upon their chiefs; when this happens a new summit is likely to be born. Thirdly, a new dimension in the technique of handling foreign affairs has developed as the result of these facts, namely the gradual merger of policy with propaganda.

[5] *Ibid.*, pp. 262–263.

POLITPROP: *The Amalgamation of Policy and Propaganda*

A description of the organizations and media for propaganda dissemination cannot do justice to the scope of the political tug-of-war between the two camps of the divided world. Conceptually, they are of secondary significance, for they constitute the conventional aspects of propaganda techniques. Far more important for an examination of the global schism is the fact that all available means and techniques are harnessed to serve the *amalgamation of propaganda and policy,* a development which has virtually replaced diplomacy and often extends beyond it. As this development is of totalitarian origin, the communists particularly excel in its use. The West, though it still persists in conceiving of propaganda and policy as two different "disciplines," has been compelled to use at least some combinations of policy and propaganda to counter the East. It is not difficult to predict that the decline of traditional diplomacy and the unlimited means of communications eventually will cause the formulation of foreign policy to merge with the means of spreading it. Political and propaganda policies will be developed and formulated in unison, and propaganda organizations will merely perform the technical functions of dissemination.

Within the framework of this study, we can only outline the problem, try to grasp its meaning, and briefly discuss some of the issues which may exemplify the policy-propaganda-approach. For the sake of brevity, in the following paragraphs the concept of policy-cum-propaganda will be referred to as *politprop.* This concept should not be confused with propaganda policy which merely directs the methods of propaganda implementation toward the target area. For example, the policy staff of an information agency explains the foreign office's position so as to avoid misinterpretation and directs the lines of emphasis or understatement of that position; it sets forth certain dos and don'ts in accordance with the wishes of the policy-makers, who are rarely trained psychologists or masters of propaganda techniques.

Politprop is vastly more. It is the technique by which policy is shaped to fit its propagandistic potential. In reverse, a propaganda approach may carry the seed of policy. Thus, there is a cross-fertilization destined finally to give birth to a compact new discipline. Althought the *politprop* technique is applicable to all important international issues, its intellectual mainsprings flow from the communist doctrine. The close connection between this doctrine and propaganda often has been pointed out, but the responsible factors have perhaps not been sufficiently clarified. Nor has their significance in policy formulation been appreciated. For this reason, an attempt will be made to sketch the philosophical background of *politprop* and to analyze two vital examples from both the Eastern and Western points of view: economic and technological competition.

In the course of its history, every nation develops a body of beliefs and views which finds eventual expression in the words of its great statesmen and philosophers. These principles, both general and specific, may be said to contain the essential elements of the nation's ideology. If these ideologies grow slowly, they result in national convictions which are not, as a rule, aggressive. Hence they are seldom exportable.

Conversely, expansionist and supra-national ideologies may have some historic roots, but their revolutionary outlook was determined by the contemporary changes in socio-technical developments. They denied national sovereignty as a factor restricting ideological incursions. Those aggressive ideologies which emanated from the concept of racial or national superiority faced severe limitations and gained only limited support from those outside the "superior race." However, a universalist doctrine which rejects nationalism and seeks to replace it with an all-encompassing belief system on behalf of the "toilers of the world" has succeeded in finding adherents in many lands.

Historically and psychologically it is understandable that those sedate national philosophies which arise from tradition do not suffer from messianic complexes as do the revolutionary ones. Therefore, the aggressive policies of an established nation usually are not universalist and, as noted earlier, have only limited aims. Conversely, the goals of revolutionary ideologies, being universalist by nature, are unlimited and endeavor to convert all "infidels" by the sword or the word. Then this lack of restraint in the conduct of international relations enabled them to seize and keep the initiative. A securely established social system, grown civilized and sophisticated, sometimes even lackadaisical, was faced with the "haunting specter" of barbarous and vigorous forces that had broken away from most traditions taken for granted by the sedate democracies. This dynamism was fired by doctrines of revolution and methods of violence or deception. Against this mixture of aggressive threat and super-Machiavellian politicking, the old-fashioned Western methods were no defense. Politically and propagandistically the West resigned itself to holding the line. The result was external containment and internal contentment — a "business as usual" approach despite a situation without precedent in human history. But for nuclear weapons, the West might have been lost, and many precious years elapsed before the predicament was fully realized.

Communist policy seeks to implement its ideological aspirations. We are aware of their nature. The doctrine, however, is two-sided: it not only states its goal, but also the reasons why such a goal is attainable. Contrasting communist blessings with capitalist shortcomings, it builds its plans upon the alleged weaknesses of the non-communist systems. It proposes the Marxist–Leninist *thesis*, sets it against the capitalist-imperialist *antithesis*, and awaits the inevitable *synthesis* dictated by the laws of dialectical materialism. The communists believe this synthesis can only be the establishment of communism (preceded by socialism) because the historical law of development provides an instrument for "scientific" forecast of the "correct" development of future events.

In the West, such theoretical maxims would hardly stand up as valid arguments for policy. Nor would a basically philosophical method of reasoning, such as dialectical materialism, be used to forecast estimates of future developments. But Marxist–Leninist principles of dialectics are as basic to communist thinking as is the Trinity for Christianity or the Nirvana for Buddhism. In simplified terms, communist dialectics holds that all phenomena are interconnected, are in continuous flux, develop in dialectical stages ("leaps"), and are propelled by the "struggle" of contradictions.

This may sound obscure to the unprepared student of politics but its connotations are clear enough to disciples of Marxism–Leninism. The philosophers of communism — perhaps Engels more than Marx, Stalin as much as Lenin, and certainly Mao Tse-tung — conceived of human development as a battle of contrasts between the declining Old and the dawning New. Lenin's examples for this battle of contrasts were the opposites of differential and integral, effect and counter-effect, positive and negative poles of electricity, joining and separation of atoms, and, most important, the class struggle. This last concept, one of the revolutionary fundamentals, provides the clue to communist *politprop* in the realm of ideology. Dialectics in this sense is not only method, it is the heart of the communist secular religion, a theory of being. It is the "unity of opposites," of theory and practice, of propaganda and policy. Mao, in his essay "On Contradictions," has further "enriched" this concept by differentiating between "antagonistic" and "non-antagonistic" contradictions.

As a thought process, dialectical materialism is perhaps more intelligible to the social scientist when studied as historical materialism, a sociological rather than philosophical theory. In Stalin's ruminations "On Dialectical and Historical Materialism," a paper of considerable influence, we find the proposition that the "material life of society, indeed its very existence, is primary and original, while its spiritual-intellectual life is merely a reflection of objective reality, a reflection of its being." In other words, "as the spiritual-intellectual life of an individual human being is a reflex of his physical state, so the spiritual-intellectual life of society is a reflex of its material conditions." According to Stalin, neither geographic nor demographic conditions are determinants but the way of making a living is, the latter being characterized by the productive forces and the conditions under which man produces. Upon this basic structure of society grows the "superstructure" (ideas, language, science, the arts, etc.).

After these preliminaries, it is necessary to apply dialectics, as the basic communist driving force, to international relations and, more specifically, the "unity of opposites" to policy and propaganda. We must surmise that the communist leadership believes in these principles as Western man believes in the ethics of Judaeo–Christian tenets. There has been no evidence whatsoever that Moscow, Peking, and their disciples have lost faith in this aspect of their secular religion: their change in methods and their promotion of a much-needed peace, being purely tactical, can be reversed at any time and their goals are outspokenly those of a communist society. In sum, it must be assumed that the doctrines of Marx, Engels, Lenin, Stalin, Mao, and lesser writers, remain the cornerstone of communist thinking, planning, and speculation.

This being so, certain conclusions are inevitable. First of all, communist long-range estimates of global developments forecast victory in their struggle for eventual communism; the "synthesis" of a classless society. Dialectical forces do not stop there, but contradictions are "non-antagonistic." (Soviet theoreticians have not stated whether a classless society will be devoid of contradictions and what the consequences of such a euphoric state of affairs might be.)

Secondly, confidence in victory rests not only on the strength of this ideology, but also on the firm belief that capitalism, imperialism, and all types of "revisionist" socialism are bound to decline and eventually perish as a result of the dialectic forces involved in the struggle. Estimates as to when this will occur are no longer so optimistic as under Khrushchev, but the communists believe that time is on their side, and they have patience. Furthermore, the Soviets now seem certain that no military action is required to stimulate the process of capitalist deterioration since this "aging" system has already reached its "highest stage, imperialism," which carries its own seeds of destruction. What they must do is demonstrate that socialism can outstrip capitalism and in this way indirectly deal it the death blow. The Chinese are much less optimistic.

It should be emphasized that the communists do not recognize the changes in the capitalist system as in any way affecting their ideological proposition. They are adamant in rejecting even the possibility of modifications that could topple their entire doctrinal construction. Democratic socialism is as repugnant to them as "monopoly capitalism" or, on the other side of the scale, Titoist revisionism. Even in the post-Stalin era there has been little room for tampering with the fundamentals, but ample room for flexibility of implementation methods.

Thirdly, Moscow and Peking believe that what is good for their respective countries is good for the world. The Kremlin's ambitions for communist leadership are, of course, founded upon the concept of the USSR as the base of world communism. Although this thesis has been compromised by the emergence of an aggressive Red China and the concept of polycentrism, it still stands as an essential element of the international movement. Peking can hardly become the Mecca of communism, though it may wind up as its Medina. In any event, the messianic ardor of the medieval Russian Church seems to have been transubstantiated into the belief that the Soviet Union can and must bring about human fulfillment not only within its frontiers but throughout the universe — and this word is used advisedly when we remember the Soviet achievements in space exploration. Protestations by Soviet leaders to the effect that communism is not exportable are simply tactical lies. For if Marxism–Leninism is to be perpetuated, it must achieve ideological expansion. Humanity outside must be "converted." The USSR's role in this mission is not that of a nation, but rather of a Moses, liberating the underdogs of the world from capitalistic servitude.

Clearly, policies formulated on the strength of these doctrines would be ineffectual unless implemented by full-scale explanation, persuasion, indoctrination, education, in sum — by propaganda. This implies neither an overt promotion of "socialism" nor revelation of the real objectives of the communist leaders. The days of crude Comintern propaganda are long gone; the rulers of the USSR are more sophisticated and have acquired a better understanding of the psychology of the West and of the new, uncommitted, underdeveloped, but nationalistic, countries. *Politprop* aimed toward the Middle East, for example, takes into account the surge of nationalistic sentiments, devises means to allegedly support such nationalism by economic and military aid, and officially ignores the local communist parties or sympathizers. Rather, it poses as friend and potential ally against the "colonialists" and "imperialists" and seeks to gain a foothold by making itself technically and economically irreplaceable and by offering its strength to counteract that of the West. The real purpose is, of course, gradual infiltration of these areas by communist ideas and personnel. Policy and propaganda go hand-in-hand. *Politprop's* strategic objectives are implemented by tactics which serve as a convenient smoke screen.

Similarly, the Western policies inaugurated by Khrushchev and continued by his successors are as good an example as those that prevailed under Stalin. They are merely better camouflaged. The strategy is "peaceful coexistence"; the method is accommodation which cedes neither ideological nor territorial positions. The peace campaign is represented as the consequence of growing Soviet power rather than its weakening; domestic ideological positions are bolstered by the dictum that Soviet successes result from the socialist system which has advanced sufficiently to permit an early move toward the "transition to communism." Peace is needed to achieve this goal; however, such relaxation of tensions is possible only because of the continuing material and technical progress of the "socialist world system."

Here is dialectics in practice: a unity of opposites, a total integration of propaganda and policy. This is *politprop* in action. Could the West forge its own *politprop*? To a certain extent, yes. There is no reason why Western policies cannot be formulated with an eye to their propagandistic effects. But so long as tradition separates policy from propaganda, so long as the ethical or philosophical premises of Western thinking exclude an intellectual base for *politprop*, there are only a few issues which can suitably inspire policies of propaganda value. Among them is economic aid.

Curiously, the United States, not the Soviet Union, created that prototype of economic *politprop*, the Marshall Plan. Some years later Moscow, not to be outdone by Washington, plagiarized the concepts of economic aid and technical assistance. Even Peking, beset by its own economic troubles, found the idea imitable. Only when we examine the motivation for such aid do the differences between the camps become evident and therewith the differences in the *politprop* concepts.

The United States proceeded from the view that post-war unrest and economic troubles were diseases and the affected nations must be provided with immunity to withstand their onslaught. The Marshall Plan concept was a "civic" action, such as might be taken by more affluent members of a community who feel (and are) responsible for the welfare of the less fortunate. It would be incorrect to deny that the decision to provide economic aid was also motivated by the knowledge that want breeds subversion. However, Americans believed it was necessary "to help other nations help themselves." True, this policy was pragmatic as well as generous, but a state is not a social-welfare agency and must look to its national interests. American policy stems from emotional as well as pragmatic sources; economic aid happens to demonstrate both traits at their best. In the last analysis, the "ideological" intent of the Marshall Plan and the technical-aid program was one not only of self-defense but also of Western ethics. This plan desired neither conquest nor profit; it wanted no more than reasonable success and perhaps some recognition that American taxpayers were being heavily assessed for the sake of improving conditions in other countries, even though many necessary improvements inside the United States had to be postponed.

Compare this position with the motivation behind communist foreign aid. For Moscow and Peking, it is a strategic objective not only to win prestige for and acceptance of a "socialist" society, but also to create a machinery for ideological, military, and economic infiltration. It is almost exclusively directed toward the neutralist nations, specifically the newly independent countries most of which are politically unsophisticated. For the Soviet Union at least, this is not too costly a means of ideological expansion. The purposes of the Kremlin are not humanitarian but "competitive"; it should be remembered that such competition is not one of traditional power politics, i.e., a struggle for markets, but primarily one for ideological prevalence. It is designed to explore strategic areas, deny their natural resources to the West, and gradually win them over to the "socialist commonwealth," thus isolating the West from crucial areas of the globe.

The difference between these two concepts of economic aid demonstrates the differences in the approach to *politprop*. Let it be emphasized that communist *politprop* is genuine while the Western one is merely a simile. That the Marshall Plan was an excellent propaganda issue is obvious, but it was not conceived for this purpose; the propaganda effect was a by-product. The United States had no intention of spending money for the diversionary maneuvers of a momentary painkiller; it attempted to eliminate the symptoms of the illness by curing the ill itself. Without exaggeration, one could say that communist foreign aid, at least from the Western point of view, was designed from the beginning either to aggravate the ill or to create it. To aid non-communist countries without laying the ground-work for revolution would be against the teachings of Lenin, who, like his spiritual fathers Marx and Engels, could not conceive of genuine accommodation between socialism and capitalism. It would be folly to attribute to any Soviet détente a change of this ideological position.

Another example of communist *politprop* is the race for techno-logical breakthroughs in connection with the disarmament campaign. As to nuclear weapons, the United States used them in World War II chiefly to avoid sacrificing hundreds of thousands of soldiers in an invasion of Japan. It also counted on the psychological effect of the new weapon to end the war earlier and, again, save untold numbers of lives. It held the weapon as a shield against a numerically superior opponent after the war and, once Moscow had developed its own nuclear devices, used it as a deterrent. But, what began as military policy became political when weapon testing by the United States, the Soviet Union, France, Great Britain, and China created conditions detrimental to human health throughout the globe because of fallout.

The Soviet "peace campaigns" directed against the West are yet another demonstration of how *politprop* works. We can distinguish two phases. The first, which was particularly virulent, was a Stalinist reaction to the fact that the United States rather than the Soviet Union possessed the atomic bomb. The second was the post-Stalinist effort to neutralize or eliminate nuclear weapons which would leave the populous communist countries with a vastly superior force of manpower and conventional weapons. Moscow's strategy was based upon *politprop* because its outcry for peace and disarmament served two purposes: as a policy it sought to obtain a period of tranquility during which to strive for the "transition to communism" while the capitalist system continued to decline as "scientifically" forecast by historical materialism; as a propaganda device it would slacken the West's alertness, portray the communist leader nation as the proto-type of a defender of peace (while condemning the "imperialists" as warmongers), thereby gaining the respect and confidence of the less-sophisticated neutralists. Indeed, if one recognizes the irreconcila-bility of the two contesting ideologies, the deviousness of communist *politprop* becomes so abundantly clear that one wonders why rational intellects, unaffected by the claims of Marxist–Leninist theoreticians, do not readily see through the deceptive front of trite appeals.

The lesson to be learned by non-communist policy-makers and propagandists is a simple one: *politprop* is here to stay, and there is nothing to prevent the West from adapting similar techniques to its own purposes. What would distinguish Western from Eastern *politprop* is the lack of revolutionary intent and a basic benevolence characteristic of mature civilizations. Apart from this broad consideration, Western *politprop* would counter the Eastern propaganda initiative which has kept the West on the defense and the neutrals wondering. If propaganda is to have a productive future in the free world, its ever closer amalgamation with policy is unavoidable.

Some Concluding Reflections

There are times in the lives of men and nations when it becomes imperative to pause, take stock, discard the obsolete, and start anew. The middle decades of our century were such a time. The problems to be solved came into focus and the changes affecting the relations among nations clearly emerged. The outlook for the second half of the century became more penetrable.

Revolutions usually are directed against petrified traditions, views, and attitudes. The trouble is that they tend to become iconoclastic and destroy the good with the bad instead of replacing the old with the new. Recognition of this probability and adjustment to changing conditions can prevent violent upheavals while vigorously stimulating evolutionary actions. We do not need revolution to prevent entrenchment in a figurative Maginot Line of traditionalist concepts of foreign affairs.

In the preceding chapters, an attempt was made to call attention to the hazards of archaic thinking under the unprecedented conditions of contemporary world politics. Conventional subject matter was purposely retained as a point of departure since it is better to chart a new course from a known position than from parts unknown. But the revolutionizing developments in the nature and technique of international relations are anything but conventional. It should therefore be useful to recapitulate the most important factors which have led to a change of substance and an eclipse of traditional principles in international relations.

There is no precedent in history for a universalist secular religion which, armed with modern means of communication, can reach all peoples of the world over the heads of their governments. Nor is there any precedent for a world-wide system of parties which overtly or covertly carries on communist business, frequently against their own nations' interests. Were it not for totalitarian ideology and organization, first fascist and then communist, the world would not now face one crisis after another.

If power *per se* were sought and contested, differences could reach eventual settlement as they have so often in the past. But a deeply ingrained concept, a philosophy of life, a quasi-religious political conviction cannot be compromised: it is an indivisible entity. Therefore no sound foreign policy can be devised by the West unless it recognizes the impact of ideology upon world politics in general and upon relations between the opposing groups in particular.

It is doubtful that the "socialist camp" ever was a monolith. In 1949, when the Chinese communists came to power, Tito already had been ousted from the Cominform. But for a few years, until Malenkov was deposed by Khrushchev and Bulganin, it appeared to be monolithic. The concept of the "socialist commonwealth" in the mid-fifties implied the replacement of a centralized rule with voluntaristic decentralization. The Kremlin leaders presumably believed that ideological impregnation and kindred attitudes toward the "imperialist camp" would hold together, without coercion, the communist-ruled countries and the leaderships of parties outside the orbit.

Speedy attainment of social and economic goals which would create the material and technical basis for the "transition to communism" (from the present state of socialism) presupposes such accommodation. It is not peace in the Western sense, but merely an extended truce during which the "socialist forces" expect to achieve the necessary strength to reach and overtake the level of capitalism while the ideological struggle continues. Moreover, the communists claim that the deterministic philosophy of dialectical and historical materialism proves "scientifically" that all other systems of human society are doomed. In view of the combination of an expected increase in communist power with the foretold decline of capitalism, the men in Moscow and Peking believe time to be on their side. Their *politprop* is formulated accordingly.

It is true that with the advent of polycentric communism and the Sino–Soviet conflict radical changes have occurred in what used to be called the international communist movement. If by movement we mean organization, then, indeed, it is questionable whether there still exists such a movement. But this equation is much too simplistic to be useful. Communism still exists — and communism is inherently international. It is no longer fashioned in the image of the Soviet Union even though Marxism–Leninism remains an influential doctrine which is adjustable to the needs of individual countries and parties. It no longer is Stalinist communism and one may sometimes doubt that it is very Marxist, but the basic Leninist elements still persist. Perhaps in future generations a type of communism may develop which is markedly different from its twentieth-century image.

We are not concerned here with the distant future, however, and, in assessing the impact of communism on foreign affairs and international relations, we cannot but reach the conclusion that the changes since Stalin, great as they are, do not substantially relieve the pressure of the communist-ruled states on world politics. The secular religion differs in different countries; there are now several communisms, but they all add up to severe disruptions of our shrinking planet. Unfortunately, the cold war is not over and the arms race continues.

The second major factor contributing new aspects to international relations is modern technology. Significant scientific and technical breakthroughs have occurred in several branches of science, particularly in communications, transportation, rocketry, space exploration and the momentous development of nuclear energy. In previous chapters, the impact of these developments on the character of national power, war, and diplomacy has been briefly described, an impact that has also affected the strategy and tactics of international communism. For, the combination of ideology and technology has produced a political monster with which all "infidel" nations must cope. Can they master or even tame it without substantially altering the very substance of their beliefs? Is it possible to maintain a *status quo* indefinitely? Is the policy of containment more than a stopgap or perhaps the Western version of "peaceful coexistence"?

The answers to these vital questions can be neither positive nor negative. They are too complex, too dependent upon a multitude of premises. But the overriding fact is that a *status quo* is an illusion and can only be a passing phase. New developments lead to new conditions which generate sudden or imperceptible changes. It is human nature to seek security, but it is human tragedy that such security, seemingly found, slips away.

In politics and international affairs, this expresses itself in never-ending sequences of undulation, comparable with the ebb and flow of the sea. The need of the individual to "adjust" himself to changing environments is paralleled by the state. If the individual fails, he is likely to suffer severe damage and so is the state. Neither the individual nor the state must necessarily sacrifice basic beliefs in order to modify their application to everyday life or practical politics. Accordingly, when the individual is confronted by a situation that threatens the very core of his existence, he first takes measures to safeguard it and then devises counter-action to guarantee his survival under the most favorable conditions. It is probable that in so doing he may be required to sacrifice some sectors of his *status quo,* but, in time, he can discover new sectors which compensate for them. It is the same with the state: its *status quo* can never be taken for granted. Stagnation would be the alternative and history proves that stagnation means decline.

More concretely, it would seem that the changing nature of world affairs has revealed the impossibility of traditional states maintaining their *status quo.* A study of the facts which have led to this situation and an evaluation of their effects on foreign policy and international relations must inevitably demonstrate that it is urgent to shed long-held concepts of policy and diplomacy and to develop new ones befitting the requirements of the changing global environment; it is necessary to reconsider not only the thinking but also the organization and coordination of the machinery for policy-making and implementation; it is essential to enhance and re-orient the education of present and future generations so as to enable citizens of the democracies to understand the problems confronting their governments.

The monster can be tamed only if it cooperates. Since there is little likelihood in the near future that it will "knuckle under," it must be mastered. This cannot be achieved by force — although force must remain in the background as evidence that we are prepared. Mastery over the monster, therefore, requires that its democratic antagonists marshal their national resources even if the sense of urgency is not so strong as in a major war when the will to survive and win generates unity and willingness to sacrifice. In an era of nuclear deterrence in which local, limited wars are fought with predominantly conventional means, possibly a long way from the belligerents' country, this feeling of resolve and purpose is hardly evident in the democracies, particularly if segments of the population disagree with their government's policy. Nor is there unity and willingness by the peoples of the democracies during a cold war or "peaceful coexistence" — there is little difference between the two terms — to sacrifice when the need for sacrifice is not obvious. This raises the old dilemma of how a democratic administration can face a centralized, totalitarian dictatorship without itself becoming dictatorial or totalitarian.

To master the monster it is necessary for the democracies to realize that we live in a twilight era where there is neither peace nor war and that, while the fate of the world hangs in the balance, peace can be achieved only by adequate preparations against aggression. A strong military establishment, a strong economy and a strong sense of unity are required. These three factors are indivisible; if one is missing, security is weakened. The question to be clarified then is: does there exist such a monster or is it imaginary? If it exists, how dangerous is it?

Opinions differ as to the nature of its threat. The view that communism is on the decline has taken hold among large sections of Western peoples and governments. Polycentric communism in Eastern Europe and the parties outside the orbit, apparent moderation in the Soviet conduct of foreign affairs, and lack of international communist organization have gained prominence over the developments in Red China where Maoist fanaticism is rampant. Moreover, there have been setbacks for the communist cause in Asia, Africa, and Latin America. Above all, the reformist movement initiated by Khrushchev in the USSR which has led to markedly different tactics in foreign relations by the Soviet leaders, has contributed to a state of euphoric expectations in Europe as well as in America despite the fact that there is no genuine evidence of basic changes in Soviet policy goals. In the light of such analyses, it is believed by many government officials and scholars that a *status quo* can be maintained. One might say that the policy of containment is competing with and can be compared to that of "peaceful coexistence." This, of course, is analysis conceived by Western minds, conceived on the assumption that Marxism–Leninism is not a political religion but only a convenient phraseology for political manipulation.

At this point one more reflection on what is called the erosion of ideology might be in order. There are some observers who go so far as to explain the ideological excesses of Red China in terms of historic development of the "realm of the middle" or nationalism. Without denying that such elements exist, it is impossible to view the irrational policies of the Mao regime as anything but the consequences of doctrinal mania. Otherwise the regime's foreign policies and internal insanities would be inexplicable. The "great proletarian cultural revolution," which probably has set back Chinese development for at least a decade, can only be diagnosed as a political-ideological schizophrenia and shows what havoc a militant religion can create. Indeed, the rational elements in Marxist–Leninist doctrine have been virtually eliminated by Mao's "thought" which is a sinicized and distorted interpretation of European Marxism whose interpretation by Lenin and Stalin was bad enough but at least showed some flashes of rationality. There can be no question, then, that ideology has not eroded in China mainland but, on the contrary, has run amuck.

In contrast, the Soviet Union presents the appearance of a sophisticated power. But has it become a traditional nation–state since the denigration of Stalin? Are its actions and policies explainable in terms of nationalism? The answer is a clear and unequivocal no. Change does not necessarily mean erosion. Change may be tactical and, in some respects, even strategic but the fundamental rationale of Soviet positions is a revolutionary world outlook. We are used to view the term revolution as indicative of bloody upheavals and even wars. This no longer is the case. The strategy of "peaceful coexistence," developed as a result of the nuclear balance of terror, is an eminently clever device for a revolution by "peaceful" means as proclaimed by Khrushchev at the 20th CPSU Congress in 1956. *Pravda*, the Soviet Communist Party organ, reminded us in early 1967 what the party — and therefore the government — of the USSR

stands for.[1] In previewing the fiftieth anniversary of the CPSU
Central Committee it was made clear that the Chinese communists
have no monopoly for revolutionary behavior. The Soviet Union was
described as waging a revolutionary war of the proletariat against
Western capitalism and imperialism, and against the bourgeois conception of the world, until the final victory of communism. The
language of this statement was almost Stalinist in tone, and it is
noticeable that, in conjunction with this position, the Kremlin leaders
also discourage reformist tendencies in the communist parties of
Eastern Europe as well as those in the West and elsewhere. Although
it is doubtful that their admonition will be heeded by the more independent parties, it serves as a reminder that with all its apparent
moderation and changes in both communist strategies and tactics,
Moscow will remain the power center of world revolution.

Nevertheless, the conflict between Moscow and Peking has greatly
embarrassed the Kremlin's foreign policy and forced it to de-empha-
size its ideological stance. Following the development of polycentric
communism, it had to postpone, for the time being at least, the goal
of unified world communism under Soviet guidance. Even the much
looser concept of the voluntaristic "socialist commonwealth" has
been fractured; the idea is not dead, but at present limited to the
Soviet–East European bloc. While Moscow was careful not to permit
its former satellites to weaken unduly their ties with Moscow, there
was no halt in the race toward more independence, at least in the
internal affairs of these countries. However, the events in Poland
and Hungary have demonstrated what the Soviet leaders will let pass
and what for them is unpardonable.

The leaders of the East European states are communists but they
also have their national interests in mind. But these interests are
coordinated with or, if necessary, subordinated to the requirements
of their communist parties. In turn, these parties are in close touch
with the CPSU. Domestic politics and, to some extent, economic
policies, have freed themselves from overweening Soviet control;

---

[1] Cf. the theses of the CPSU Central Committee of June 25, 1967, "On the 50th
Anniversary of the Great October Socialist Revolution."

countries like Romania have gone to great lengths to demonstrate their independence of action. However, it would be self-deception to assume that important foreign and military policy decisions could be made against Soviet interests. Nor is it likely that the USSR would permit any of these states to quit the Warsaw Pact organization. This is particularly so in the strategic northern tier of Eastern Europe, comprising Poland, East Germany, and Czechoslovakia and, to some extent, Hungary. But on the whole, the entire area is a Soviet security sphere, a consideration which unquestionably is as important for the Kremlin as is the maintenance of an ideological stance. Yugoslavia, it should be noted, is not a part of this Soviet *cordon sanitaire*. Indeed, its League of Communists has now decided to remain merely the guide and mentor of the country and leave government to the proper specialized authorities, while elsewhere in Eastern Europe the parties still are in command of governments.

Important changes have occurred in the "socialist camp" since the advent of Khrushchev. They may be for better or worse but they indicate movement and, so far as the Soviet bloc is concerned, adjustment. They have greatly confused many Western interpreters of political events who were married to the concept of Stalinist communism and could not accept as genuine any other communism. But even they would not deny that the flexibility and increasing sophistication of post-Stalinist Soviet communism plus the emergence of an extremely aggressive and politically irrational Red China do not presage happy times ahead. In the words of Lenin, "What is to be done?"

Individuals and countries must roll with the punches. They must either go forward or decline. If the democracies insist on their *status quo,* time and fate will by-pass them. To obtain the New, they must relinquish the Old. In the lives of men nothing is permanent; the only immutable is change itself. It follows that in order not to lose such vital ingredients of democracy as the freedom and dignity of the individual, lesser privileges can and should be sacrificed. For example, the maintenance of a strong national economy need not necessarily be built upon the foundations of luxury and hedonism. The preservation of peacetime budgeting under conditions of nuclear stalemate is not necessarily the safest approach to national security. The liberty of the individual to do as he pleases must be subjected to and limited by communal and national responsibilities without abridging his freedom of expression. The self-interest of one nation has to be restricted by the requirements of allied or like-minded states and such restriction may be even tighter if the nation commands a leading position. The business of a country, be it political, economic, social, or technical, can no longer be conducted with haphazard *laissez-faire* individualism; it must be planned to meet the totalitarian threat.

These may seem to be unpopular suggestions, yet they propose remedies against democratic calcification and demonstrate the need for new departures toward vigorous policies. In the last analysis, the stalemate affecting East–West relations is not only of a technological nature; it is one in which the rejuvenation of policies and actions shares equal importance.

The revolutionary convulsions of the globe have led to a rapid deterioration of traditional relations among nations. In the new world emerging, the West must match the vigor of communist brains and brawn. It has the resources to do so, but must develop an awareness of the nature of the threat it faces and channel its counter-measures to meet the core of the danger rather than its periphery. Most of all, it must throw an intellectual switch from the nineteenth to the twentieth century and prepare for the twenty-first. Once this is accomplished, the ideological and technological stalemate will no longer put the West in a purely defensive position. Knowing more of our adversaries than we do now, we would be better prepared to counter their moves or anticipate them. Perhaps, once this is appreciated on the other side of the Curtains, an accommodation might be obtained that is more than temporary. We cannot expect a "kingdom of heaven on earth," imperfect as we are. But we can hope for a long-range evolution which would eliminate futility and restore sanity. Admittedly, this hope is vague, yet it points to the only possible solution of the permanent crisis which disorients relations among nations and perpetuates that political no-man's-land in which we dare not make war and cannot achieve peace.

Bibliography

Contemporary World Politics

GYORGY, A., and P. A. TOMA. *Basic Issues in International Relations.* Boston: Allyn and Bacon, 1967.

HOLSTI, K. J. *International Politics: A Framework for Analysis.* Englewood Cliffs, N.J.: Prentice–Hall, 1967.

KULSKI, W. W. *International Politics in a Revolutionary Age.* Philadelphia: J. B. Lippincott, 1964.

LONDON, K. *The Making of Foreign Policy: East and West.* Philadelphia: J. B. Lippincott, 1965.

MACRIDIS, R. C. (ed.). *Foreign Policy in World Politics.* 3rd ed. Englewood Cliffs, N.J.: Prentice–Hall, 1967.

MCNEAL, R. H. (ed.). *International Relations Among Communists.* Englewood Cliffs, N.J.: Prentice–Hall, 1967.

OLSON, W. C., and F. A. SONDERMANN (eds.). *The Theory and Practice of International Relations.* 2nd ed. Englewood Cliffs, N.J.: Prentice–Hall, 1966.

ROSENAU, J. N. (ed.). *International Politics and Foreign Policy.* New York: The Free Press, 1961.

SETON–WATSON, H. *Neither War Nor Peace: The Struggle for Power in the Post War World.* New York: F. A. Praeger, 1960.

SNYDER, R. C., H. W. BRUCK, and B. SAPIN (eds.). *Foreign Policy Decision-Making.* New York: The Free Press, 1962.

SPANIER, J. W. *World Politics in an Age of Revolution.* New York: F. A. Praeger, 1967.

SPROUT, H. and M. *Foundations of International Politics.* Princeton, N.J.: Van Nostrand, 1962.

STOESSINGER, J. G. *The Might of Nations: World Politics in Our Time.* 2nd ed. New York: Random House, 1965.

VAN DYKE, V. *International Politics.* 2nd ed. New York: Appleton–Century–Crofts, 1966.

Communism and Ideology

BLACK, C. E., and T. P. THORNTON (eds.). *Communism and Revolution.* Princeton, N.J.: Princeton University Press, 1964.

BORKENAU, F. *World Communism*. Ann Arbor, Mich.: University of Michigan Press, 1962.

BRZEZINSKI, Z. K. *Ideology and Power in Soviet Politics*. New York: F. A. Praeger, 1962.

COHEN, A. A. *The Communism of Mao Tse-tung*. Chicago: University of Chicago Press, 1964.

DALLIN, A. (ed.). *Diversity in International Communism*. New York: Columbia University Press, 1963.

DANIELS, R. V. *The Nature of Communism*. New York: Vintage Books, 1963.

DRACHKOVITCH, M. (ed.). *Marxism in the Modern World*. Stanford, Calif.: published for the Hoover Institution on War, Revolution, and Peace, by Stanford University Press, 1965.

———. *Marxist Ideology in the Contemporary World*. New York: published for the Hoover Institution on War, Revolution, and Peace, Stanford University, Stanford, California, by F. A. Praeger, 1966.

GRIFFITH, W. E. (ed.). *Communism in Europe*. Cambridge, Mass.: The MIT Press, 1964.

GYORGY, A., and G. D. BLACKWOOD. *Ideologies in World Affairs*. Boston: Blaisdell Publishing Company, 1967.

GYORGY, A. (ed.). *Issues of World Communism*. Princeton, N.J.: Van Nostrand, 1966.

HUNT, R. N. C. *The Theory and Practice of Communism*. Baltimore: Penguin Books, 1963.

LOWENTHAL, R. *World Communism*. New York: Oxford University Press, 1964.

MEYER, A. G. *Leninism*. New York: F. A. Praeger, 1962.

———. *Marxism*. Cambridge, Mass.: Harvard University Press, 1954.

RAMUNDO, B. A. *Peaceful Coexistence: International Law in the Building of Communism*. Baltimore: The Johns Hopkins Press, 1967.

RUBINSTEIN, A. Z. *Communist Political Systems*. Englewood Cliffs, N.J.: Prentice–Hall, 1966.

TREADGOLD, R. W. (ed.). *Soviet and Chinese Communism: Similarities and Differences*. Seattle, Washington: University of Washington Press, 1967.

Foreign Policies of the Western Alliance

CRABB, C. V., JR. *American Foreign Policy in the Nuclear Age*. 2nd ed. New York: Harper and Row, 1965.

GERBERDING, W. *United States Foreign Policy: Perspectives and Analysis.* New York: McGraw–Hill, 1966.

GROSSNER, A. *French Foreign Policy Under De Gaulle.* Translated from French by L. A. Pattison. Boston: Little, Brown and Co., 1967.

HARTMAN, F. H. *Germany Between East and West: The Reunification Problem.* Englewood Cliffs, N.J.: Prentice–Hall, 1965.

JACOBSON, H. K. (ed.). *America's Foreign Policy.* Rev. ed. New York: Random House, 1965.

KULSKI, W. W. *De Gaulle and the World: The Foreign Policy of the Fifth French Republic.* Syracuse, N.Y.: Syracuse University, 1966.

MORLEY, J. W. *Japan and Korea: America's Allies in the Pacific.* New York: Walker and Co., 1965.

RICHARDSON, J. L. *Germany and the Atlantic Alliance.* Cambridge, Mass.: Harvard University Press, 1966.

SEABURG, P. *Power, Freedom, and Diplomacy: The Foreign Policy of the United States of America.* New York: Random House, 1963.

SPANIER, J. *American Foreign Policy Since World War II.* 2nd rev. ed. New York: F. A. Praeger, 1965.

WALTZ, K. N. *Foreign Policy and Democratic Politics: The American and British Experience.* Boston: Little, Brown and Co., 1967.

WOODHOUSE, C. M. *British Foreign Policy Since the Second World War.* New York: F. A. Praeger, 1962.

YOUNGER, K. G. *Changing Perspectives in British Foreign Policy.* New York: Oxford University Press, 1964.

Soviet Foreign Policy

ASPATURIAN, V. V. *The Soviet Union in the World Communist System.* Stanford, Calif.: published for the Hoover Institution on War, Revolution, and Peace, by Stanford University Press, 1966.

DALLIN, D. *Soviet Foreign Policy After Stalin.* Philadelphia: J. B. Lippincott, 1961.

LIBRACH, J. *The Rise of the Soviet Empire.* Rev. ed. New York: F. A. Praeger, 1966.

MACKINTOSH, J. M. *Strategy and Tactics of Soviet Foreign Policy.* New York: Oxford University Press, 1963.

McLANE, C. B. *Soviet Strategies in Asia under Lenin and Stalin.* Princeton, N.J.: Princeton University Press, 1966.

RUBINSTEIN, A. Z. (ed.). *The Foreign Policy of the Soviet Union*. 2nd ed. New York: Random House, 1966.

SHULMAN, M. *Stalin's Foreign Policy Reappraised*. New York: Atheneum Publishers, 1965.

WARTH, R. D. *Soviet Russia in World Politics*. New York: Twayne Publishers, Inc., 1963.

Chinese Foreign Policy

BLUM, R., edited by D. BARNETT. *The U.S. and China in World Affairs*. New York: published for the Council on Foreign Relations by McGraw–Hill, 1966.

BOYD, R. G. *Communist China's Foreign Policy*. New York: F. A. Praeger, 1962.

BUCHAN, A. (ed.). *China and the Peace of Asia*. New York: F. A. Praeger, 1965.

HALPERN, A. M. (ed.). *Policies Toward China: Views from Six Continents*. New York: published for the Council on Foreign Relations by McGraw–Hill, 1965.

HINTON, H. C. *Communist China in World Politics*. Boston: Houghton Mifflin, 1966.

NORTH, R. C. *Chinese Communism*. New York: McGraw–Hill, 1966.

The Sino–Soviet Conflict

DOOLIN, D. J. *Predatorial Claims in the Sino–Soviet Conflict*. Stanford, Calif.: The Hoover Institution, 1965.

GRIFFITH, W. E. *The Sino–Soviet Rift*. Cambridge, Mass.: The MIT Press, 1964.

——. *Sino–Soviet Relations, 1964–1965*. Cambridge, Mass.: The MIT Press, 1967.

HONEY, P. J. *Communism in North Vietnam: Its Role in the Sino–Soviet Dispute*. Cambridge, Mass.: The MIT Press, 1963.

HUDSON, G. F., R. LOWENTHAL, and R. MACFARQUHAR. *The Sino–Soviet Dispute*. New York: F. A. Praeger, 1961.

LONDON, K. (ed.). *Unity and Contradiction: Major Aspects of Sino–Soviet Relations*. New York: F. A. Praeger, 1962.

MEHNERT, K. *Peking and Moscow*. New York: Mentor Press, 1964.

NORTH, R. C. *Moscow and Chinese Communists.* 2nd rev. ed. Stanford, Calif.: Stanford University Press, 1963.

ZAGORIA, D. S. *The Sino–Soviet Conflict, 1956–1961.* New York: Atheneum Publishers, 1964.

Eastern Europe

BENES, V., A. GYORGY, and G. STAMBUK. *Eastern European Government and Politics.* New York: Harper and Row, 1966.

BROMKE, A. *The Communist States at the Crossroads between Moscow and Peking.* New York: F. A. Praeger, 1965.

BROWN, J. F. *The New Eastern Europe: The Khrushchev Era and After.* New York: F. A. Praeger, 1966.

BURKS, R. V. *The Dynamics of Communism in Eastern Europe.* Princeton, N.J.: Princeton University Press, 1961.

BYRNES, R. F. (ed.). *Eastern Europe and the U.S.* Englewood Cliffs, N.J.: Prentice–Hall, 1967.

FISCHER–GALATI, S. A. (ed.). *Eastern Europe in the Sixties.* New York: F. A. Praeger, 1963.

LONDON, K. (ed.). *Eastern Europe in Transition.* Baltimore: The Johns Hopkins Press, 1966.

SKILLING, H. G. *The Governments of Communist East Europe.* New York: Thomas Y. Crowell, 1966.

Communism and the Third World

BRZEZINSKI, Z. K. (ed.). *Africa and the Communist World.* Stanford, Calif.: published for the Hoover Institution on War, Revolution, and Peace, by Stanford University Press, 1963.

KAUTSKY, J. H. (ed.). *Political Change in Underdeveloped Countries: Nationalism and Communism.* New York: John Wiley, 1962.

KURZMAN, D. *Subversion of the Innocents: Patterns of Communist Penetration in Africa, the Middle East, and Asia.* New York: Random House, 1963.

LONDON, K. (ed.). *New Nations in a Divided World: The International Relations of the Afro–Asian States.* New York: F. A. Praeger, 1963.

POPPINO, R. E. *International Communism in Latin America: A History of the Movement, 1917–1963.* New York: The Free Press, 1964.

SCALAPINO, R. A. (ed.). *The Communist Revolution in Asia.* Englewood Cliffs, N.J.: Prentice–Hall, 1965.

SCHATTEN, F. *Communism in Africa.* New York: F. A. Praeger, 1966.

THORNTON, T. P. (ed.). *The Third World in Soviet Perspective.* Princeton, N.J.: Princeton University Press, 1964.

WORSLEY, P. *The Third World.* Chicago: University of Chicago Press, 1964.

Cold War Economics

AMES, E. *Soviet Economic Processes.* Homewood, Ill.: Richard D. Irwin, Inc., 1965.

BERGSON, A., and S. KUZNETS (eds.). *Economic Trends in the Soviet Union.* Cambridge, Mass.: Harvard University Press, 1963.

FEIS, H. *Foreign Aid and Foreign Policy.* New York: St. Martin's Press, 1964.

GOLDMAN, M. *Soviet Foreign Aid.* New York: F. A. Praeger, 1966.

HOLZMAN, F. D. (ed.). *Readings on the Soviet Economy.* Chicago: Rand McNally and Co., 1962.

KASER, M. *Comecon.* London: Oxford University Press, 1965.

MASON, E. S. *Foreign Aid and Foreign Policy.* New York: published for the Council on Foreign Relations by Harper and Row, 1964.

NOVE, A. *The Soviet Economy: An Introduction.* New York: F. A. Praeger, 1962.

PLOSS, S. I. *Conflict and Decision-Making in Soviet Russia: A Case Study of Agricultural Policy, 1953–1963.* Princeton, N.J.: Princeton University Press, 1965.

SAWYER, C. A. *Communist Trade with Developing Countries, 1955–65.* New York: F. A. Praeger, 1966.

SCHWARTZ, H. *The Soviet Economy Since Stalin.* Philadelphia: J. B. Lippincott, 1965.

SPULBER, N. *Soviet Strategy for Economic Growth.* Bloomington, Ind.: Indiana University Press, 1964.

U.S. CONGRESS, JOINT ECONOMIC COMMITTEE. *Dimensions of Soviet Economic Power.* Washington: U.S. Government Printing Office, 1962.

——. *Current Economic Indicators for the U.S.S.R.* Washington: U.S. Government Printing Office, 1965.

——. *New Directions in the Soviet Economy.* Washington: U.S. Government Printing Office, 1966.

——. *An Economic Profile of Mainland China.* 2 vols. Washington: U.S. Government Printing Office, 1967.

The United Nations

BLAISDELL, D. C. *International Organization.* New York: The Ronald Press Co., 1966.

CLAUDE, I. L. *The Changing United Nations.* New York: Random House and Alfred A. Knopf, 1967.

DALLIN, A. *The Soviet Union at the United Nations.* New York: F. A. Praeger, 1962.

GOODSPEED, S. S. *The Nature and Function of International Organization.* 2nd ed. New York: Oxford University Press, 1967.

LARUS, J. (ed.). *From Collective Security to Preventive Diplomacy.* New York: John Wiley, 1965.

PADELFORD, N. J., and L. M. GOODRICH (eds.). *The United Nations in the Balance.* New York: F. A. Praeger, 1965.

Disarmament

BRENNAN, D. G. (ed.). *Arms Control, Disarmament and National Security.* New York: Braziller, 1961.

CLEMENS, W. C. *Soviet Disarmament Policy, 1917–1963: An Annotated Bibliography.* Stanford, Calif.: Stanford University Press, 1965.

DALLIN, A., et al. *The Soviet Union and Disarmament: An Appraisal of Soviet Attitudes and Intentions.* New York: F. A. Praeger, 1964.

HALPERIN, M. H. *Sino–Soviet Relations and Arms Control.* Cambridge, Mass.: The MIT Press, 1967.

HALPERIN, M. H., and D. H. PERKINS. *Communist China and Arms Control.* New York: F. A. Praeger, 1965.

SCHELLING, T. C. *Arms and Influence.* New Haven, Conn.: Yale University Press, 1966.

WOLFERS, A., et al. *The United States in a Disarmed World.* Baltimore: The Johns Hopkins Press, 1966.

Protective Alliances

BUCHAN, A. *NATO in the 1960's.* Rev. ed. New York: F. A. Praeger, 1963.

CERNY, K. H., and H. W. BRIEFS (eds.). *NATO in Quest of Cohesion.* New York: published for the Hoover Institution on War, Revolution, and Peace, by F. A. Praeger, 1965.

COTTRELL, A. J., and J. E. DOUGHERTY. *The Politics of the Atlantic Alliance.* New York: F. A. Praeger, 1964.

FURNISS, E. S., JR. (ed.). *The Western Alliance: Its Status and Prospects.* Chicago: University of Chicago Press, 1966.

GRZYBOWSKI, K. *The Socialist Commonwealth of Nations: Organizations and Institutions.* New Haven, Conn.: Yale University Press, 1964.

LAWSON, R. C. (ed.). *International Regional Organizations: Constitutional Foundations.* New York: F. A. Praeger, 1962.

MODELSKI, G. (ed.). *SEATO.* Vancouver: Publication Centre, University of British Columbia, 1963.

STANLEY, T. W. *NATO in Transition: The Future of the Atlantic Alliance.* New York: published for the Council on Foreign Relations by F. A. Praeger, 1965.

THOMAS, A. V., and A. J. THOMAS. *The Organization of American States.* Dallas: Southern Methodist University Press, 1963.

War and Peace in the Nuclear Age

ARON, R. *The Great Debate: Theories of Nuclear Strategy.* Garden City, New York: Doubleday and Company, Inc., 1965.

BRODIE, B. *Strategy in the Missile Age.* Princeton, N.J.: Princeton University Press, 1959.

——. *Escalation and the Nuclear Option.* Princeton, N.J.: Princeton University Press, 1966.

BROWN, N. *Nuclear War: The Impending Strategic Deadlock.* New York: F. A. Praeger, 1965.

DINERSTEIN, H. S. *War and the Soviet Union; Nuclear Weapons and the Revolution in Soviet Military and Political Thinking.* Rev. ed. New York: F. A. Praeger, 1962.

GARTHOFF, R. L. *Soviet Military Policy: A Historical Analysis.* New York: F. A. Praeger, 1966.

——. *Soviet Strategy in the Nuclear Age.* Rev. ed. New York: F. A. Praeger, 1962.

HALPERIN, M. *China and the Bomb.* New York: F. A. Praeger, 1965.

HEILBRUNN, O. *Conventional Warfare in the Nuclear Age.* New York: F. A. Praeger, 1965.

HORELICK, A. L., and M. RUSH. *Strategic Power and Soviet Foreign Policy.* Chicago: University of Chicago Press, 1966.

HSIEH, A. L. *Communist China's Strategy in the Nuclear Era.* Englewood Cliffs, N.J.: Prentice–Hall, 1962.

KISSINGER, H. A. (ed.). *Problems of National Strategy.* New York: F. A. Praeger, 1965.

KNORR, K. *On the Uses of Military Power in the Nuclear Age.* Princeton, N.J.: Princeton University Press, 1966.

KOLKOWICZ, R. *The Soviet Military and the Communist Party.* Princeton, N.J.: Princeton University Press, 1967.

WOLFE, T. W. *Soviet Strategy at the Crossroads.* Cambridge, Mass.: Harvard University Press, 1965.

Intelligence

DULLES, A. W. *The Craft of Intelligence.* New York: Harper and Row, 1963.

DE GRAMONT, S. *The Secret War: The Story of International Espionage Since 1945.* New York: G. P. Putnam's Sons, 1962.

HILSMAN, R. *Strategic Intelligence and National Decisions.* Glencoe, Ill.: The Free Press, 1956.

KENT, S. *Strategic Intelligence.* Princeton, N.J.: Princeton University Press, 1966.

KNORR, K. E. *Foreign Intelligence and the Social Sciences.* Princeton, N.J.: Princeton University Press, 1964.

PLATT, W. *Strategic Intelligence Production: Basic Principles.* New York: F. A. Praeger, 1957.

RANSOM, H. H. *Central Intelligence and National Security.* Cambridge, Mass.: Harvard University Press, 1958.

Diplomacy

IKLÉ, F. C. *How Nations Negotiate.* New York: Harper and Row, 1964.

JOHNSON, E. A. J. (ed.). *The Dimensions of Diplomacy,* by McGeorge

Bundy (and others). Baltimore: The Johns Hopkins Press, 1964.

KERTESZ, S. D. *The Quest for Peace Through Diplomacy.* Englewood Cliffs, N.J.: Prentice–Hall, 1967.

KERTESZ, S. D., and M. A. FITZSIMMONS. *Diplomacy in a Changing World.* South Bend, Ind.: University of Notre Dame Press, 1961.

KLINEBERG, O. *The Human Dimension in International Relations.* New York: Holt and Rinehart, 1964.

LALL, A. *Modern International Negotiation.* New York: Columbia University Press, 1966.

NICOLSON, H. G. *Diplomacy.* 3rd ed. London: Oxford University Press, 1963.

PEARSON, L. B. *Diplomacy in the Nuclear Age.* Cambridge, Mass.: Harvard University Press, 1959.

SATOW, E. M. *A Guide to Diplomatic Practice.* 4th ed., edited by N. Bland. London: Longmans, Green, 1958.

Propaganda

BARGHOORN, F. C. *The Soviet Cultural Offensive.* Princeton, N.J.: Princeton University Press, 1960.

———. *Soviet Foreign Propaganda.* Princeton, N.J.: Princeton University Press, 1964.

BROWN, J. A. *Techniques of Persuasion: From Propaganda to Brainwashing.* Baltimore: Penguin Books, 1963.

CLEWS, J. C. *Communist Propaganda Techniques.* New York: F. A. Praeger, 1964.

FRANKEL, C. *The Neglected Aspect of Foreign Affairs: American Educational and Cultural Policy Abroad.* Washington: Brookings Institution, 1966.

GORDON, G. N., I. FALK, and W. HODAPP. *The Idea Invaders.* New York: Hastings House, 1963.

JOYCE, W. *The Propaganda Gap.* New York: Harper and Row, 1963.

LIFTON, R. J. *Thought Reform and the Psychology of Totalism: A Study of "Brainwashing" in China.* New York: W. W. Norton, 1961.

MARTIN, L. J. *International Propaganda: Its Legal and Diplomatic Control.* Minneapolis, Minn.: University of Minnesota Press, 1958.

PASSIN, H. *China's Cultural Diplomacy.* New York: F. A. Praeger, 1963.

QUALTER, T. H. *Propaganda and Psychological Warfare*. New York: Random House, 1962.

U.S. CONGRESS, HOUSE COMMITTEE ON FOREIGN AFFAIRS. *Modern Communications and Foreign Policy*, Report #5 of *Winning the Cold War: The U.S. Ideological Offensive*. Washington: U.S. Government Printing Office, 1967.

WHITAKER, U. J. (ed.). *Propaganda and International Relations*. San Francisco: Chandler Publishing House, 1963.

WHITTON, J. B. *Propaganda and the Cold War: A Princeton University Symposium*. Washington: Public Affairs Press, 1963.

YU, F. T. C. *Mass Persuasion in Communist China*. New York: F. A. Praeger, 1964.

Africa: communism, spread of, 87
  nationalism in, 11
  Soviet aid to, 80
Afro–Asian bloc: constitutions of, 67
  foreign aid to, 73
  neutrality, 11
Albania: economic freedom, 57
  in Greece, support of communists, 119
  independence from Moscow, 97
  Soviet support, 110
  22nd Communist Party Congress, 127
Alliances: against Soviet encroachment, 107
  economic, 60
  forming, 9–12
  post war, trade, 57–58
  protective, 98–115
  See also NATO, SEATO, etc.
Anglo–Iraqi Agreement, 107
Anti-ballistic missile system, 94, 122
ANZUS treaty (1951), 104
  and SEATO treaty, 106
Arab–Israeli war (1967), 82
Arab League, 107, 116–117
Arab states, communist sympathies, 17–18
Arms control, 93–98
Asia: communism, spread of, 87
  de-nuclearized zone, 94
  economic socialism, 75
  ethnic minorities, 49
  religion in, 60
  Soviet aid to, 80
Aswan dam, 82
Atlantic Charter (1941), 115
Atom bomb, 90–91, 122, 124
Atomic age, 6
  technological advances, 10
Australia: ANZUS treaty, 104
  in SEATO, 104
Austro–Hungarian empire, balance of power, 90
Autarky, 87–89
Azerbaijan, Soviet activities in, 107, 118

Baghdad Pact, 106–108
Baguio conference, 104
Balance of power, 9, 72, 89–91
Balance of terror, 93

Balanced economy, 58–59
Baltic states, loss of independence, 110
Bandung principles, 127n.
Basic Law (West Germany), 141–142
Bay of Pigs, CIA and, 174
Belgium: balanced economy, 59
  and Locarno Pact, 92
  NATO and, 100
  Brussels Treaty, 100
Berlin blockade, 99, 119, 202
Bilateral agreements, 10
Bipartisan international policy, 65
Bipolar power concentration, 5
Bipolarity, political, 10–12
Birth control, 46
Bogotá Conference (1948), 100
British Empire-Commonwealth, 59
Brussels Treaty (1948), 100
Buddhism, religious minority, 50
Bulganin, ouster of Malenkov, 218
Bulgaria: and CEMA, 111
  in Greece, support of communists, 119
  population growth, 46
Burma, SEATO treaty, 106

Cambodia, and SEATO treaty, 106
Canada, and NATO, 100
Capitalism, laissez-faire, 55
CEMA, 57, 110–113
  and eastern European economy, 76
CENTO, 106–109
  trade relations, 57–58
Central Intelligence Agency (US), 167, 175–177
Central Europe, Soviet seizure, 99
Central Treaty Organization. See CENTO.
Ceylon, and Pacific security, 104
Chapultepec Pact, 116
Chiang Kai-shek, 150
China. See Red China.
Christians, as religious minority, 50
Churchill, Sir Winston Spencer:
  Atlantic Charter, 115
  and de Gaulle, 103
Classless society, and minorities, 49
Clausewitz, Karl von, 13, 90
Climate, and national strengths, 38–40
Climatic psychology, 39

Coalition, international policies, 65
Cold war, Moscow–Peking, 4. *See also*
　　Moscow–Peking axis.
Collective security, 91–93, 96
Colombo Plan, 105
Colonialism: disappearing, 59
　and economic assistance, 61
　Western Europe/U.S., 79–80
COMECON, 57, 111
Cominform, 110
　and Tito, 218
Comintern, propaganda from, 212
Common Market, 27
　and CEMA, 112
　France and, 4
　and NATO, 101
Communication, East–West, lack of, 7
Communications techniques, 6
Communism: Five Year Plans, 56
　and foreign aid, 79
　　for political reasons, 82
　impact of, 219
　internationality of, 18
　in Middle East, 37
　neo-Leninist concepts, 25–26
　spread of, since World War II, 87
　types of, 16
　and West, outstripping, 97–98
Communist economy, qualifying, 82
Communist party: Central Committee
　　rules, 147
　ideology of, 15, 209
　and neutralism, 88
　Politburo, 147
　rules Soviet, 146
　Stalin's denigration, 16, 222
　20th CPSU Congress, 4, 124, 125–
　　126, 222
　21st CPSU Congress, 28, 53, 111–112
　22nd CPSU Congress, 127
Communist states, and minorities, 49
Conference of Communist and Workers
　　Parties, 127
Conformity, 25, 28
Confucianism, religious minority, 50–51
Congo (Brazzaville), neo-colonialism, 17
Congress of Vienna, 10, 187, 196
Constitutional law, 67
　and foreign policy, 132
Constitutional philosophies, 67–68
Council of Mutual Economic Assistance,
　　57, 111
Cuban missile crisis, 125
Cultural diplomacy, 203
Cultural relations, as propaganda, 203–
　　205
Culture, national, 204
Cyprus, UN in, 120

Czechoslovakia: and CEMA, 111
　German minorities in, 49
　and Locarno Pact, 92
　Soviet influence, 110, 224
　Soviet seizure, 99
　and Warsaw Pact, 113

Defense measures, and foreign policy, 13
Defense potential, and foreign policy,
　　121
Defense strategy, Western, 95–96
de Gaulle, General Charles:
　on Common Market, 4
　foreign policy, 133, 140
　hatred of U.S. and Great Britain, 103
　national grandeur, 4
　national security, 159
　NATO, 102–104
Democracy: and domestic politics, 64
　foreign policy and, 132–133
　international relations, 65
　majority will, 66
Demography, 44–48
Denmark, and NATO, 100
Depopulation, and power ratio, 47
Deterrence of power, 10–11
Dialectical materialism, 16
Dictatorships, and domestic policies, 64.
　　See also Totalitarian states.
Diplomacy, 187–193
　concepts of, 187–188, 199–200
　cultural, 203
　envoys plenipotentiary, 189
　lip service to customs, 16
　personal, 198
　and propaganda, 188, 199–216
　summit conferences, 196–197, 198
　types of, 199–206
　Western dilemma of, 198
　Western style, 192–193
　Wilsonian concept, 187
Diplomats: Eastern bloc, 192–193
　free world, independence of, 190
　modern, 188–189, 191
　personality of, 22–31
　training, 192
　Western, freedom of action, 191
Disarmament, 93–98
　and economic upheaval, 95
Domestic policy, and foreign policy, 123
Dulles, John Foster, 82
Dunkirk Treaty (1947), 100

East, power in, 145–151
East Germany: and CEMA, 111
　economic freedom, 57
　intelligence system, 179
　People's Army, 113

Soviet influence, 110, 224
and Warsaw Pact, 113
East–West cultural exchange, 204
East–West negotiations, 193–198
Eastern bloc, and national security, 86
and newly-independent countries, 17
Eastern Europe: economy of, 58
and CEMA, 71
ethnic minorities, 49
intelligence system, 179
polycentric communism, 4, 221
security problem, 97
trade, Western Europe, 57
Economic aid, 66
Economic analysis, 83
Economic assistance, 60–61
Economic freedom, 57
Economic geography, 55–62
Economic individualism, 72–73
Economic influence, U.S./Great Britain, 73
Economic liberalism, 73
Economic and Social Council of the United Nations, 77
Economic socialism, 75
Economic stability, 61
Economic status, 62
Economic systems, and foreign affairs, 72
Economic upheaval, and disarmament, 95
Economic warfare, 72
Economy, cold war, 72–85
communist, qualifying, 82
domestic, and foreign affairs, 72
Red China, 61–62
U.S./Soviet, 61
Education: polytechnical, 53
Red China, 54–55
Soviet, 53
Soviet theses, 26
technology and, 51–55
Egypt: Arab League, 107
Baghdad Pact, 108
Soviet aid to, 81
Eisenhower, Dwight D.:
on diplomacy, 196
Khrushchev conference, 197
national security, 154
Entente cordiale, 10
Environmental changes, 6
Envoys plenipotentiary, 189
Estonia, Soviet incorporation, 110
Ethical concepts, Western, 5
Ethnic minorities, 49
EURATOM, and CEMA, 112
Europe: de-nuclearized zone, 94
ethnic minorities, 49

national security, 86
population growth, 44–45
European Free Trade Association. *See* Outer Seven.
European Payment Union, 112
European Recovery Program. *See* Marshall Plan.
Export–Import Bank, 77
Exports/imports, 60, 75

Federal Republic of Germany. *See* West Germany.
Food supply, 46
Foreign affairs, 13–31
bipolar conduct, 187–198
communism, impact of, 219
domestic economy and, 72
intangible hazards, 30
leadership in, 27–31
public opinion and, 68–69
Foreign aid: Red China, 78–79, 91
Soviet, 78–79, 81–83
United States, 72–73, 76–85
See also Economic aid.
Foreign policy, 13–18
aspects of, 13
constitutional law and, 132
defense measure, 13
defense potential, 121
diplomats' domain, 187
domestic policies and, 123
formulation: France, 133, 139–143
Great Britain, 133, 137–139
Japan, 143–145
Red China, 149–151
Soviet Union, 145–149
United States, 133, 134–137
West Germany, 141–143
intelligence system and, 163
non-communist, 17
prime objective, 13
of revolutionary governments, 2
war as continuation of, 13, 90
Foreign relations, economic systems and, 72
France: Brussels Treaty (1948), 100
Common Market, 4
communist unrest, 99
cultural relations, 203
de Gaulle and NATO, 102–104
Dunkirk Treaty (1949), 100
foreign policy, 133, 139–143
geopolitics, 35
group pressures, 65
"guided democracy," 140
intelligence system, 178
Locarno Pact, 92
national security, 159

and NATO, 100, 102–104
Nazi aggression, 99
nuclear development, 103
nuclear weapons treaty, unsigned, 94
population, 47
SEATO, 104
Soviet conferences, 197
U.S. aid to, 77
Western power, 139–141
Free enterprise system, 72, 73
French Union, disintegration of, 59

Gaza strip, UN in, 120
Geneva Convention (1955), 197
Geopolitics, 34–36
German–Russian entente (World War II), 36
cultural program, 203
Germany: East. *See* East Germany.
cultural program, 203
geopolitics, 35–36
Locarno Pact, 92
Nazi: attacks Soviet, 99
demography, 44
and geopolitics, 35, 37
population growth, 46–47
race superiority theory, 63
unilateral aggression, 99
Gosplan, 75
Great Britain: Baghdad Pact, 107
balance of power, 90
Brussels Treaty, 100
cultural relations, 203
Dunkirk Treaty (1947), 100
economic influence, 72–73
foreign policy, 133, 137–139
group pressures, 65
Industrial Revolution, 51
intelligence system, 167, 177–178
Locarno Pact, 92
NATO, 4, 100
Nazi aggression, 99
SEATO, 104
security policy, 152, 157–159
Soviet conferences, 197
U.S. aid to, 77
Western power, 137–139
Great Society program (U.S.), 130
Greece: Communists in, 119
Cyprus civil war, 120
NATO, 100
Soviet aggression, 99
U.S. aid to, 77
Gross National Product, U.S./Soviet, 83
Group pressures, 65
Guatemala, CIA and, 177

Hague Convention (1907), 88
Haushofer, Karl, and geopolitics, 35–36, 38
Hitler, Adolf:
foreign policy, 13
and geopolitics, 37
German minority groups, 49
violation of Locarno Pact (1936), 92
Holy alliance, 10, 90
Hull, Cordell, 69
Hungary: Soviet influence, 224
Soviet seizure, 99
Warsaw Pact, 113
Hydrogen bomb, 90–91, 122

Iceland: and NATO, 100
Soviet aid to, 80
Ideological empires, 2
Ideological schism, 8–12
Ideology, East/West, 15
Imperialism, 4, 91, 95
communist, 63
stigma of, for U.S., 81
India: neutrality, 12
non-alignment policy, 106n.
Pacific security, 104
Pakistani War (1965), 109
religion in, 50
Indochina, SEATO treaty, 106
Indonesia: Pacific security, 104
SEATO treaty, 106
Indo–Pakistani War (1965), 109
Industrial decentralization, 34
Industrial development, 33
Industrial Revolution (England), 51
Information: freedom of, 70
and propaganda, 200–201
See also Intelligence.
Information services, as propaganda, 201–202
"Inner Six." *See* Common Market.
Insecurity, 28
Intelligence: clandestine, 172–173
evaluation of, 165–166
fact-finding, 164–165
historical investigation, 164
mass communications, 170–172
and national leaders, 170
organizational aspects, 174–186
political and military, 163–186
research projects, 165
sources of, 168
strategic, 166–168, 176–177, 183, 185–186
theoretical aspects, 163–164
Intelligence systems: Eastern bloc, 179
France, 178
Great Britain, 177–178

Moscow–Peking, 182
NATO, 179–180
Red China, 183–186
Soviet, 180–183
United States, 167, 172, 174–177
West Germany, 179
Inter-American Pact of Chapultepec, 116
International Bank for Reconstruction and Development, 77
International Monetary Fund, 77
International organizations, 115–120
International policy, bipartisan and coalition, 65
International Red Cross, 9
International relations:
   changing aspects, 1–8
   and communism, impact of, 219
   deteriorating, 190
   and education, 26
   ideologies and, 63
   modern technology and, 219
   psychopathology in, 19–31
International state system, 8–12
International Student Union, 182
International trade, 60
   political economy and, 72
International Trade Organization, 77
Iran: CIA and, 177
   CENTO, 108
   Soviet aggression, 99
   Soviet aid to, 81
   Soviets in, 118
Iraq: Arab League, 107
   Baghdad Pact, 107
   revolution in (1958), 108
   Turkish Pact, 107
Islam, religious minority, 50
Islamic countries, isolation of, 8
Isolation, 87–89
   of Asia, 8
Israel, hatred of, 11–12
Italy: communist unrest, 99
   demography, 44
   and geopolitics, 35
   NATO, 100
   religious minorities in, 50
   Fascist: and Locarno Pact, 92
      population growth, 46
      unilateral aggression, 99

Jackson, Senator Henry M., 154–155
Japan: cultural relations, 203
   demography, 44
   foreign policy, 143–145
   group pressures, 65
   isolation of, 8
   national security, 159
   unilateral aggression, 99
U.S. security treaty, 104
   Western power, 143–145
Jews, religious minority, 50
Johnson, Lyndon B., 60
   Great Society program, 130
   national security, 155, 157
Jordan, Baghdad Pact, 108

Kashmir conflict, 109
Kennedy, John F.
   Cuban missile crisis, 124
   foreign aid program, 78
   Khrushchev conference, 197
   national security, 155, 157
Kjellen, Rudolf, and geopolitics, 36
Khrushchev, Nikita:
   Cuban missile crisis, 124
   denigration of Stalin, 16, 222
   educational program, 53
   Eisenhower conference, 197
   fall of, 133
   foreign aid, 80
   Kennedy conference, 197
   on nuclear war, 124
   ouster of Malenkov, 218
   "peaceful revolution," 222
   philosophy of, 211
   pragmatic communism, 103
   reform movement, 221
   Sputnik I, 126
   and Marshall Tito, 110
   torpedoing of Paris Conference, 197
   Western policies, 212
   and Marshal Zhukov, 130
Khrushchevism, 115
Korean War, UN and, 115, 119
Kuomintang, 150

Laos, SEATO treaty, 106
Latin America:
   communism, spread of, 27
   communist setbacks, 221
   de-nuclearized zone, 94
   Soviet aid to, 80
Latvia, Soviet incorporation, 110
Leadership: communist, 25, 53
   in foreign affairs, 23–31
League of Nations: Covenant of, 91
   end of, 115
   established, 8
   failure of, 92
   Soviet membership, 99
Lend–Lease program, 76, 77
Lenin, V. I.: on imperialism, 125
   philosophy of, 210
Liberty, East/West concepts of, 28–30
Liebermanism, 82
Lithuania, Soviet incorporation, 110

241

Locarno Pact (1925), 92–93, 115
Luxemburg, and NATO, 100

MacArthur, General Douglas, 147
Mackinder, Sir Halford 35–36, 37
Magsaysay, President Ramon, 105
Malenkov, G., ousted, 218
Mali, neocolonialism, 17
Manila Conference (1954), 104
Manila Treaty, 105
Mao Tse-tung: birth control, 46
  and CEMA, 76
  Chinese economy, 61–62
  foreign policy, 150–151
  interpretation of doctrine, 84, 85
  official position, 150
  peaceful coexistence, 93
Marshall Plan, 77, 78, 100
  as propaganda, 202, 213–214
Marxism–Leninism:
  communist imperialism, 63
  conformity, 28
  confused issues, 44
  constitutional law, 132
  contemporary technology, 51
  dialectical materialism, 16
  economic policies determined by, 84
  interpretation, 17
  peaceful competition, 15
  Soviet leadership, 53
Middle East: communist pressure, 37
  ethnic minorities, 49
  nationalism in, 11–12, 37
  Soviet aid to, 80
  Soviets in, 107
Mikoyan, A., on nuclear war, 124
Minorities, 48–51
Molotov, V., 148
Moscow–Peking axis, 4, 7
  foreign aid, 73
  intelligence system, 182
  Soviet foreign policy, 223
  Vietnam war, 89
Moslems, as religious minority, 50
Mutual Defense Treaty (1951), 104

Nasser, Abdel Gamal, Soviet aid, 81
Nation–individualism, 4–9
National culture, 204
National interest, East/West concepts, 12
National mind, 41–44
National minorities, 48–51
National objectives, 13–14
National power, metamorphoses of, 32–62
National security, 86–102
  and intelligence, 163

See also Security policy.
National Security Act of 1947 (U.S.),
  153, 154n., 174, 177
National Security Council (U.S.), 154–
  157, 175
Nationalism, 17
  Africa/Near East, 11–12
  Middle East, 37
  prejudices and stereotypes, 83
Natural resources, 33
NATO, 100–101
  Belgian headquarters, 103
  de Gaulle and, 102–104
  geopolitical concepts, 36
  intelligence systems, 179–180
  and SEATO, compared, 106
  trade relations, 57–58
  Warsaw Pact and, 113
Near East: nationalism in, 11–12
  Soviet aid to, 81
Neo-colonialism, 17
Netherlands: balanced economy, 59
  and NATO, 100
Neutral powers, 9
Neutral states, and East/West trade,
  60–61
  economic assistance to, 60–61
  national security, 86
Neutralism, 87–89
Neutrality: Afro–Asian, 11
  and neutralism, 88
  in United Nations, 12
New Communist Man, 20–21, 25, 29
New Deal, 74
New Zealand: ANZUS treaty, 104
  in SEATO, 104
News dissemination, and propaganda,
  201
Nicolson, Harold, concept of diplomacy,
  188
Nonviolent combat, 129
North Atlantic Treaty Organization.
  See NATO.
North Korea, and CEMA, 112
North Vietnam, and CEMA, 112
Norway, and NATO, 100
Nuclear age, power in, 32–71
Nuclear war: possibility of, 126
  Red China and, 127–128
  See also World War III.
Nuclear weapons, 90–91
  banned, in outer space, 94
  cost of, 122
  U.S./Soviet race, 93

October Revolution (Russia), 50, 200
Office of Strategic Services (U.S.), 174
Organization of American States, 100

Outer Mongolia, and CEMA, 112
"Outer Seven," 57
  and CEMA, 112
  and NATO, 101
Outer space, nuclear weapons banned, 94

Pacific Charter, 105
Palestine, problem of, 107
Pakistan: Baghdad Pact, 107
  CENTO, 108
  ethnic minorities in, 50
  Indian war (1965), 109
  Pacific security, 104
  Red China, 109
  SEATO, 104
  Soviet aid, 81
  Turkish alliance, 107
Panch Shila principles, 127
Paris Conference (1960), 197
Pasha, Nuri, 108
Peace: communist concept, 18
  in nuclear age, 121–131
Peace campaigns, and propaganda, 215
Peaceful coexistence, 3, 79, 221
  by arms control, 95
  communist interpretation, 87
  Moscow's concept, 18
  Red China and, 93, 127–128
  Soviet drive for, 124
  Soviet policy, 89
Peaceful revolution, 222
People's Army (East Germany), 113
Permanent revolution, 148
Personal diplomacy, 198
Philippines, and Pacific security, 104
  SEATO, 104, 105–106
  U.S. treaty, 104
Point Four Program (U.S.), 77–78
  SEATO treaty, 105
Poland, and CEMA, 111
  German minorities in, 49
  Locarno Pact, 92
  Soviet influence in, 224
  Warsaw Pact, 113
Policy, and propaganda, 207–216
Policy planning, organizational aspects, 174–186
Politburo, 47
Political bipolarity, 10–12
Political economy, bipolar, 72–76
  communist, 56
  Western concepts, 57
Political freedom, and economic liberalism, 73
Political geography, 34–37, 52
Political ideologies, era of, 6
  contest between, 18

  and religion, 42
Political philosophies, 42–43, 73
Political science, 1
Political states, and economic status, 62
Political warfare, and psychological warfare, 205–206
  Soviet (1945), 200
Politprop, 207–216
Polycentric communism, 4, 221
Polytechnical education, 53
Population, world, estimated, 47
Population growth, 44–48
Portugal, defense strategy, 96
  and NATO, 100
Power, bipolar, rigidity of, 90
  ingredients of, 32–71
  struggle for, 14
  traditional elements, 32
Power concentration, bipolar, 5
Prejudices, 23–24, 27, 69
  influences of, 66–67
  in international relations, 41
Preventive war, 121
Propaganda, 71, 198
  Comintern, 212
  concepts and types, 199–206
  cultural relations as, 203–205
  and diplomacy, 188, 199–216
  information and, 200–201
  Nazi/Fascist, 200
  and policy, 207–216
  psychological warfare and, 205–206
  U.S./Soviet, 202
Propaganda media, diversity in, 200
Protective alliances, 98–115
Protestants, as religious minority, 50
Psychological warfare, and political warfare, 205–206
  and propaganda, 205
Public opinion, totalitarian countries, 70
Public opinion polls, 68

Quirino, President E., 104

Racial superiority theory, 63
Rapacki Plan (1958), 94
Ratzel, Frederick, and geopolitics, 35–36
Red China: birth control, 46
  break with Moscow, 93
  and CEMA, 76, 112
  cultural revolution, 85
  Eastern power, 149–151
  economy of, 61–62, 83–85
  education in, 54–55
  ethnic minorities, 49
  foreign aid by, 78–79, 81
  foreign policy, 149–151

243

geopolitics, 35
ideological excesses, 222
incentive earnings, 75
insecurity in, 29
intelligence system, 183–186
irrationality of, 224
nuclear war, 126
nuclear weapons, 90–91
nuclear weapons treaty, unsigned, 94
Pakistan and, 109
peaceful coexistence, 93, 127
population growth, 46
relations with Soviet Union, 3–5
scientific development, 54–55
security policy, 152, 159
security problem posed by, 97
Soviet foreign aid to, 83
Soviet military treaty, 110
Tibet overrun by, 81
trade with Soviet Union, 57
Vietnam war, 128
Red Cross, 9
Regional security pacts, 117
Religion, 25, 217
in Asia, 50
contemporary science and, 51
minority groups, 50
modern life concepts, 6
political ideologies and, 42
in Red China, 50
in Soviet Union, 50
Revolutionary nations, 1–5
Rhineland, militarization of (1936), 92
Rio de Janeiro treaty (1947), 100
Rocket development, 126
Rocket missiles, 122
Romania, and CEMA, 76, 111
Communist Party Congress (1960),
127
independence from Moscow, 97
population growth, 46
religion in, 50
trade with West, 57
Roosevelt, Franklin D., and Atlantic
Charter, 115
and de Gaulle, 103
national security, 157
Russia, See Soviet Russia.
Tsarist, 35, 36
population, 47

Saudi Arabia, Baghdad Pact, 108
Science, East/West, 21
contemporary, 51–55
geopolitics as a, 37
Scientific development, Red China, 55
SEATO, 104–106
and NATO, compared, 106

trade relations, 57–58
SEATO Treaty, 107–108
Security, collective, 91–93
Security Council. See United Nations.
Security policy, 160
formulation: France, 159
Great Britain, 152, 157–159
Japan, 159
Red China, 152, 159
Soviet Union, 152, 159
United States, 152, 153–157
West Germany, 159
Sino–Soviet conflict, 16, 93. See also
Moscow–Peking axis.
Sino–Soviet Treaty of Mutual Assist-
ance, 111n.
Social sciences, fluidity of, 7
Socialism, social and economic system,
56
Socialist camp, 16
changes in, 224
foreign aid and, 82
isolation and indoctrination, 71
international dealings, 43
non-monolithic, 218
to outstrip West, 97–98
Society, Western, 98
South Asia, ethnic minorities, 49
South Korea, communist invasion, 93
Southeast Asia Treaty Organization.
See SEATO.
Soviet: A bomb threat, 90
aggressiveness, post World War II,
93, 99
Albania and, 110
anti-ballistic missile system, 94
balanced economy, 58–59
Baltic states, occupation of, 110
Berlin blockade, 119
CEMA, 110–113
CENTO, 109
communist aggression, support of, 93
conflict with Red China, 93
Constitution (1936), 67, 68
Cuban missile crisis, 125
cultural relations, 203
Czechoslovakia, 110
diplomacy, 192, 194–195
Eastern power, 145–149
economic development, 61
economic isolation, 76
economic system, coordinated, 58
educational program, 53
educational theses, 28
ethnic minorities, 49
export/imports, 75
foreign aid: 78–79, 82
Near East, 81

neutrals, 73
Red China, 83
unrestricted, 81
foreign policy, 145–149
French conferences, 197
geopolitics, 35
Germany attacks, 99
Great Britain, conferences, 197
gross national product, 83
incentive earnings, 75
influence of, Eastern Europe, 97
  on Warsaw Pact countries, 224
intelligence system, 168, 180–183
Iran, 118
Korean war, 119
Marshall Plan, emulates, 79, 213–214
membership in League of Nations, 99
Middle East activities, 107
minorities in, 49
NATO's policy and strategy, 101
neo-capitalistic, 82
nuclear weapons, 90–91
Poland, 110
political warfare, 200
population growth, 46
propaganda by, 202
puppet regimes, 109
Red China, 3–5
  a security problem, 97
  trade with, 57
Red China military treaty, 110
religion in, 50
science, post Stalinist, 21
security policy, 152, 159
security problems, 97
Soviet zone of Germany, 110
Sputnik I, 126
superpower, 11
treaty network, 110–111
Turkish non-aggression treaty, 107
UN veto, 92–93
Vietnam war, 128
Western European trade, 57
world power, 7
World War II casualties, 47
Yugoslav relations, 110
Space exploration, 51, 126
Spain, religious minorities, 50
Sputnik I, 126
Stalin, Josef, 21
anti-imperialist line, 99
denigration, 16, 222
economic aid, blocks, 78–79
on imperialism, 125
philosophy of, 210
Soviet Constitution (1936), 67, 68
and Marshal Zhukov, 130
Strategic intelligence, 166–168, 176–

177, 183, 185–186
Suez, problem of, 107
Sukarno, President, "guided democracy," 140
Summit conferences, shortcomings, 198
Switzerland, neutrality of, 88
Syria, Baghdad Pact, 108

Taoism, religious minority, 50
Technology, contemporary, 51–55
Test Ban Treaty, 94
Thailand, in SEATO, 104, 106
  Pacific security, 104
Tibet, isolation of, 8
  Red China engulfs, 81
Tito, Josef Broz, 110
  "national" communism, 16
  ousted by Cominform, 218
  Soviet support, 110
Totalitarian states, 15
  diplomacy, concept of, 188
  foreign policy, 132–133
Totalitarianism, 7, 63
  and contemporary technology, 51
Trade, East-West blocs, 57
Trade fairs, as propaganda, 205
Traditional nations, 1–5
Treaty of Economic, Social and Cultural Collaboration and Collective Self-Defense (1948), 100
Treaty of Locarno (1925), 92–93
Trotsky, Leon. permanent revolution, 148
Truman, Harry S., foreign aid program, 78n.
Turkey, and CENTO, 108
  Cyprus civil war, 120
  Iran pact, 107
  NATO, 100
  Pakistan alliance, 107
  Soviet aggression, 99
  Soviet aid to, 81
  Soviet non-aggression treaty, 107
  U.S. aid to, 77

United Arab Republic. See Egypt.
United Kingdom. See Great Britain.
United Nations, Charter of, 115–116
  cooperation, lack of, 92
  and Cyprus, 120
  Gaza strip, 120
  Greece, communists in, 119
  Korean war, 115, 119
  national security policies, 161
  population growth studies, 45
  prejudice and stereotypes, 41
  Soviet intransigence, 118
  Soviet veto, 92–93

245

United States, anti-ballistic missile system, 94
  ANZUS treaty, 104
  Baghdad Pact, 108
  colonialism, 80
  Cuban missile crisis, 125
  cultural relations, 203
  economic conditions, 61
  economic influences, 72–73
  foreign aid program, 72–73, 76–85
  foreign policy, 133, 134–137
  Great Society program, 130
  gross national product, 83
  group pressures, 65
  "imperialism," 81
  India, support of, 107
  intelligence system, 167–172, 174–177
  Japanese security treaty, 104
  minorities in, 48
  NATO, 100
  nuclear weapons, 90–91
  overseas trade, 74
  Philippine treaty, 104
  Politprop, 213
  propaganda by, 202
  rocket development, 126
  SEATO, 104, 105
  security policy, 152, 153–157
  trade, Eastern bloc, 57, 60
  Vietnam war, 89, 128, 130
  Western power, 134–137
UNRRA, 76, 77

Vandenburg Resolution, 100
Vienna Conference (1961), 197
Vietnam, and SEATO treaty, 106
Vietnam war, 89, 128, 130

War, abolishing, 121
  concept of, in new technology, 123
  national security, 86–87
  in nuclear age, 18, 121–131
  political/psychological, 205–206
War of liberation, 89

Warsaw Treaty Organization, 111, 112–114
  Soviet influence on members, 224
West, power in, 132–145
West Germany, Basic Law, 141–142
  Constitution, 141
  foreign policy, 141–143
  group pressures, 65
  intelligence services, 179
  national security, 159
  NATO, 100
  Western power, 141
Western bloc, and national security, 86
  newly-independent countries, and, 17
Western Europe, colonialism, 79–80
  communist trade with, 57
  demographic future, 47–48
  economic policy, 74–75
Western European Union (1954), 100
  and Warsaw Pact, 113
Western society, 98
Wilson, Woodrow, diplomacy, concepts of, 187
  Fourteen Points, 115
World economics, comparison, 55–56
World Federation of Trade Unions, 182
World Peace Council, 182
World politics, ideologization of, 43
World War I, postwar effects, 6
  postwar technological revolution, 37
  prewar alliances, 10
World War II, alliances, 10
World War III, futility of, 18, 123–124, 128
Woytinsky, W. S., 46

Yugoslavia, break with Cominform, 16
  CEMA, 112
  in Greece, support of communists, 117
  independence of Moscow, 97
  Soviet aid to, 80, 110
  Soviet influence, 224

Zanzibar, neo-colonialism, 17
Zhukov, Marshal, G. K., 130

A B C D E F G H I J   5 4 3 2 1 7 0 6 9 8 7